PE

GONE

Margaret was born in Sydney. Her great ambition was to see the world and in 1966 she left Australia for a twelve-month working holiday. She returned after thirty years.

During that time she lived on three continents and travelled extensively. Her first job was as a 'Golden Girl' for the Australian government in the UK, followed by a career in oil and later aluminium in the Middle East. She also helped to establish Al Noor, the first school for disabled children in Dubai.

Margaret now spends her time writing, helping on dinosaur digs, and doing voluntary work raising funds for disabled children.

Margaret Wilcox

GONE

A MOTHER'S 14-YEAR SEARCH FOR HER ABDUCTED DAUGHTER

PENGUIN BOOKS

PENGUIN

Published by the Penguin Group
Penguin Group (Australia)
250 Camberwell Road, Camberwell, Victoria 3124, Australia
(a division of Pearson Australia Group Pty Ltd)
Penguin Group (USA) Inc.
375 Hudson Street, New York, New York 10014, USA
Penguin Group (Canada)
90 Eglinton Avenue East, Suite 700, Toronto, Canada ON M4P 2Y3
(a division of Pearson Penguin Canada Inc.)
Penguin Books Ltd
80 Strand, London WC2R 0RL England
Penguin Ireland
25 St Stephen's Green, Dublin 2, Ireland
(a division of Penguin Books Ltd)
Penguin Books India Pvt Ltd
11 Community Centre, Panchsheel Park, New Delhi – 110 017, India
Penguin Group (NZ)
67 Apollo Drive, Rosedale, North Shore 0632, New Zealand
(a division of Pearson New Zealand Ltd)
Penguin Books (South Africa) (Pty) Ltd
24 Sturdee Avenue, Rosebank, Johannesburg 2196, South Africa

Penguin Books Ltd, Registered Offices: 80 Strand, London, WC2R 0RL, England

First published by Penguin Group (Australia), 2008
This edition published by Penguin Group (Australia), 2009

13 5 7 9 10 8 6 4 2

Text copyright © Margaret Wilcox 2008

Design by Claire Wilson, based on an original design
by Megan Baker © Penguin Group (Australia)
Typeset in 11/17 Sabon by Post Pre-press Group, Brisbane, Queensland
Printed and bound in Australia by McPherson's Printing Group, Maryborough, Victoria

National Library of Australia
Cataloguing-in-Publication data:

Wilcox, Margaret
Gone: A mother's 14-year search for her abducted daughter / author, Margaret Wilcox
2nd ed.
978 014 301073 9 (pbk)

362.8297092

penguin.com.au

For my darling daughter

Tanya

Contents

Tanya

LONDON
Short-lived freedom: December 1977

As the British Airways aircraft circled over Heathrow I could only catch brief glimpses of the familiar landscape below through heavy grey clouds and dappled light. I leaned across to make sure Tanya's seat belt was secure. I couldn't help thinking that except for her exotic colouring she looked like a typical little English three-year-old, in her brown double-breasted topcoat with its velvet trim on the collar, cuffs and pockets. It wasn't her silky brown hair or green eyes that distinguished her but the pale-honey colour of her skin. She had managed our two-and-a-half-hour flight from Malaga in her usual placid manner and, while bemused by the strangeness of the experience and the enclosed environment, she did not fuss or complain, although she seemed a little quiet. This was the first flight she had been on since our trip from Australia to Spain when she was six weeks old. My concerns about her being scared, not wanting to sit still for over two hours or suffering discomfort in her ears were all unfounded.

'We are nearly there, sweetheart. When the aeroplane's big wheels touch the ground it could be a bit bumpy, and there might be a lot of noise.'

'Like fireworks, Mummy?'

'Well, no. Just like a lot of big bus engines all being noisy at once.'

'Will it take long?'

'No, not very long. Then we'll get off and collect our bags. There's nothing to be afraid of, Mummy is here.'

I squeezed her warm and trusting little hand. She had managed to deal with the flight like a seasoned traveller.

It was a typical London November day, cold and raining, so after clearing immigration and customs I added a matching brown hat and woollen gloves to Tanya's already bulky clothing. We were now equipped to find a taxi and head for the hotel.

Tanya sat contentedly during the forty-minute drive to central London. Thrilled to be able to explain the unfamiliar things in our new surroundings, I pointed out the big red buses, the policemen in their quaint hats, the blinking yellow lights and the 'lollypop' men at school crossings. I also noticed several billboards advertising *Swan Lake* at the Coliseum Theatre. Tanya loved dancing, especially ballet, so already wondering how I would entertain a small child for the next forty-eight hours I decided a matinee the following day would be a perfect interlude.

This brief two-night stopover in London was to allow us to gather our strength before the long twenty-eight-hour flight home to Australia. The following morning I decided to take Tanya to

Whiteleys department store to see Santa Claus. This would be a special treat and hopefully make her happy in our new environment, particularly after the past few days when, because of my distracted frame of mind, my behaviour had sometimes been uncharacteristically erratic. Tanya knew about Santa Claus but the custom of jolly fat men with white beards, dressed up in red suits and big black boots, was not followed in Spain. This would be a new experience for her.

Although Tanya was not frightened when she sat on Santa's knee, I couldn't get her to smile for the camera. Even the antics of the professional photographer failed to arouse any animation on her small face. As the queue lengthened I saw his flashlight capture a sullen snapshot. Then Santa gave her a small plastic doll but she showed no interest and just wanted to come back to me. Sadly I collected a receipt for the picture and pushed it into the bottom of my bag, feeling the exercise had been a waste of time. I had no intention of ever returning to collect the photograph and disappointed with Tanya's response, I decided it was time to move on.

In the taxi on the way to the theatre I was surprised when Tanya wanted to sit on my lap. She then complained about walking a short distance to the box office. This was very unusual for my independent, energetic little girl. The only tickets available were in the upper circle, which meant climbing several flights of stairs.

'Come on darling, hang onto the handrail while we go up the stairs.'

'No. I don't want to go up the stairs.'

'But we are going to see the pretty girls dancing,' I pleaded.

However, as her little jelly legs folded under her she insisted, 'No. I want to go home.'

'But all the girls in their pretty tutus are ready to dance for you.'

To my dismay Tanya refused to move. I picked her up, together with our parcels, and under the weight of winter clothing stumbled up the flights of stairs. Scurrying people bumping into me and pushing past made my ordeal worse. I stopped a couple of times to rest, so by the time we reached our seats, hot and exhausted, the heavy red velvet curtains were beginning to open. While making sure Tanya was comfortable and had an uninterrupted view of the stage I was aware that people were staring at us. Were they surprised at seeing a three-year-old in the audience, or were they afraid she would make a noise or be disruptive? If so, they did not know my angelic daughter. A few minutes after Tchaikovsky's melodious notes drifted up from the orchestra pit and the curtains had fully opened, Tanya asked to sit on my knee. Within ten minutes she was curled up on my lap and fast asleep. As I cuddled her lethargic little form, I was completely baffled by her behaviour. All I had wanted was to see Tanya's joy as she watched her first live performance. My earlier fear of her also wanting to dance to the music now seemed foolish and I felt cheated.

The ballet continued but I could not focus on it. All I could do through my bitter disappointment was wonder why Tanya was acting so strangely. Here, for me, was one of ballet's most beautiful love stories, with its impending tragedy unfolding, and Tanya slept through the entire performance. Surely she wasn't jet-lagged after such a short flight? But what else could be wrong?

Was it that she was homesick, missing the familiarity of our house and her daily routine, including the Spanish cartoons she watched on television even though the language was foreign? Was this sudden thrust into a new city and culture the problem? The tension I had felt during the past couple of days had undoubtedly affected my demeanour and perhaps Tanya was now reacting to this. Even though I had carefully organised our escape for many months in my head, when it came to enacting the plan my lack of self-confidence shone like a beacon. Would the neighbours see me leaving the house with suitcases and try to stop me? Would the immigration officers refuse to let us pass through their net at the airport? Would Hadi return from his business trip unexpectedly before the plane left the tarmac? These were some of the worries that had plagued my every minute.

I smoothed Tanya's soft, fine hair with my free hand. A mother's instinct is usually accurate and she can sense her child's mood. The bond between mother and child is so strong it is sometimes difficult to know where the mother's feelings end and the child's begin. But this was altogether a new experience for me and I couldn't understand Tanya's disinterest and sullen state.

When the ballet ended I gently woke Tanya and carried her down the stairs. Even the suggestion of an ice-cream did not raise any enthusiasm so we returned to the bleak isolation of our hotel.

That evening Tanya was scratchy, whimpering and generally out of sorts. At first I put this down to the strange environment of a hotel, the noise and bustle of London, and the climate change from sunny Spain. Even her appetite was non-existent. My attempts to obtain food for a small child in a London businessman's hotel were not treated enthusiastically or with any sympathy, but room service did eventually agree to send a soft-boiled egg and some bread and butter. They need not have bothered. Even these were left untouched and all Tanya wanted to do was cuddle up in my lap.

While we both sat huddled on the bed I gently placed my hand on her forehead and realised that her temperature was higher than normal. This new discovery concerned me so I asked to see the hotel doctor.

His visit was brief.

'So this is the little lady who is off-colour?'

'Yes. She just hasn't been herself. Listless, not interested in food, and her temperature is higher than it should be.'

'Hello Tanya. I'm just going to put this little thing under your arm for a minute, and have a look at your neck. Hmm. A little rash here, and some swollen glands. Easy to see why you are not feeling very well. You've got measles!'

No wonder she has been crotchety, I thought.

'How long are you in the hotel for, Mrs Wilcox?'

'We are flying to Australia tomorrow.'

'Not any more, I'm afraid.'

'What do you mean?'

'Tanya will have to be kept in a dark room, and she won't be able to fly for three weeks. I will give you a prescription, which the concierge can get for you. She'll be fine, just keep her warm.'

As I slowly closed the door behind the doctor I was in shock at this incredible news. Tanya had never been ill before. Might she get worse than she already was? Had taking her out in the cold exacerbated her condition? I wondered guiltily. How would I cope? Where could I go?

On the one hand I was relieved that Tanya's unusual behaviour had a genuine medical basis and was not because she was away from her everyday surroundings. But on the other hand how would I manage with an ill three-year-old in a London hotel for three weeks? How would I keep the room dark, as the doctor had ordered, and prepare her food, and what about laundry? How could I entertain her in this small ordinary room with no view and no facilities?

The one comfort she did have was 'Lambie'.

When Tanya was born in Sydney my mother gave her a lamb-skin to sleep on. This was the fleece of a baby lamb and covered the base of her crib. It was generally known that the natural fibres of the fleece allowed babies to breathe even if they were lying face down. It was also very soft and comfortable, and could be used in any climate and laundered like any other bed linen. Lambie had become Tanya's security blanket and now, three-and-a-half years later, despite being torn, tattered and almost half its original size, it hardly left her side. It had comforted her through teething problems and minor illnesses, and always went to bed with her. Lambie was very much part and parcel of this wee person.

Now I needed my own security blanket, but how would I find it? My first inclination was to telephone my very dear friend Maureen, but she had recently moved to a new house and I did not know its whereabouts.

Maureen and I had met nine years earlier in Libya, where we both worked for the American oil company Occidental. Maureen, although English, had lived in Canada for fourteen years prior to this, which gave her a distinctive and charming mid-Atlantic accent. I was only twenty-four when we met but the decade of years separating us went unnoticed; as single career girls, and both rather conservative, we struck up an instant and enduring friendship. Maureen's honesty and integrity were apparent from the beginning – the way she would look at me over the top of her glasses when I suggested anything a little daring or out of line – but she also possessed a fun-loving nature and a good sense of humour.

During those years in Libya Maureen and I became very close friends, sharing events foreign to both of us. We made all our own clothes and were excited by the exotic fabrics we found in the markets. Because of our shared love of cooking we swapped recipes and culinary hints. Our discovery of the local butchers' shops, where the animal's head as well as its carcass or parts of its carcass were displayed on the flat wooden counter, punctuated by hundreds of flies, shocked us. The shoe shops dazzled us and, overwhelmed by the elegance and beauty of the Italian shoes, we bought several pairs without enough money to pay for them. The shop owner would give us the shoes and tell us *mah'lesch* – 'pay me tomorrow' – and we did. What a wonderful system. On other occasions we did not know how to react when offered syrupy tea or Coca Cola by a shopkeeper we had never seen before. We learned to deal with local customs, such as discovering that we should spread our flour on white paper and leave it in the sun for a few minutes before using it, in order to get rid of the weevils. Then there were the many trips to Rome, Malta and Tunis, as well as adventures in the Libyan desert, which were all part of our wonderful times together. We also shared the bad times – news of misfortune, illness and even death that took place far away in our respective home countries. When my father died, it was Maureen who was at my side to comfort me.

Maureen was still employed by Occidental but now worked in the London office. On Monday morning when I telephoned the company her secretary informed me that Maureen was on leave and I could not, under any circumstances, be given her home telephone number. I asked to be transferred to Bob Macalister, a vice president, Maureen's ex-boss and a mutual friend. Bob and his family, whom I knew well from our days in Libya, were now also living in London, where Bob ran Occidental's newly acquired North Sea oil concession. After a brief conversation about the family and their new life in London, Bob told me Maureen had not been well and was on sick leave. Knowing she would be pleased to hear from her old friend, he gave me her telephone number.

Maureen was surprised to hear I was in London. I was equally surprised and shocked to hear that she was at home on prolonged leave, currently undergoing neurological tests for a possible brain tumour. We were both in trouble. Maureen, in her most generous and caring way, immediately suggested Tanya and I leave the confines of our hotel and stay with her. She had just moved to a new area, Claygate, hadn't unpacked, was unable to do anything herself but the beds were accessible. Once we overcame my prime concern of Tanya being infectious and thereby possibly compounding Maureen's problems, relief at the opportunity to leave the hotel poured through me. Hidden away in the county of Surrey we could at least be in a homely environment where I could take care of Tanya in a more normal manner.

Hurriedly I telephoned Australia to advise my mother there had been a glitch in my plans. I cancelled our onward air bookings then found a capacious London taxi to take our belongings to Maureen's new home at Elm Road.

In the cold grey drizzle the long taxi ride from central London to Claygate – some eighteen miles – was slow and tedious through the city's crammed suburbs and heavy traffic, but Tanya eventually slept in the warmth and comfort of the back seat.

We arrived at Maureen's two-up and two-down terrace house opposite the local school. In uncustomary housecoat and slippers and looking extremely pale, her tall, slim figure welcomed us. As Maureen had never married, I knew she might feel awkward with a small child in her midst, but after directing me to deposit our belongings in the spare bedroom and showing me the layout of the house she crept back to bed. I put some of Tanya's toys around the room, placed Lambie on her bed and settled down to read her a story.

Packing cases were scattered throughout all the rooms, makeshift curtains – obviously emergency arrangements – hung at the small windows and the floor was bare, but the kitchen was functional and the television was unpacked. The disarray did not bother me for one second, but the steep narrow stairs down from the bedrooms to the living area were a great concern. Our home in Malaga also had stairs but they were wide, with gentle risers, and a solid rail for

Tanya to hold. I would have to be particularly watchful of my small child on this potentially lethal staircase.

The following day, which continued to be cold and wet, the new carpet arrived. The men worked diligently in every room of the house at once, leaving Maureen, Tanya and me marooned in the kitchen, where we sat on the bench like the Three Graces, unable to move. Boxes and odds and ends from the other rooms accentuated the already small confines of the kitchen. Fortunately there was a toilet and basin next to the laundry, which adjoined the kitchen. As tedious as this situation was, we were able to laugh about it and I was relieved to be with someone I could trust. Thankfully, the carpet-layers finished the whole house in one day and after I unpacked some of the offending boxes everything looked much brighter.

Two days later the ambulance came to take Maureen to Atkinson Morley Hospital. Tanya and I stood forlornly at the front door to wave goodbye. It was surreal to see my dear, vivacious, independent friend being led away by two strangers. She was being admitted to undergo more tests, which meant more waiting and more uncertainty. I felt tremendous concern for her but, knowing her strength and determination, her English stiff upper lip, I could not envisage anything except a positive outcome. Much later, when her diagnosis revealed viral polyneuritis, it was such a relief to know that she did not have a brain tumour, but her recovery was long and slow.

Several cold, wet, monotonous days followed Maureen's departure, the highlight being when the milkman arrived each morning. He not only delivered milk but also bread, eggs, yoghurt and an array of other small necessities. This, together with the huge shopping expedition I undertook before Maureen left for hospital, would keep us well stocked in food while we waited out our quarantine.

Tanya and I mostly retreated to the warmth of the small sitting room, where we watched television, coloured and pasted pictures and read her favourite stories. I also made several telephone calls to close friends in England to tell them of our situation. They all expressed surprise, except Alice, my English eighty-year-old surrogate 'mum'.

When I first left Australia for a working holiday, which I thought would last eighteen months, I was given Alice and Pop's contact details in Southend-on-Sea in England. Dorothy, my mother's best friend, advised her parents of my imminent arrival and relayed the message that they would be delighted to hear from me. Over the years, Alice and Pop became my English 'family'. After Pop died, I asked Alice to visit us in Malaga. She had stayed for two weeks, some twelve months before my recent flight to London, and on her last day had issued a mysterious but emphatic warning. This was the first time the thought of escape was planted in my mind.

Now as I ticked off each day on the calendar, waiting anxiously for our three weeks in hiding to pass, the ringing of the telephone interrupted my musing. It was Alice.

Breathless and alarmed, she asked, 'Do you know Hadi's in England?'

'What do you mean?'

'He's just left my house. He's looking everywhere for you.'

'But how on earth did he find you?'

Alice explained that Hadi had gone to the local police station in Southend-on-Sea and told the officer in attendance that he was looking for an elderly lady called Alice, who had been burgled a year earlier. The burglary had taken place just before Alice's visit with us in Spain. Alice had no idea what else Hadi had told the officer but he had been given her address and directions to her house!

I explained to Alice that he couldn't possibly find Tanya and me because he didn't know we were in London. In any case, even if he did, apart from the thousands of hotels in England, I had friends all over the country with whom I could be staying, from the Isle of Wight in the south to Sheffield in the north. Also, until I arrived in London and spoke to Maureen, I didn't have her new address or even know to which suburb she had just moved.

Secretly concealed in Maureen's anonymous terrace house on the outskirts of suburban London, I felt completely safe. Nobody, other than Maureen's next-door neighbour and the milkman, knew where Tanya and I were. My mother in Australia and a couple of friends in England had the telephone number but no address or location. In spite of this, each time the piercing ring of the telephone echoed through the house I hesitated before answering it, always apprehensive until I knew who was on the other end. I kept reassuring myself that I had left absolutely no trace of where Tanya and I had been or where we were hiding in this sprawling city of twelve million people. Surely nobody would find us at Elm Road.

Although anxious at first after hearing of my husband's arrival in England, I again settled into our dreary routine over the next couple of days, confident Tanya and I were safely hidden.

A small calendar, comprising picturesque scenes of England that were so familiar to me, hung from a rusty drawing pin on the kitchen wall. Each time I looked at it and marvelled how anyone managed to find so many sunny days to capture these photos, I mentally crossed off the days. Our departure date for Australia slowly drew closer. The thought of being on a Qantas aircraft heading for the safety of my family, far away from my prison in Spain, was continually in my mind. The further away we could be the better. To my relief Tanya's happy, energetic demeanour was slowly returning. At the same time this brought new problems – how to occupy her, for instance – and I wondered how I could keep her imprisoned inside for much longer.

Three days later, and for the first time in a week, the sun came out. In spite of its insipid December colour and lack of warmth, it was a welcome relief from the rain. I was even contemplating taking Tanya out into the damp, miniscule back garden when there was a knock at the front door. It was about the time the milkman normally arrived with his parcel of fresh produce. Making sure Tanya was well away from any possible draught, I opened the door and was surprised to see a man in a heavy brown winter coat and brown hat. As I gazed at this stranger, thinking he had the wrong house, my surprise turned to fear.

When I looked more closely, and heard his voice, I realised it was Hadi.

Margaret

LIBYA
Valentine's Day aftermath: 1969

It was 14 February 1969, one week after my twenty-fifth birthday. As I carefully dressed for my first party since arriving in Libya, I had no idea the evening would shape the next twenty-three years of my life. The Valentine's Day party was crowded and noisy when I arrived. A group of thirty to forty expatriates were gathered in a sparsely furnished apartment in the Garden City area of Tripoli. Apart from a few Americans and Italians, most of the guests were British. I was certainly the only Australian, and at that time, several days after my arrival from London to work for the American oil company, Occidental, I thought I was the only Australian in town.

My attention was distracted from the group I had joined by the dominating voice and laughter of the man standing directly behind me. He was talking about Hong Kong, my favourite city, and hearing someone talk so enthusiastically about the place aroused my interest immediately. I was mentally transported back to that wonderful city. I had spent a short time there on my way from Australia to England three years earlier and was enchanted by its exotic character, which was so different from anything I had previously experienced. English colonial-style buildings overlooked the harbour at that time; the skyscrapers were a later addition. The water was a moving mass of craft of every size, all jostling for position – junks with their romantic ballooning sails gliding up and down, large tankers and cruise liners, and passenger ferries crossing from one side of the harbour to the other. The streets were crowded with a curious mix of people: men in business suits hurrying among beautiful, slim women in jewel-coloured cheongsams; and Chinese male and female workers in traditional dark blue or grey cotton work clothes – loose trousers, flowing collarless shirts and flat black shoes – many of them balancing bundles suspended from the ends of bamboo poles. The unfamiliar smell of garlic and burnt soy sauce emanated from the cooking of Chinese delicacies in the small roadside stalls. The odour of waste from inefficient drains accosted my senses, and the pungent fumes from fuel that powered both street and sea traffic were always present. I was mesmerised by the sights and sounds, the colour and vibrancy, of this captivating city.

Drifting back from my reverie, I turned and made brief eye contact with the owner of the voice.

Cheekily I asked, 'When were you in Hong Kong?'

'I arrived back this morning,' came the friendly reply.

I found myself looking at a particularly handsome man, attractive in an unusual way. Naughty green eyes sparkled as he spoke and his skin colour, a deep honey tone, looked more the result of the sun than any inherent ethnic characteristic. He was tall and well built. Although his hair was in short supply, growing only on the lower circumference of his head, leaving a completely bald, smooth, shiny top, it was not unattractive. It was dark with just a tiny speck of grey at the temples. His clothes, although casual and well coordinated, were obviously very expensive, probably Italian. I couldn't quite work out his accent; it wasn't Italian, it certainly wasn't English – although his English was faultless, even including colloquial expressions – and it didn't seem German, although his appearance seemed more German than anything else. His name, Hadi Senussi, did not serve to enlighten me either.

After listening to a number of his amusing stories and jokes it was clear that he was an interesting man, a very colourful character who enjoyed life, was well travelled and immensely entertaining, but I knew nothing more about him. However, by the end of the evening I was confident I would hear from him again.

Sure enough the following morning, during the frantic rush of a busy office, I received a telephone call from Hadi with an invitation to dinner that evening at The Swann, which I subsequently learned was reputedly the best restaurant in Tripoli. Later in the day, I relayed the events of the previous evening and the morning's invitation to Maureen. She raised one eyebrow, in her conservative way, and said something like, 'You've done well.'

Not having any idea what she was talking about, I looked back at her in confusion. Maureen went on to explain that 'Senussi' was the name of the royal family, with King Idris, the ruler of Libya, as its head. Hadi, a distant member of the royal family, was well known as a prominent and successful businessman. I was surprised to hear this, as he certainly didn't have the physical appearance of a local and would have passed anywhere as a European.

When Hadi collected me that evening he arrived with a small bunch of gardenias, one of my favourite flowers. He looked immaculate in his tailored linen suit and colourful silk tie, and his manners were impeccable. Ever since my arrival in Libya I had heard that it was considered wrong for Western girls to socialise with the local men. They certainly shouldn't date them and the few girls who did were considered cheap and disgraceful. Here I was, barely three weeks after my arrival, about to break this unwritten rule. Everything appeared perfect right now, but what was I to expect later in the evening?

The Swann was situated by the water in Giorgimpopoli, the American residential part of town, and lit by candlelight it was very romantic. As we entered there was soft music playing in the background. A welcoming and efficient Italian, presumably the owner, who was on first-name terms with Hadi, met us at the door. A number of Western diners also acknowledged Hadi as we passed through the room. At the end of an amusing, enjoyable evening, and relaxed after sharing an expensive bottle of wine, the prohibitions I had been warned of were long forgotten. The restaurant, with its delicious food and fine wines, later became a regular favourite dining spot for us.

As a recent arrival in Tripoli I was grateful to Hadi for kindly showing me around the city, taking me to the best places to shop, explaining some of the local customs, and generally being helpful. He was very social and over the months that followed I regularly accompanied him to glamorous diplomatic and corporate functions. He never wore local dress and always looked so handsome, whether in a dinner suit or casual attire. With his green eyes he looked more European than Arabic. His only friends I met were Western and he appeared to move exclusively in expatriate circles. If at first I was conscious about the stigma attached to dating a local, the fact that Hadi was so Westernised and so accepted among my colleagues soon convinced me that the difference in our backgrounds was not an issue.

Hadi also introduced me to another new experience, the desert, and this was for me the start of a lasting love affair with this beautiful terrain. During our excursions into the Sahara I was amazed at its kaleidoscope of colours, the magic contours of its soft, flowing sand and the razor-sharp edges at the rim of the dunes. The soft rustle of wind formed waves on this inland sea, which were decorated with the tracks of lizards and the twisting trails of small snakes. Infrequently, after rain, the ground became a carpet of green and hyacinth-like flowers popped up like mushrooms. In this pristine, silent environment – such a contrast to the noise and bustle of Tripoli – I was happy and content.

Our friendship continued. Some months later, unaware of the intricacies of Arab culture and the importance of being introduced to family members, I was curious when Hadi suggested we visit his farm. We were on our way back to Tripoli after lunch at Sabratha, one of Libya's impressive Roman-ruin sites, and had to pass the farm on our way.

We arrived at a set of large metal gates that hid the farm from the main road and the outside world. The family owned several farms, but this one on the shores of the Mediterranean Sea, with its private beach, was where Hadi's mother lived during the summer months. Hadi called out to one of the farmhands to open the gate. I never saw Hadi open or close the gates himself; this always puzzled me and I wondered if it was due to his adherence to some sort of Arab hierarchy. An avenue of pomegranate trees with their small, red, bell-like flowers lined the driveway to the house. As our visit was unscheduled, I sat in the car while Hadi crossed the verandah and went inside to announce our arrival to his mother.

Hadi returned and led me into the dark interior – the wooden shutters were closed to keep out the afternoon heat – then left me in the middle of what seemed like a sitting room, sparsely furnished by Western standards. I could hear him speaking loudly in Arabic in what seemed like a teasing manner. After several minutes he returned, pushing his embarrassed mother in front of him. All I could see behind her blue-patterned baracan was weathered skin and one aged, watery eye. Her hands, clutching her baracan tightly around her face, were sun-tanned and tattooed in an inky blue. Her body, bundled in traditional baggy pantaloons, long dress and goodness knows what else under her baracan, was well rounded. Hadi pushed her towards me as her raucous voice objected and her torso pulled back. This charade continued for several minutes, orchestrated by an exchange of Arabic. Slowly I was offered a coarse, tattooed hand to shake. I placed both my hands around it in a gentle caress. More Arabic and then Om Saad left the room; to prepare tea, I was told.

Over time, even without a common language, we grew to understand each other. The baracan was discarded but Om Saad always wore a thin cotton scarf covering most of her hair. Once unveiled, the inky blue tattoos on her forehead, nose and chin were revealed. The fresh smell of Lily of the Valley talcum powder accompanied her aura of resignation. Nobody seemed to know how old she was, but as Hadi was thirty-five, with a twenty-five-year gap between him and his next oldest sibling, I guessed she would have been close to eighty.

Every Friday after our beach barbecues we would stop to have supper with Om Saad, but she would never eat with us at the table. She would simply sit on cushions on the floor in the adjoining room. The only place the three us were ever together was in the kitchen. She taught me to prepare a number of Libyan recipes and laughed unashamedly when Hadi, as translator, pressed her for precise measurements instead of 'a handful of this' and 'a lump of that'.

Whenever we visited Om Saad we always left laden with food, both in our stomachs and in boxes to take home. She was clearly an adoring mother and Hadi, in her eyes I was sure, could do no wrong. However, if ever any hint of disagreement arose between Hadi and me she would immediately take my side and shout at Hadi, often waving a forceful, podgy finger in front of his face. In spite of the language barrier we developed a warm affection for each other.

This was far from a normal Libyan family. Hadi's youngest sister, Aminah, had been a teacher in an Italian school before she married and she only wore European clothes, almost unheard of in this Muslim society. I also learned that Hadi, over the years, had had numerous European girlfriends, and I presumed Om Saad was accustomed to this and therefore readily accepted my presence.

After six months of dating, Hadi made overtures of marriage. Not being at all gracious I simply laughed at this proposal and advised him I had absolutely no intention of getting married and was very happy as a single career woman. My desire to broaden my experience, see more of the world and learn new things was paramount. I had not been in a serious relationship before and felt incapable of making a decision of such magnitude; I still had some growing to do. Hadi was certainly important in my life. He was the most interesting and charming man I had been out with and I loved being with him. He was fun, generous and gregarious. But marrying Hadi would mean living permanently in Libya, a very long way from Australia and my family. This was a major concern to me and I was far happier to maintain the status quo.

I thought Hadi might sever our friendship on hearing this as, before we met, he had broken an eight-year engagement to an English girl, and being of an age – ten years my senior – where he was expected to be married, he may not have wanted to waste any more time on someone so uninterested. But I genuinely hoped this would not be the case.

We continued to see each other. I had been in Tripoli for almost eight months when, on the last day of August, Hadi drove me home after a barbecue for a group of twenty-five of my colleagues and other expatriates at his farm. Some thirty kilometres out of town, the farm was a perfect location for the beach parties that had become a regular Friday feature. Although Occidental and all the other oil-related companies were predominantly American-owned, it was necessary for them to follow the Muslim working week – six days, Saturday to Thursday, with Friday as the day of rest. Hadi would supply all the food for these gatherings, including whole lambs for the spit, and the guests, mainly American, always brought extra goodies and an ample supply of alcohol. At the end of the day after the guests had left Hadi would talk with the farm workers for a while then we would visit his mother in the house. When we arrived back in Tripoli, on this occasion, it was almost midnight before Hadi left me at my apartment building.

Knowing that after a few hours sleep I would be due at my office for a day's work, my preparations for bed were rapid. Sleep came easily after the long sojourn at the beach in the hot summer sun. In the dark of night I was awoken from a deep sleep by a strange noise. The sounds of tanks and guns were familiar to me only from movies and television, and when they seemed to be coming from just outside my bedroom I thought I must have been dreaming. Lying very still in bed, I could hear men shouting in Arabic and the noise of marching feet. As the noise increased, and seemed to come even closer, I decided to get up and take a look from my bedroom balcony. In the narrow side street below, the guards from the American Embassy next door were being led away at gunpoint by soldiers in Libyan army fatigues. This was a very strange exercise to be taking place at two o'clock in the morning, I thought.

After a few minutes one of the armed soldiers on the opposite side of the lane looked up and saw me on the balcony. He pointed his gun in what seemed like my direction and started shouting in Arabic. He couldn't possibly be talking to me, I thought. What was I doing wrong? As I continued to watch he slowly walked across the narrow lane, gun still aimed, until he was standing directly below my first-floor balcony. By now the tip of his gun seemed to be only inches from my nose and there was no mistaking that the angry stream of Arabic was directed at me. I stumbled back inside and locked the French wooden shutters, totally confused and somewhat fearful of these events.

I decided it might be a good idea to change out of my pyjamas and get dressed. Only minutes later my doorbell rang. Still in my bedroom and frozen to the spot, I was certain the soldiers had come either to shoot or arrest me. Panic now took hold as I knew there was no way to escape. When the bell continued ringing, I decided it was better to get this over as quickly as possible so with shaking hands I roughly pulled up the covers on my bed and reluctantly moved to the door. When I opened it, to my huge relief an Englishman was standing on the other side. He introduced himself as a neighbour from the third floor and explained he was looking for anyone in the building with a telephone. Private telephones in Tripoli in 1969 were practically non-existent and he was endeavouring to make a call to the British Embassy to establish what was going on. After I had explained that I did not have a telephone, my neighbour left to continue his search, giving me his apartment number and inviting me to join him and his flatmate at any time should I wish to do so.

The virtually empty building, mainly occupied by single men who spent most of their time in the desert and came to Tripoli for a couple of days a month only, had taken on an eerie quality that unnerved me. There was certainly no sleep for the remainder of that night. The local radio station played nothing but military music, and the one television station – relayed from Wheelus, the American army base a few kilometres out of town – only operated for a couple of hours each night and was long closed. Around seven in the morning, which I thought a reasonable hour in the unlikely event that anyone had slept, I made my way to my newly acquainted neighbour's flat. He had located a telephone in the building but none of his calls had proved informative. Nobody knew what was happening.

Hadi, with his contacts and connections, would surely know. After establishing the whereabouts of the phone, I went to make a call. Unfortunately this time Hadi was unable to enlighten me. In reply to my questions, such as, 'Have the Egyptians taken over?' and 'Have the Israelis invaded?' Hadi simply said, 'Stay inside and don't go out of your flat.'

I did not have a death wish so I was unlikely to do anything to the contrary. Hadi was clearly very nervous about this conversation and kept making excuses to end it. Expatriates were always discussing rumours about telephones being tapped and I now suspected that Hadi might know those stories to be true. When the Wheelus Air Base news finally aired later that day the entire slot was devoted to Rocky Marciano, the world heavyweight-boxing champion – not a word about Libya.

Tense waiting and anticipation filled the next few days. Every hour I tuned into the BBC World Service, the only English radio available, to hear if Libya had made the headline news, but there was not a single word about the country. I made various efforts to keep myself occupied but it was impossible. Try as I could there was no way I could concentrate enough to catch up on my unanswered correspondence. What could I possibly say while caught in this vacuum of ignorance and uncertainty? How long could we survive locked up behind four walls, and for what purpose? Who would release us? How could I get word to anyone? And whom would I contact anyway?

The streets were deserted except for the occasional tank and the sound of gunfire in the distance. I knew the houseboy would certainly not arrive so to help pass the time I decided to wash the white marble floors and to my surprise they came up even cleaner than usual. There was also the unexpected opportunity to finish a party dress I was making, if I could put my mind to it for long enough.

The curfew eventually lifted after a couple of days, for one hour each morning to allow everyone to buy bread and other small necessities. On the first morning, Hadi arrived on my doorstep with a mountain of bread, pasta, sugar and a huge packet of washing powder. As he was always a stickler for cleanliness, I could only surmise that, at the very least, he wanted me to be clean if I was blown up or shot! To my great disappointment he still did not know what had happened or the reason for the unrest. One thing he did know, however, was that the elderly, beloved King Idris was safely out of the country. Most of Hadi's family were in Tripoli but thankfully his mother was tucked away safely at the farm. With my emergency rations unceremoniously deposited on the kitchen table, Hadi rushed back home in order to obey the one-hour curfew. A week later we learned that a revolution led by Colonel Gaddafi and his army had overthrown the government in Libya.

On approximately the fourth day of the trouble and in the midst of the curfew my doorbell rang again. This time it was not the bell of my apartment front door that was ringing, but the security door downstairs at street level. Gingerly I peeped through the bedroom shutters and could see it was my boss – the president of Occidental Oil. What on earth was he doing at my residence? I rushed down the stairs and opened the heavy wooden door, where Bob Espey, not quite his usual relaxed self, was hurried and to the point. As president of Libya's largest oil company he had managed to obtain a special pass that allowed him to break the curfew and go to his office. Being ever-generous, he had also obtained a pass for me! As his secretary, I was the only member of the staff in Libya who knew the code to operate the scrambling machine. I alone, and my counterpart at the American end, could send and interpret highly confidential messages. The code, which was committed to memory, was changed regularly. Messages were mainly of a technical or financial nature, relating to the running of the oilfields, but on this occasion I felt the text would be of a very different nature.

Bob drove his big, ostentatious, black Cadillac through the deserted streets, finally stopping the car at the entrance of the Mitchell Cott's Building, the home of Occidental's offices in Tripoli. We were met by a group of young soldiers, all heavily armed and looking decidedly unfriendly. Leaving the car at the front of the building, not normally a parking zone, Bob almost dragged me up the steps, flashing our passes along the way. There was much loud talking in Arabic, the soldiers uncertain that they should allow us into the building. There were no lights in the foyer, only another group of armed soldiers. Once inside we made our way up the stairs, not wanting to risk being stuck in the lift.

On arrival at our floor level, Bob went into his spacious office and I moved towards the tiny secure room in the corner behind my office where the scrambling machine lived. At first the soldiers did not want me to unlock the room but eventually we somehow persuaded them that the oil would stop flowing if I didn't get in. I sat at the machine, the air thick from the September heat and the odour of three bodies in a confined space with no air-conditioning. With an armed soldier flanking me on either side I prayed that they couldn't understand English. Bob had relayed to me in the car the message he wanted sent and my fingers visibly trembled as I proceeded to type. Not even Bob knew what had taken place in the country but he realised the importance of sending a holding message to our head office in Bakersfield in California.

Once my task was completed we made preparations to leave. We were instructed not to take anything with us but for some reason Bob had seen fit to collect from his office a round, silver-coloured alarm clock with two bells on top, which he carried by its handle. This attracted great interest from the soldiers, who inspected it very carefully, turning it over and over before finally deciding it was not of state interest, handing it back and allowing us to leave the building and proceed to the car. To this day I have no idea what Bob's reason was for removing the clock.

The curfew continued except for the one-hour suspension each morning to enable the purchase of food and essential provisions from corner shops. Apart from the gravediggers and workers at the spaghetti factory, who were requested over the local radio to return to their respective workplaces, everything else was at a standstill. Several days later Hadi came to deliver his daily supply of rations but somehow managed to miss the departure time that conformity to the curfew required. At least there was now someone to share the long, boring hours of confinement.

The curfew was eventually lifted during daylight hours only, and we all got back to work. Nobody knew what would happen under the new regime or had any idea what to expect from one day to the next. One thing, however, was certain. The old regime was definitely gone and members of the former government who were still in Libya were put in prison. Fortunately King Idris was in Egypt with his family, and most members of the government were also abroad enjoying the end of their summer vacation. Colonel Gaddafi and the members of the Revolutionary Command Council had no doubt cleverly timed the coup to coincide with these absences.

Libya, under King Idris's long reign, had been peaceful and prosperous. He was a mild, religious man and it appeared his people loved him. Now the atmosphere was very different. Rumours that many prominent Libyans had been put in gaol, that expatriates – declared as spies – were being thrown out of the country overnight, and that businesses and private properties were being appropriated on a daily basis, along with the establishment of the new government run by Gaddafi and his Revolutionary Command Council, all fostered an atmosphere of fear. There were many suppositions among the expatriate community. The usual conspiracy theories surfaced and speculation was rife. Some thought Egypt was behind the revolution, some thought it was America, and some argued it was Russia. Apart from the fact that a revolution had taken place, there was little else reported. We were left to gather information from any source we could find and draw our own conclusions, not knowing whether they were correct or not.

Neither Hadi nor any member of his family had been arrested but undoubtedly they were very nervous about their future. Nothing for them would ever be the same again.

Several weeks after the revolution I received the news that my father in Australia had suffered a heart attack, been admitted to hospital and had died several hours later. Because my passport had been lodged with the Ministry of Labour to renew my work permit, it was impossible for me to leave the country and get home in time for the funeral. Occidental tried every day to retrieve my passport but with everything now in the hands of the new Revolutionary Command Council it was almost impossible to get anything from the new 'government'.

Immediately on receipt of my passport I flew to Sydney to be with my mother and sister Kim. My mother was in a terrible state of shock and grief and I spent the next few days trying to sort out the tragic situation. My father had always taken care of everything and my mother didn't even know how to manage a chequebook. The city house they lived in came with my father's work and my mother and Kim would have to move, which would mean organising a change of school for Kim. She was only thirteen years old – I had been an only child for twelve years before she was born.

To my amazement Hadi followed me to Sydney, arriving unexpectedly a week later. To my further astonishment he brought with him a certificate from the British Embassy in Libya certifying that he had never been married. This, as he informed me, was necessary for a Muslim to marry outside his country. Was this a proposal?

My flippant attitude to Hadi's earlier proposal had now changed. When he had posed the prospect of marriage some months earlier I was still looking forward to broadening my experience of the world. However, the revolution in Libya, and the death of my father only nine weeks later, changed my life and outlook forever. For the first time I realised how uncertain and tenuous life can be. It was not just about fun and adventure and I had to become more responsible. Here was a man I loved, a man who loved me and wanted to protect me, and in my hour of despair had flown halfway around the world to prove it. Why should I hesitate any longer?

On 7 January 1970 Hadi and I were married in my childhood home, the caretaker's residence of the Sydney Law Courts at Queens Square. The building was commissioned in 1819 by Governor Macquarie to house convicts, and was still being used to deal with criminals. I had only ever known those courtrooms when I joined my father, or some other friendly face, when they were required to check on some small detail after hours. It was here that I played games with my young friends who visited on the weekends, and held noisy parties with older friends when I was grown up. The courtrooms were wonderful places for such occasions, with plenty of room to dance, no neighbours to complain about the noise, and containing nothing that could be damaged. Over a decade later, in 1984, while I still lived overseas, the building was changed to the Hyde Park Barracks Museum.

During our marriage ceremony in the family sitting room, surrounded by my mother, sister and a small group of family friends, I couldn't help but think the Muslim mullah with his long cream gown and burgundy fez looked out of place. The only thing he and Hadi had in common, from my perspective, was that they conversed in Arabic. The service was in English but its content was foreign to everyone except Hadi. My family and friends looked bemused by the whole affair. Kim, in particular, appeared confused and bewildered, and displayed a certain scorn for Hadi, which I attributed to her age and the grief of losing our father.

The wedding was a last-minute affair and far from an organised event. In the first place, up until a few days earlier I had had no thoughts of marriage. Secondly, and more importantly, I was preoccupied with relocating my mother and thirteen-year-old sister. Daddy's death at the age of fifty-five was totally unexpected and our home of over twenty years would be repossessed, as it came with his job. Providing for my reduced family was paramount and my wedding seemed a somewhat inconvenient intrusion and interruption.

Naturally at this time my mother was distraught with grief, her world seemingly at an end with no view to the future. I couldn't help visualising her in more normal times with her happy and friendly disposition. I had always marvelled at this side of her personality, which belied the traumatic beginnings of her life. Her father died when she was four years old and her mother died when she was ten, leaving her and her twelve-year-old brother. They were both put into orphanages but at the age of twelve my mother was sent to childless relatives in New Zealand, whom she had never met. Not ever would she elaborate on this period of her life other than to say how terribly strict Aunty Annie and Uncle Roo were, and that they would make her do most of the housework and chores. But then she would tell funny stories of how she sat on the window sill of her upstairs bedroom reading by a street light because they would not let her have a light on, and how eventually she would sneak out at night and run off to meet a friend. But she was so unhappy that at the age of sixteen she escaped from the house and stowed away on a ship bound for Australia. We have a newspaper clipping of her bedraggled arrival back in Sydney.

Now at forty-eight she again had to face life alone, a situation made worse by her first-born daughter marrying and returning to live overseas. I couldn't bear the thought of my mother and sister being evicted from their home again and it seemed that my one option to ensure their security was to buy them a house. The only way I could pay for this was to return to Libya to earn inflated oil dollars.

As a woman in 1970, in spite of my substantial salary, I experienced enormous difficulty trying to obtain a mortgage. Eventually I succeeded in securing both a mortgage and a house. Relieved at accomplishing my mission, the eventual day of our departure for Tripoli arrived. My mother and sister moved into their new home several weeks after Hadi and I left Sydney.

Hong Kong of course had to feature in our honeymoon, it being so much part of our initial meeting and a place we both loved. Hadi had booked a suite at the luxurious Peninsula hotel overlooking the harbour and on our arrival the hotel provided a Rolls Royce to collect us from the airport. During the next few days we shopped, were invited to a private box at the Happy Valley racetrack, and dined in the rooftop restaurant of the Mandarin hotel, overlooking the lights of the harbour. Everything was perfect.

Our next stopover was in India, ostensibly to break the flight but also to include a visit to the romantic Taj Mahal. The journey to Agra from New Delhi was uncomfortable and cramped in the back seat of a small dusty Ambassador hire-car. It was a cold morning and bumping over pot-holed roads, while dodging cows, oxen and stray children, I wondered if the two-hundred-kilometre trip from the capital to the seat of the old Mogul Empire was worth it. But as Hadi and I walked through the stone entrance and saw the shimmering white marble edifice at the far end of the long, narrow channel of water that runs to the base of the tomb, I was instantly enthralled.

My complaints about the cold were immediately forgotten as this renowned expression of love came into view. As most visitors know, the Mogul Emperor, Shah Jahan, constructed this magnificent mausoleum for his beloved second wife. The tomb was built on the bend of the Jamuna River to enable Shah Jahan to view it from his palace further upstream. It was easy to see why this structure is one of the Seven Wonders of the World and why it took twenty-two years to build. As we slowly walked hand-in-hand beside the shallow slip of water towards the front of the tomb, the refined elegance of the whole building was dramatically revealed, with its main central dome surrounded by four smaller onion-shaped domes and flanked by four minarets. The entire vision was sheathed in gleaming white marble. Not wanting to rush the experience but anxious to see more we walked up the steps and entered the central chamber. Again every visible element was covered in white marble. The only light that entered, other than through the open archways, came through pierced latticework and scrollwork in the marble. Delicate flower patterns and calligraphic verses from the Koran were inlaid with precious gems such as agate, amethyst, coral, garnet and onyx. Persian and Turkish motifs were evident and signified just two of the many countries from where the original craftsmen came in 1631.

On this winter's day there were no other tourists and we enjoyed the privacy as well as the splendour. Slowly we meandered through the archways and along the passageways, overwhelmed by the magnificence of this dedication to love. We left the tomb, impassioned by the atmosphere, and entered the formal walled garden where the sallow sun seemed to give greater warmth.

Reluctantly we looked at our watches and saw it was time to leave, so Hadi went to find our driver. I waited in the peace and quiet of the gardens surrounding the building and, sitting on an old stone wall, recalled the unplanned events of recent weeks. While watching my handsome husband of eleven days disappearing to the other side of the lawn I was deep in thought, grateful for the brief period of quiet contemplation after the turmoil I had been through.

Feeling relaxed but somewhat weary we climbed into the car, only to find that our driver was anxious to take us shopping before we returned to Delhi. In spite of our protestations we were transported to a secluded part of town where, hidden from view behind a drab exterior, we found ourselves in a rather palatial jewellery store. The first object produced was a twenty-five centimetre tall, solid gold elephant complete with howdah, encrusted with diamonds and precious stones of every colour. It had been specially crafted for the World Fair that year and was a magnificent piece of art. After we oohed and aahed over the elephant, objects and jewellery of every description were rapidly presented, none of which remotely interested us. A lot of fast-talking in Urdu followed, especially after I showed no interest in their diamonds. Foolishly, after dismissing the diamonds, I made the mistake of saying that I loved emeralds.

Next thing we were in a tiny, private room at the rear of the shop where 'father', the owner of the business, appeared. He was a small, charming, elderly man, and blind. He dismissed everyone from our presence except one son. The four of us chatted easily and sipped tea. Before the tea was finished a hushed instruction was given from father to son and in no time the most beautiful emerald ring I had ever seen was placed in front of me. Without missing a beat, the old man explained its history. Because of the enormous taxes the maharajahs had been compelled to pay recently, many were forced to sell off parts of their estates, including jewellery, to meet their debts. The three small perfectly matched emeralds and the twelve diamonds surrounding them had come from a maharajah's pin and had been crafted on these premises into the ring.

Whether the story was true or not I didn't care, the stones and the ring were exquisite. Hadi slipped the ring onto my finger and said if his wife liked it then she must have it. I was overcome by his generosity. I couldn't believe how lucky I was to have fallen in love and married this wonderful man who truly loved me, and who wanted me to be completely happy. What a profound life we would share. After collecting a receipt, including a history of the ring's background, we happily commenced the long drive back to Delhi in the afterglow of the wonders of the Taj.

All this exotic happiness was short-lived. We flew from Delhi to Rome to connect with our flight home to Tripoli and to my horror our first argument came in Rome airport at the end of our brief honeymoon.

A tall dark man in a pilot's uniform entered the first-class lounge where we were enjoying a cup of coffee and waiting for our onward flight. He reminded me of a very kind man I had been seated next to on the flight to Djakarta during my recent trip home to Australia. The rapid pace and mixed emotions of the past month had temporarily erased my memory of the incident. Now I turned to my husband to share the story with him.

My travelling companion on that earlier flight had been in civilian clothes but it transpired that he was a captain with Garuda Airlines returning to his home base. Our arrival in Djakarta was scheduled for about eleven o'clock in the evening and as my hotel was in the centre of town, a considerable distance from the airport, he had offered to give me a lift as it was on his way and his driver was meeting him at the terminal. This I gratefully accepted, as I had never been to Indonesia before, knew it to be somewhat unsafe for a young lone female at night, and a friendly face was most welcome. We agreed to meet outside the customs hall but unfortunately I didn't make it that far.

As I presented my passport to the surly immigration officer he abruptly enquired why I didn't have a visa. Dumbfounded, I stupidly said I didn't know I needed one. The next instant I was led away from the bustle of the arrivals hall to a deserted area at the rear of the terminal. I found myself in a back room surrounded by several uniformed men. All other rooms and offices were either closed or in darkness. The only signs of life were the guards standing around me, the majority with cigarettes hanging from their tight lips. It was a small cramped room with an overhead light emitting a dim, eerie glow. Most of the officers were armed, and I wasn't sure if they spoke English. As I sat at the small table their officious expressions and aggressive gestures made me feel like a wanted criminal.

The interrogation began and their dilemma was revealed. They could not allow me to enter the country without a visa, there were no more flights leaving until the following morning and the airport was about to close for the night, so what would they do with me in the meantime? The merry-go-round of questions continued for at least half an hour and I was trying not to think of the prospect of spending the night alone in an empty airport. Its atmosphere and the people servicing it so far had been hostile, abrupt and unwelcoming. The discussions, which I could not understand, were becoming more heated and the frustration was clearly mounting.

My spirits immediately lifted with the appearance of my newly acquainted pilot friend at the door. At least he could act as an interpreter. When I failed to meet him outside the customs hall he had come looking for me. God does move in mysterious ways and this night he was certainly looking out for me.

There was much shouting, arguing and general confusion between the agitated officers and my new friend, while I sat silently not knowing what was going on, but very relieved that someone seemed to be on my side. Eventually a compromise was reached and I was granted an emergency visa that allowed me to stay overnight in Djakarta then depart the following day to continue my journey home. My new friend had given up over an hour of his time to extract me from the clutches of bureaucracy and deliver me to the Marriott Hotel as promised.

Understandably, my gratitude for this man's kindness was immense. However, when I related the story to Hadi I couldn't believe the outburst of anger that followed. What did I think I was doing speaking to a strange man, and how dare I let him drive me to the hotel? The tirade continued. No wife of his would act in this way. Who had he married – a cheap street girl? These words from the warm, generous, urbane man I thought I knew came as a complete shock. I was not only embarrassed by his outburst in a public place but also horrified that he would behave like this. His shouting attracted the attention of the other passengers, and his palpable anger seemed to pervade every corner of the small, quiet room.

Why had such an innocent story elicited such rage?

I could only think back over the events I had just described. The pilot had been so kind to look after me and had inconvenienced himself by waiting around Djakarta airport for so long. If he hadn't been there what would have happened to me? Just because he was a man, did this make him 'off limits'? Was I not supposed to talk to any other men? Wasn't marriage about love, trust and respect? Yes, I was now Hadi's wife but what did he think he was doing speaking to me in this accusatory manner? And what was he accusing me of?

I had never seen anyone so angry before. I couldn't believe how his whole face changed – a black shadow fell across his countenance and he looked like a complete stranger. If this were what he thought marriage was about I would end it right now. I knew he was used to giving orders to his staff and to the labourers employed at his farms, but I was his wife! I had witnessed local men arguing and shouting at each other in Tripoli but they weren't educated, sophisticated people like Hadi. Did he think he owned me? I would not tolerate this behaviour.

It didn't take me long to decide what I had to do. I turned to Hadi and as calmly as I could, given my emotional state, threatened to leave him right there and then. Demanding my air ticket, I said I would not fly to Tripoli with him and there was no way I would entertain marriage to someone who behaved in such a manner. I slipped off my diamond wedding ring of eleven days, and the beautiful emerald and diamond ring we had purchased in Agra after our visit to the Taj Mahal, and held them out for his taking. Hadi simply ignored this gesture and continued to argue his case.

Brought up in a happy, loving family, I had never witnessed conduct like this; moreover I had never heard my father even raise his voice. He could get angry, and I had stirred that anger once or twice, but I was always punished by the withdrawal of treats or freedoms, never ever by shouting or vulgar behaviour. Certainly I had never heard my parents exchange cross words. Once, as a nineteen-year-old, I was taken aside by a slightly older friend who advised me that my family was not typical – in normal households there were usually fights and arguments, she explained. I assumed she was being somewhat theatrical, her over-dramatic self, and I paid little attention. Was the scene I had just experienced with Hadi an example of what she had warned me about?

I was totally confused by this change in Hadi's personality. Here I was on the starting blocks of my dream life with the man I loved, after a perfect honeymoon, and in less than two weeks it was disintegrating. Had I made a mistake in marrying this man? In retrospect, I must have felt a sense of wounded pride. If I walked away now I would be admitting failure and, deep down, I didn't believe that I had made the wrong choice. Part of a conversation I'd recently had with a friend while visiting Sydney sprang to mind. Marriage, she had told me bluntly, was all about compromise.

I wrestled to find some common ground. Then it came to me. Hadi's anger was not directed at me at all; it was at his staff. He owned a large travel agency serving most of the oil companies in Tripoli and his Italian manager, Bruno, had made all the arrangements for my trip to Australia. My mind raced back to a conversation with Bruno some weeks before.

During a social outing he had asked me, 'Aren't you afraid of Hadi?'

'Of course not,' I had laughed. 'Why?'

'Because all his staff members, including myself, are terrified of him,' Bruno replied.

'I can't believe that. He's never done anything to frighten me.'

Now it seemed reasonable to assume that Bruno was the one who had precipitated Hadi's outburst. Yes, it was totally Bruno's fault for not advising me of the need for an Indonesian visa, and had resulted in the circumstances in which I found myself on arrival in Djakarta. He had completely jeopardised my trip by displaying total incompetence and thereby embarrassing and annoying Hadi. Now I understood. Bruno's inefficiency had not only disconcerted Hadi but in his view had endangered his new wife. This incompetence and threat to my wellbeing was what had really upset Hadi, I rationalised, not my silly story at all.

Feeling sorry that Hadi had been put in this untenable position and knowing he would see it as losing face, I defused the situation by gently agreeing that my actions in Djakarta were perhaps a little rash. There was no further discussion. We joined the flight to Tripoli and I quietly reflected on this unsavoury incident and the future on which I was embarking.

In hindsight I realise how naïve I was. I was twenty-five years old but had never experienced a long-term relationship. I had been devastated by Hadi's behaviour but looked for reasons to excuse it. He had pursued me to the other side of the world and I was flattered by what I perceived as concern and attention. Not once did it ever occur to me that these attractive qualities might mask an obsessive and controlling nature.

Somehow during the flight from Rome to Tripoli, Hadi managed to appease my sadness and anger. He was always able to find a clever way of doing that.

Miramar Hotel Hongkong 15.1.70

TRIPOLI
Living a secret marriage: 1970

Back in Libya, Hadi and I knew we had to keep our marriage secret. We could not tell anyone except Hadi's mother and his youngest sister, Aminah. Hadi also had two older brothers and an older sister but I had not met them and believed he hardly ever saw them. If they were to be told it was not a decision in which I played any part. Being more traditional in their ways, they were not part of our married life. At the time of our marriage, Hadi had not spoken to his eldest brother for seven years. This was something I had great difficulty understanding. How could anyone not speak to a family member for that long, no matter what the disagreement was about?

One of the first edicts Gaddafi imposed after the revolution was that locals could no longer marry foreigners. We were aware that

Hadi, as a Senussi, was probably being watched by the secret police, but as we were moving to live in a multistorey, multi-entrance apartment building on the seafront, they were unlikely to make the connection that we were living together. Hadi left for his office at a different time than I left for mine and he also came home later than I did. I didn't change my surname and continued to work and go about my life on a daily basis as before. By continuing in this manner, we felt safe that our marriage would remain a secret. It appeared I was the same single working girl I was previously. I also regarded Hadi's reputation as a playboy as an added protective shield. People would not suspect that he had settled down with an unknown foreigner.

Our plans were to leave Libya as soon as possible and make our home in Europe. Before we could do this it was necessary to ensure that we secure sufficient funds outside the country to lead our new life. After the revolution, transferring any money out of Libya was illegal, so we smuggled it out in the best and safest way possible, but knew this would obviously take a little time.

Public entertainment of any kind had ceased and we relied entirely on our friends for any social life. Apart from my work colleagues I knew few other people so when Hadi said he wanted me to meet an American friend with his new English wife, without giving me any further details, I did not know what to expect. I had no idea that a lifelong friendship was about to commence. When I met Bill and Christine it was a welcome surprise. They were virtually neighbours; our apartment block comprised three towers and we lived in one of the end towers while Bill and Christine lived in the centre one. Bill had worked for Oasis Oil for over twenty years and had known Hadi for most of that time. He had not lived in America for twenty-five years. His first wife was Italian and now lived in Rome with their two teenage children. Christine, his second wife, was in her early twenties, slim and almost as tall as I was, with beautiful, flowing auburn hair, and large laughing eyes. She had met Bill while working as a flight attendant with British Caledonia.

We warmed to each other immediately as two young brides venturing cautiously into a new phase of our lives in an exotic and challenging part of the world. But most of all we were able to laugh at the absurdities of life in Tripoli: no water when you were expecting eight people for dinner, no electricity when we were in the middle of baking or the daily wash, and sometimes not being able to buy the most basic commodity because 'the ship had not come in'. Although sometimes difficult, we loved our life in Tripoli – the tranquillity of its white sandy beaches, where we held picnics and barbecues; the beauty of the desert that would spring to life after the tiniest drop of rain; and the company of an array of cosmopolitan, sometimes eccentric, friends, colleagues and neighbours.

Although life in general was very unsettled there was one promise I wanted to keep. Blair Cook, a very dear friend from London, had been looking forward to visiting me in Tripoli since my arrival some sixteen months before. We had met four years earlier, in March 1966, just after my arrival in London, when I was chosen as one of the ten Golden Girls working for the Australian High Commission to promote Australian primary products in the United Kingdom. Blair had been part of the interviewing panel at Australia House in London and during the ensuing twelve months became 'mother' to our team. She was tall and statuesque, with red hair and a peaches-and-cream complexion, offset by a pair of sparkling eyes. As the Australian Golden Girls continuously toured the United Kingdom, sometimes alone, sometimes in pairs and less frequently as an entire team of ten, Blair was our manager, a pillar of efficiency who arranged our travel, accommodation, briefings and debriefings for each assignment, and frequently joined us in the field when major promotions were undertaken.

The ten of us were in our early twenties, from different areas of Australia, with different professions but all having the same aim – to see the world. Few of us had had experience in public relations but we were all proudly Australian and our staunch patriotism ensured that we made a conscientious effort, whether we were promoting Kangaroo butter in a Scottish supermarket, Hannimax cameras in an Irish department store, or Australian wool at the York Races when the International Wool Secretariat sponsored the main race. After long days at trade fairs or delivering boxes of Australian apples or pears to orphanages or nursing homes, we changed to our more formal uniform to attend cocktail parties or special dinners organised in honour of Australian trade in Britain. Although it was taxing work, long hours and constant travel, we enjoyed every minute of it and made fun of our difficult predicaments and situations.

Being alone in a foreign country and a long way from home, we took every opportunity to meet up, sometimes driving a hundred miles to have dinner together. The British thought we were insane as they view distances quite differently on their small island and, in those days, many had not ventured beyond their own village. On one occasion one of our group, Georgie, and I were returning from such a dinner when our car ran out of petrol. It was one o'clock in the morning in the wilds of Scotland, not a situation one would choose. Fortunately as we sat in the cold on the side of the road discussing what we might do, a policeman drove by. When he heard of our plight he drove to the next village, woke the owner of the general store and came back with a jerry can of petrol. This didn't put us off at all; we just made sure on future occasions the car was full of petrol.

Stories like this were not relayed to Blair of course. We knew she would probably see the funny side of the situation, but we were not supposed to be driving around the countryside in the early hours of the morning and our safety was ultimately her responsibility. However, with her beautiful smile, happy disposition and wicked sense of humour she was just what a slightly homesick girl in a foreign country needed and it was always a delight to see her. Without fail she was available to advise us what to do in new or awkward situations, check our golden uniforms, straighten our berets, which had been created by a well-known hat designer of the time, Age Thurrup, or smooth our tailored shirts and jackets. Heaven help us though if we were less than perfect in any part of our dress or grooming – limp hair or an imperfect manicure were simply not tolerated. We all loved Blair dearly and after my contract with Australia House ended I regarded her as a staunch friend and we remained in close contact.

Four years later and married for only five months, I had invited Blair to Tripoli and eagerly awaited her arrival. Her great passion was Greek and Roman ruins, and the wonders of Sabratha and Leptis Magna on the shores of Libya were among the few she had not visited. In spite of the recent revolution with all its restrictions, Hadi was able to obtain a week's visa for her. Tourists were not welcome in Libya so the Roman ruins of Sabratha and Leptis Magna stood deserted in all their magnificent glory on the edge of the Mediterranean – with no fence, no guards and certainly no guides or other tourists in sight.

Sabratha, sixty-five kilometres west of Tripoli and almost completely excavated, was my favourite. Perched on the shoreline, majestically hiding the secrets of its past, the highlight is the theatre with its semicircular auditorium facing the sea. Once seating up to five thousand people, it is the largest in North Africa. At the back of the stage, Corinthian columns in various colours tower twelve metres high, resembling the front of a three-storey palace. At the foot of the stage is a marble relief of the Three Graces, the goddesses of joy, charm and beauty, who reputedly had the power to endow artists and poets with the ability to create beautiful works of art. In the total area of the ruins only one complete mosaic remained – the head of Neptune with his elaborate ringlets made of small brightly coloured tiles. At the baths, where the terracotta pipes and drains that formed part of the advanced water-supply system are still intact, it was amusing to show visitors the thirty-seat latrine. No visit to Sabratha was complete without a stop at the small family-run Italian restaurant with its delicious food and warm atmosphere. Housed in an adjacent villa, its tables were placed on a verandah overlooking the ruins, the golden sand and the calm sapphire-blue sea.

Twice the distance and in the opposite direction from Tripoli was Leptis Magna, one of the world's best-preserved archaeological sites. A city of matchless grace and beauty in 200 AD but sacked by Barbarian vandals in 455 AD, wide colonnaded streets had once led down to the port. There were two separate forums, or public squares, one with a Christian basilica next to it. In the market place were stone tables – some still retaining the marks used for measuring cloth. The once luxurious baths, featuring rooms offering cold, tepid or hot conditions, were all finely detailed with marble sculptures and columns. Hadi's father, as a political prisoner under the Italians, had worked on the excavation of this ancient hillside metropolis in the 1920s. All these years later, still only one-tenth of the original city was exposed.

Hadi and I visited both these archaeological sites regularly, and loved to speculate that we might find a Roman coin or some ancient artefact poking out of the sand, which was possible and not uncommon for the lucky fossicker in those days.

We watched as Blair's British Caledonia aircraft slowly taxied to a stop in front of the terminal building. The structure always reminded me more of a Nissen hut than an airport. Although square instead of semicircular, it was so temporary looking, and with a tin roof and squalid appearance, it was not a welcoming place. In fact, with its lack of air-conditioning, heavy odour of unwashed bodies and surly-faced officials, it was quite unnerving. The lack of females was also evident, as in many Arab locations, and if there were one visible she was generally lurking in a corner, swathed behind a full-length, white woollen baracan covering her from head to foot, with only one eye peeping out in order to view her world. Unless they were labourers or in uniform, the local men wore exactly the same covering but often with their heads uncovered, the baracan crossing in front, draped around their shoulders and a burgundy fez-like cap on their heads. For the men, both eyes were always exposed.

After glancing around at these depressing surrounds I looked up to see a vision of pink across the tarmac at the top of the airline steps. There was my beautiful Blair, like a luxurious powder puff in a pale rose-coloured linen suit with the ruffles from her pink chiffon blouse bubbling down the front, all offset by a large pink hat and matching parasol. She glided swan-like down the steps to the heat of the tarmac. This was a vision reminiscent of Ascot rather than a sandy, dusty terminal in the middle of the Libyan desert. But Blair's beaming smile and jolly disposition assured me that she had not noticed any of her surroundings.

The week Blair spent with us was a very happy one, highlighted by the farewell party we held, which coincided with the evening in June when Edward Heath won the election in Britain and took up his first term as prime minister. Everyone was happy and life seemed wonderful. The only comment I recall Blair making about

Hadi before she left was that I would certainly have my hands full – whatever that meant!

The days immediately after Blair's departure were lonely and I missed her bright, happy disposition every time I walked through the front door. But life soon returned to normal: going to the office six days a week – only a five-minute walk from our apartment – barbecues and swimming at the farm on Fridays, and occasionally visiting friends in the evening. This was our routine, week in and week out.

From time to time, I would suggest to Hadi that I do the shopping as his working days were busy and usually longer than mine. I was aware that it was customary for Arab men to buy the food and other necessities for the home. This prevented their woman from making contact with strangers or being seen by other men, and allowed them to spend the long hours necessary to prepare their traditional meals. But I was not a local woman. I knew Hadi wanted to shield me from any outside unpleasantness so he always insisted that it was too hot for me to be outside, too dirty, too noisy, that he knew the vendors and they would give him better produce, and finally it was for my own protection. Because I had many things to attend to in my limited time at home, I accepted his apparent concern, even though I believed it to be ill-founded.

One incident did unsettle me and the other girls in the office. Miniskirts were the height of fashion at the time, but living in a Muslim country where the local custom dictated decorum, no woman would copy the extremes that were worn in London unless she had no respect for the culture, and certainly no sense. The story of a secretary from another oil company who was picked up by the police as she walked down the main street spread through town very quickly. She was wearing a London-style miniskirt and they took her to the police station where her legs were painted black.

A welcome variation to our routine came when Dave, a colleague from Occidental, invited me to a birthday party he was giving for his wife. This was the first time I had been invited to their house and I was excited, particularly by the implication that I had been accepted as a member of their group. Everyone knew I was 'dating' Hadi and the invitation automatically included him. By the time we arrived at Dave's villa the party was already under way and Hadi knew most of the American guests. It was a welcome change to be in such a festive atmosphere.

On our recent trip back from Australia, I had purchased a length of silvery slate-blue Thai silk. Another stopover in New Delhi inspired me to fashion it into a trouser suit – slim, straight pants topped with a long-sleeved collarless Nehru jacket to which I had added small, silk-covered buttons. With this plain ensemble I wore a long silver chain with a square, silver Koran holder I had found in the old souk (market). Hadi, always looking handsome, wore a pale-blue linen suit and a white, body-hugging, short-sleeved Swiss cotton shirt, and smelt like a spring flower with an abundant use of Christian Dior Eau Sauvage aftershave. By comparison the other guests looked more casual, the women in brightly coloured gathered skirts or crimplene trousers and the men all without jackets.

In the dining room a delicious buffet was set up, with two large fillets of beef as the centrepiece, with a selection of sauces, including one based on *jalapeños* – the hot chillies of which the Texans were so fond. Numerous colourful salads, cold meats and small jacket potatoes completed the array. The sweet smell of barbecued corn crept in from the kitchen. A bar stocked with ample homemade brew took up an entire wall in the games room, while lively music echoed from the dance area and happy chatter filled the house. The relaxed fun and gaiety that existed behind those closed doors in the hidden depths of Giorgimpopoli were a relief from the austere martial law that was in evidence outside on the streets of Tripoli.

At one stage of the evening loud laughter drew my gaze to the other side of the room, only to see Hadi in full swing, telling a story to the surrounding group. Captivated by his elaborate hand gestures and engaging manner his audience hung on every word, waiting for the next sentence. His blinding smile lit up everything around him and emphasised the deep dimples on his handsome face. How proud I was of my congenial, urbane husband.

Everyone had a good time. Later in the evening Alan, a geologist from the company, asked me to dance. He was an excellent dancer and we took to the floor, executing our versions of the 'twist'. It seemed like only minutes later that the music changed to a slower pace. Before I had time to catch my breath, Hadi stormed across the floor and pulled me from the room by my arm, leaving Alan marooned. Without any explanation, we were through the front door and headed for the car.

'What on earth are you doing?' I trembled.

'How dare you dance with another man and let him hold you so close.'

'But we were only dancing.'

'I saw the way he was holding you, and the way you looked at him.'

'He is a colleague and a married man. What are you talking about?'

'That is no way for a married woman to behave. It is not acceptable.'

I was so shocked by this outburst I didn't know what to say or how to react. It was all so stupid and embarrassing. The silence on our drive home was overpowering and in my dazed state, I tried to fathom what had really upset Hadi. I searched for an explanation. It finally came to me. He had just returned from a long business trip to the Far East where the outcome of the negotiations had not been to his expectations or liking. This extraordinary behaviour at the party must surely be a result of his fatigue, jet lag and frustration. Perhaps the business discussions had been even more difficult and disappointing than he had led me to believe. Also, as a Senussi living in Tripoli after the revolution with secret police everywhere, there was the ongoing political strain that he underwent on a daily basis. All these things gave me excuses for what I thought was his irrational behaviour.

Tanya

LIBYA – TAIWAN
Wonderful news: 1973

By the summer of 1973 Hadi and I had smuggled enough money out of Libya to fund our future life in Europe and felt we could safely cut our ties and leave Libya permanently. I had also discharged the mortgage on Mummy's home, so that was no longer an issue.

Earlier on a trip to Spain we had purchased a two-bedroom apartment in Eden Roc, a building on the promenade in Marbella above the calm blue shores of the Costa del Sol. The apartment was brand-new and could only be described as luxurious. It had a long balcony running along the front overlooking the Mediterranean and on a sunny day Gibraltar was in clear view. This would be our temporary home in Spain until we could build our dream villa.

At this time Marbella was the jewel of Andalusia, and made famous in the early seventies by the jet set. A small fishing village, nestled at the foot of the Coin Mountains, it was particularly appealing because of its very attractive microclimate. In the mid-1950s Prince Alfonso Zu Hohenlohe had established the Marbella Club on the outskirts of the village, which catered to the rich and famous and brought renown to the area. Puerto Banus, with its extravagant and glamorous marina harbouring luxury yachts such as those belonging to shipping magnates Niarchos and Onassis, not to mention billionaires such as Adnan Kashoggi, was another international drawcard of this charming haven.

In spite of all the wealth that Marbella was attracting, the population was small and it still retained the charm of an old village, with its local growers' market in one area and in another Orange Square, where people congregated under the citrus trees for coffee and conversation. The locals were happy and looked prosperous, and the atmosphere reflected an easy, international holiday spirit. There were already a number of foreigners who had moved there either to try to find work in a more congenial atmosphere or simply to retire in the sun. For all these reasons it seemed like an ideal place for us to live. By contrast, the much larger centre of Malaga, an ancient port city to the east, was still creating its economic base and was home to many gypsies.

I handed in my resignation to Occidental and the removalist company was booked to ship our personal effects to Spain. On the day the packers came, my friend and neighbour Christine called in to help. There were men in each of the rooms packing and removing everything in sight so Christine's extra pair of eyes was a godsend. It was only a stroke of luck that took me into the bedroom in time to see one of the packers laboriously wrapping the wastepaper basket, complete with rustling rubbish. It wouldn't have really mattered if those cast-off scraps of paper had travelled to Spain but I couldn't help the horrible thought of the outcome if it had been the kitchen bin. It was a reminder of the cultural differences and how amazing it is that people can be so similar and yet so very different.

All was well until Christine anxiously called me to the front door. Here I saw our large American refrigerator being manoeuvred down the steep narrow stairs because it was too big to fit in the small lift. The heavy appliance was balanced on one man's back as several labourers in front and several behind took the weight. Then I saw it. A rope was tied around the fridge but also looped around the principal carrier's neck! There was so much shouting and directing going on by the men, all in Arabic, that I didn't dare open my mouth to interfere. We were on the tenth floor! Christine and I shot alarmed glances at each other and decided to return inside and pray.

Now devoid of most of our furniture and furnishings, that evening we went to Maureen's place for a final supper and to borrow a few essentials to get us by before flying out of Tripoli the following day.

After four years in Libya it seemed strange to be leaving for the last time, severing ties to a system where Hadi had influence and could arrange almost anything. I was used to the surly locals, the dirty dusty backstreets and the inevitable power cuts and water shortages. But I would miss the friendliness of some of the Libyans and their warmth. Our office tea boy, Ali, for example couldn't speak a word of English but his big toothless smile and greeting, *keif haalik* – 'How are you?' – each morning was genuine. Just before my first Christmas Day in Tripoli, Ali handed me a thumbed white envelope then hurriedly left my office. On opening the envelope, a card with the salutation 'Happy Birthday Grandmother' greeted me! Ali's name, in scratchy Arabic, was inside. It took pride of place among my Christmas cards and was valued more than most.

I would miss the beauty of the desert, which I had grown to love, the wonder of the Roman ruins at Sabratha and Leptis Magna, and the delicious taste of borek, the deep-fried crispy batter containing minced meat and sometimes an egg, which we bought every time we visited the old crumbling souk. But most of all I would miss our friends.

We flew to Marbella where we stayed for only a few days to deposit some of our personal belongings before flying on to Hong Kong. Hadi had won a tender for the supply of goods (that he had sourced from Hong Kong) to the Libyan government, and it was now necessary to finalise the contracts. Our stay in Hong Kong did not go according to plan when suppliers suddenly reneged on agreements made with Hadi some weeks before. This placed him in a precarious situation and we went on to Taiwan to try and set up alternative suppliers.

After bartering and haggling in tiny rooms in the back alleys of Taipei, it finally looked as though we were going to be able to fulfil our million-dollar contract. However, for the local bank to honour the letter of credit made out by the Libyan government, the document details would have to be changed to reflect the change in the suppliers' names. The quickest way this could be done was for Hadi to fly back to Tripoli, have the alterations made, and return to Taipei. I was left to wait in our hotel on the outskirts of the city.

Hadi had no sooner arrived in Tripoli when, on 6 October 1973, the Egyptian and Syrian armies attacked Israel. With the Yom Kippur War raging, all commercial air traffic in the Middle East ceased. Although the Arabs had the advantage of surprise – Yom Kippur (Day of Atonement) is the holiest and quietest day of the Jewish year – it wasn't long before Golda Meir's army took the lead. After Gaddafi's rise to power, Libya, for its part, had been financing the modernisation of the Egyptian army for several years as well as supplying them with French-built Mirage jet fighters. Fortunately, after two weeks of war the United Nations managed a ceasefire and commercial flights over the area recommenced.

Taipei in 1973 offered very little to the Western visitor. Once you had seen the Palace Museum, which was full of wonderful treasures including the largest collection of Chinese porcelain in the world, the Grand Hotel built in traditional Chinese palace style with its vermilion pillars, stately archways and tiled roof, and a small selection of souvenir shops near the American army base, there was little else to do.

Hadi had been gone for about five days and I sat, totally bored, in our hotel looking at the view. Thankfully our room was on the side overlooking the paddy fields rather than the unattractive buildings on the other side, but the view was not inspiring. The valley floor, stretching to the distant mountains, was flat and uninteresting, and not far from our hotel a murky brown river ran sluggishly like a drab ribbon across my view, reminiscent of the open sewers that criss-crossed the city. Autumn was well established and the grey cloudy sky added to the bleak scene. In the distance a couple of farmers trudged behind lumbering oxen, engaged in ploughing the muddy soil. Three or four trees relieved the dreary landscape but they were now bereft of leaves and there was not a bird in sight.

No matter how hard I tried to be positive this depressing view did nothing to lift my spirits. In spite of the cold I decided I would go for a walk as there was a shopping area not far from the hotel. The pavements were dirty and uneven, and along the edges, at intermittent intervals, stood transformer boxes, with electrical sparks dancing out in all directions as you passed. The streets were constantly crowded with people walking at a much slower pace than my own brisk step, and invariably headed in the opposite direction.

As I approached the entrance of a department store it looked like a welcome escape. But after a short time inside its stuffy interior, being pushed by the crush of humanity, I felt decidedly light-headed and in need of fresh air. I returned to the throngs on the pavement and remember being bustled along.

The next thing I knew I was seated in the rear of a car with a Chinese man on either side of me and two more in the front. Confused, I was aware of my head almost touching the roof of the small vehicle, a problem not shared by my companions. Crammed into the back seat, the men at my side were partially turned towards me, their bodies concealing the door handles. We were speeding along a main road in an area I had never seen before and none of my 'companions' spoke English. Pinned between my two 'escorts' I had no means of escape.

While the minutes passed, I struggled to gather my thoughts. My first realisation was that I had no identification as my passport was safely back at the hotel. As my head started to clear I didn't panic, but knew I needed to do some quick thinking. If we stopped at a red light and I created a scene what would that accomplish? People might look and be puzzled, even curious, but it was highly unlikely they would do anything to help me. Not a soul in the world except Hadi knew where I was, or worse, would know I was missing. There was no way of knowing how long it would be before Hadi returned to Taipei to find I was gone.

How had I landed in this situation? As we passed block after block and intersection after intersection I didn't dare think what my destiny might be. I could only wonder why on earth these four men would want to kidnap a very tall Western woman who made them look like dwarfs?

With a screech of brakes the car pulled up in front of a large, white multistorey building. I was dragged out of the car, marched through a glass door, and deposited at a desk behind which stood a young Chinese girl dressed in white. Hasty discussions in Chinese took place while I stood in the centre of the huddle feeling superfluous. The girl addressed me in broken English but by the time I discovered I was at the American hospital, my captors had gone!

A few minutes later I was ushered into a small consultancy room, where a young Chinese doctor stood and extended his hand. His manner was warm and the fact that he spoke English was a great relief. He explained that he had studied medicine and acupuncture in Taiwan but had completed his medical training in America. After he told me that I had been brought to the hospital because I had collapsed in the street, he questioned me thoroughly. Had I ever fainted before? No. Could I be pregnant? No.

After hours spent in different sections of the hospital, undergoing many tests, which all proved negative, the doctor said there was only one more test he could do. Another half hour or so later he announced that I was pregnant!

The hospital kindly arranged for a taxi to take me back to the hotel. This revelation had come as a complete shock as I had noticed no change in my monthly cycle. It transpired that I had been suffering some blood loss due to another problem, which was subsequently cured by the doctor. In the hotel I sat lost in thought, unable to share my exciting news with anyone.

Telephone communication with Libya from Taiwan was very difficult at that time. There was a six-hour time difference, added to which I had no idea where Hadi was staying. If he didn't know this wonderful news I could not tell anyone else; that would not be right. I wondered how he would react. Would he be as excited as I was? After all we hadn't planned for this to happen at this time. Now life would be complete, a new home in a new country, a new baby for us both to love and share, and the freedom to celebrate a new life as a family.

The Yom Kippur War ended and Hadi returned to Taiwan and was delighted to hear that he was going to become a father.

Because of problems with the various suppliers, our few days in Taiwan stretched to weeks, and then into months. We moved into a small apartment, I became Hadi's secretary, and continued to visit the young Chinese doctor, who oversaw my pregnancy. By the time I was in my eighth month, Hadi decided I should return to Australia for the birth. Although I had complete faith in my local doctor, the thought of having my baby at home in Australia was a far more exciting prospect. With my mother at my side for advice and guidance, no language problems and a familiar environment, everything would be perfect. Arriving home four weeks prior to the birth would also allow me time to shop for the baby's needs and not be restricted to what I could find in Taipei. There was the added bonus that the instructions would be in English!

The only negative in this plan was that Hadi would have to return to Taiwan the day after depositing me at home. It was also possible he would not make it back to Sydney for the birth despite assuring me that he would. Together we flew to Sydney and the welcoming arms of my mother, but Hadi returned to Taipei after two days to complete his contract.

Mummy and I had a wonderful time in those next couple of weeks, visiting baby shops, meeting friends for lunch, enjoying quality time together and relaxing at home. Because of the abundant nursery shopping Mummy had already done before my arrival there was little more to do, but we loved looking for new acquisitions.

Lying in bed on the night before the baby was due, I thought back to all the difficulties I had had four years earlier securing this house for my mother and sister. Originally, I was looking for a two-bedroom property but ultimately, in spite of the additional expense, was forced to buy a three-bedroom house. As Kim was now seventeen and living away from home, it meant that Mummy and I each had our own room and temporarily used Kim's bedroom, to her delight, as the nursery. As is so often the case, situations fraught with difficulties at the time often turn out for the best.

At two o'clock in the morning I gently woke my mother to say I thought it was time to go to the hospital. Mummy quietly suggested we should have a cup of tea and wait a while. This idea alarmed me, as I was afraid I might give birth in the taxi! Bowing to my mother's better judgement we arrived at the hospital some hours later. In 1974, arriving at a maternity hospital with one's mother was not altogether normal. The two nurses at the desk, after noting my name as Wilcox, asked who my companion was. Noting she was my mother and also a Wilcox, they then questioned me about the father. When I replied he was overseas on business the sneering glances between the two nurses were obvious. By this time I didn't care, I just wanted them to complete the paper work as quickly as possible.

Still using my maiden name after Hadi and I married had raised eyebrows before, when booking into hotels for example, but by now I was used to it. Originally, the reason had been to conceal our marriage from the Libyan authorities, and even though we had now left Libya, changing my name was not a priority. All my official documents were still in my maiden name and apart from receiving the occasional odd glance, it was easier to leave things as they were.

Our beautiful healthy daughter was born much later that day, and my mother and I remained at the Royal Women's Hospital in Paddington for eight days – a period of time unheard of now – the nurses' curiosity about the absent father still unabated.

May is my favourite month in Sydney. The warmth of the summer sun is still evident but the intense heat has disappeared and you know the onset of the winter chill is just around the corner. The clouds also seem to disappear leaving clear, pale-blue skies. It was just one of these mornings when I had to bathe Tanya for the first time. I was terrified. I used every excuse I could possibly think of but my mother, knowing her eldest daughter too well, simply made all the preparations on the dining-room table. She had spread two soft, sparkling white towels with pink embroidery on a white sheet. A tiny terry-towelling jumpsuit, a clean nappy and plastic protective pants sat next to the baby soap and moisturising cream. Before my arrival in Sydney Mummy bought a blow-up baby's bath, the likes of which I had never seen! Its bright yellow oval shape with sausage-like sides looked like a miniature whitewater-rafting dinghy. At least it could not hold much more than a cup of water, I thought with great relief. The gentle morning sun was streaming in through the lace curtains behind the table creating a scene I will never forget.

With much cajoling Mummy persuaded me to undress Tanya. To my amazement, the wet plastic acted like a magnet, and between the crux of my arm and Tanya's tiny slippery body, there was no space left in the bath for Tanya to roll or slip. To our delight Tanya loved the experience and we spent far more time oohing and aahing than we should have. Morning baths became the highlight of our day. It was at these special times that I really missed Hadi and was sad that he was absent for the first important events in his daughter's life.

Kim had returned for the weekend from her job in the ski-fields in order to meet her new niece. She joined Mummy and me on our regular walks through the nearby park, proudly pushing the pram. The leaves had not fallen from the trees but their gold and rusty tones embraced us with their warmth and added to our glow of happiness. At a slow, casual pace Kim, Mummy and I walked for hours. There is a large duck pond in Centennial Park and this was our favourite destination, where we would sit and gaze at Tanya as though she were the only baby in the world. I am sure Mummy's stature increased every time she saw someone glance sideways at the pram.

I also wondered if Kim's joy and excitement about her new niece might temper her attitude towards Hadi. After their first meeting following Daddy's death, she had avoided him whenever possible and treated him with disdain when she could not. Even though she was now four years older, the contempt she had displayed for him earlier still seemed as strong. Was this the reason she was not living at home during my visit, I wondered? Would this hostility ever disappear? Surely it would ease, given more time and maturity on her part.

With all the chaos of a newborn baby, and frequent visits from friends, the days passed quickly. When Tanya was five weeks old Hadi arrived back in Sydney to welcome his new daughter. A week later, after obtaining her first passport, we flew to Spain.

Alice & Tanya

SPAIN
The dream unravels: 1974–1977

Over the three and a half years I lived in Spain, Doctor Benjamin Spock was my saviour. Without his book on childcare, which I purchased in Sydney when Tanya was born, I would have been completely lost. I did not know anyone and did not speak Spanish, so he helped me with teething, temperatures, tantrums and all the anxieties of a new parent. Apart from this 'bible', I was completely on my own. If it wasn't in Doctor Spock's book, I did my best and prayed. I longed to pick up the telephone and ask my mother for advice, or even reassurance, but long-distance telephone calls from Spain to Australia were difficult and expensive in those days. Mobile phones and facsimiles were still many years away. There was no such thing as direct-dial; we placed all calls through an operator with no idea how long it would take to be connected. On good days it could take several minutes, on a bad day it might take hours. So to call my mother in Australia to ask childcare questions was not an option.

Marbella, where we lived for the first eight months, although very beautiful, was a small fishing village and offered little in the way of services and entertainment. Even visits to the paediatrician were a forty-minute drive. We could see the blue Mediterranean stretch endlessly from the narrow strip of sand below our apartment balcony, which was delightful, but there was little space for Tanya to explore once she was mobile. For all these reasons we decided to move, although we kept the apartment as a weekend retreat.

When Hadi returned from one of his visits to Malaga and announced he had found us a new six-bedroom home, I was delighted. Malaga, the capital of the Costa del Sol, is a port city some sixty-four kilometres from Marbella. The house was a traditional Spanish villa built around an enclosed courtyard, ideal for harnessing a curious toddler. It was remarkably similar to an Arab house, except for the Spanish archways and ornate black metal bars on all the windows and doors. At the front of the house was an ample lawn and garden that captured the fading afternoon sun. I was excited about our new home in a new town, a new neighbourhood, and the chance to make new friends and hoped that the daily palette of my life would be infused with new colour and movement.

The move to Malaga did not fulfil my hopes. The house was in an old, established suburb, where all the homes were large, mostly two-storeyed and surrounded by high fences. Apart from the neighbours on one side, who had school-age children, I was virtually unaware of another soul. A car driving down our street was a rare occurrence and I never saw people out walking. After several months I wondered where everyone was. The only sounds

I heard were the children next door arriving home from school and, every couple of months, the ringing of a bell by a man who rode his bicycle around the streets looking for business sharpening scissors and knives. Where could all the residents be? They were clearly very private, maintaining an anonymity that seemed impenetrable. The men might be at work but where were the women? Did they stay locked behind the high fences like the women in Libya? Did they drive each time they went out? In the end I assumed that the majority were elderly and, like most Spaniards of their generation, did not work but instead spent much of their time at home. By comparison Marbella, with its village atmosphere, seemed like a bustling and lively community.

After our arrival in Spain I noticed a change in Hadi's demeanour but put this down to our changed circumstances, which he would adapt to over time. We just needed a chance to settle. But there was one incident that struck a fundamental nerve. It was not linked to the strange behavioural patterns that I had recently witnessed but something that gave me a surprising insight into Hadi's basic values. From time to time this episode came back to bother me like an irritating itch.

Before we left Libya, having decided the Costa del Sol was to be our future home, we made a number of reconnaissance trips. In addition to the apartment in Marbella for our own use, Hadi was keen to acquire additional properties as investments. One of these was a large parcel of rural land in an area called Calahonda, on the outskirts of Marbella. Originally, the land comprised several family farms but now it was for sale as one lot. We returned to Libya and during Hadi's animated description of the land and the area in general, an American friend, John, became curious and showed interest in also investing in the area. Marbella was the latest destination for jetsetters in the early 1970s and development was proceeding at an ever-increasing rate. Hadi and John eventually came to an agreement to purchase the land in Calahonda jointly, Hadi owning the major share with seventy-five per cent. Everyone was happy, especially me, as John was my colleague and a close friend, as was his English wife, Valerie. In fact, I had made her wedding dress when they married. With an investment in Spain, they were sure to spend time visiting, especially once Hadi and I were living there permanently.

Barely more than two years after that happy partnership formed, Hadi and I were settling into our new Spanish environment. One morning Hadi returned home from visiting the municipal offices, Tanya was sleeping and we were discussing the difficulties of obtaining legal title for property in Spain.

From the outset I knew the price of the Calahonda parcel of land as well as the percentage share agreement between Hadi and John. Mathematics was always one of my strong points but despite many jottings and calculations, I couldn't understand Hadi's figures. Local taxes were due on the land and we were checking the sums. The less I understood Hadi's calculations the more agitated he became. Again and again, he went over the figures. Totally frustrated he went back to the original sale and John's input.

'But what do you mean he gave you twenty-five thousand dollars? The total price was only fifty thousand,' I queried.

'That's correct,' Hadi sighed.

'But John only bought a twenty-five per cent share, which would be twelve and half thousand dollars.'

'No. He agreed to buy twenty-five per cent for twenty-five thousand. That was our deal.'

'But you only paid fifty thousand dollars for the lot. You can't do that – it's cheating. It's dishonest. He's our friend.'

'No, it's business. I found the land and he agreed to buy it at my price.'

I couldn't believe what I was hearing. That was the beginning of a huge argument about honesty and ethics and ended with Hadi telling me I was a stupid woman who knew nothing about business. He jumped up, stormed out and slammed the door behind him. I was left to question my feelings of trust, belief and respect for Hadi, which at that moment were lying in tatters at my feet.

In Libya I had generally welcomed Hadi's wish to do the daily shopping. While working full time in Tripoli, I had plenty to occupy myself without worrying about this daily chore. When we lived in Marbella while Tanya was a small baby and I was adjusting to motherhood I was grateful for his help. But slowly over time I became frustrated with the routine. It became apparent that Hadi was of the view that, as an Arab man and head of the household, the daily shopping was his task exclusively. Whenever I suggested I join him on these trips he always had an excuse why I couldn't. The market was too dirty to take Tanya, it was too crowded, too hot, too cold, or it would interfere with her morning nap. He aggressively denied me even brief escapes from the house. When I suggested I would walk to the local shop to buy some basic commodity, Hadi would guard this as his right. It was not worth an argument or making him angry for such a trivial need so, after a time, I seldom suggested it. I had no desire to create friction and therefore trigger one of his furious outbursts so I let the matter drop. Irrespective of whether we needed anything or not, Hadi went off to town every morning to have a coffee in one of the many small bars where local men congregated to gossip and chat.

The beauty of the Costa del Sol together with its Mediterranean climate attracted many foreign retirees, especially from England, and it became obvious that we should look for friendships from among this group. These residents were somewhat out of our age bracket but at least there was no language barrier. The prospect of life at thirty with only seventy-year-olds as friends was a new concept and did not fill me with great enthusiasm. However, when Hadi told me about some ex-professional women who had formed a small group I was immediately interested. They had retired with their husbands to the coast, away from their native homelands, and in addition to playing golf or tennis met every four to six weeks for lunch. Hadi met them during one of his outings and they asked him if I would like to join them.

The long-awaited call from Vera eventually came. It was strange meeting her over the telephone but she sounded very friendly and her happy voice belied her age. As I excitedly dressed for the first outing by myself since our arrival in Spain I was sure this was the beginning of a new era for me, an opportunity to meet other women, make new friends and end my isolation. We were to gather in a small restaurant in the centre of Malaga. Vera informed me six other women were coming and were all looking forward to meeting me.

Tanya was over a year old but still had an afternoon nap after lunch so I knew she would be asleep for some of my absence. I kissed Tanya and Hadi goodbye and assured Hadi I would be back as quickly as I could. Over several months, on the two occasions when I met this group, I was delighted to learn things about the new country in which we lived. A recently opened shop that sold English produce, a second-hand bookshop specialising in foreign books, how much you should tip the gardener, all this information I had no other means of discovering. To my bitter disappointment after those initial two happy gatherings, Hadi's attitude changed. He complained about looking after Tanya, complained that I had been gone too long, and quizzed me endlessly about who was there and where I had been. After the second outing, he always found an excuse why I couldn't see the women for lunch, or even join them for a quick coffee at the end of their meal. It wasn't long before their invitations dwindled and then stopped altogether. I was back to my isolation. My attempt to establish a small pool of friends had been thwarted by Hadi's anger and hostility, and the brief flood of comfort I had started to experience immediately evaporated.

Several more months passed in our new home, and by this time everything had found its rightful place and all the alterations we needed had been made. There was little for me to do except prepare our meals, look after Tanya and supervise the housekeeper. I was bored and lonely and desperate to get away from the house and explore our new environment.

'Hadi, why don't we go into Malaga for a walk and look at the shops?'

'What do you need?'

'I don't need anything but I thought it would be nice to go out for a while.'

'Why would you want to go into the dirty, hot, congested streets with lots of people pushing and shoving?'

'If we go in the afternoon it won't be too hot, and it won't be as crowded.'

'Why would you want to subject Tanya to all that discomfort and other people's germs? She could catch something.'

'I'm sure she'll be fine. All the other children seem to be okay.'

'That is the problem – all the other children. You don't know what they have. Here you have a wonderful home and fresh air, Tanya has all her toys and is happy. Why would you want to parade yourself around the dirty streets of Malaga?'

'I just thought it would be nice to go out for a change.'

'That's your problem. You always want to go out. You are a mother now. Your duty is here in the home, not running around the streets of Malaga. You have everything here and you are still not happy. Other women would envy what you have.'

'I only wanted to explore a little bit of our new city.'

'There will be plenty of time when Tanya is older. You don't see these other women going off to walk the streets.' Hadi gestured with his hands to indicate our neighbours.

That is how our conversations went. I knew not to continue any further. Once Hadi had made up his mind you couldn't change it and to proceed would only end up with him shouting and scream-ing and going into one of his moods. Maybe he was right. I was no longer a career girl. Maybe I was expecting too much.

The weeks were long and repetitive for me and I felt caged being in the house day in and day out. Social outings for us were almost non-existent, which, after our non-stop social whirl before Tanya was born, was a huge readjustment. The other big change was that neither of us worked. The house was our sole domain.

When I first met Hadi he told me he would retire when he was forty, but as I had never heard of such an outrageous idea I thought he was joking. In my world, people worked until they were at least sixty and often long beyond that age. By the time we reached Malaga, Hadi was in his forty-first year, the prime of his life, but he never worked another day.

It was difficult to comprehend the sullen, introverted person Hadi had become since our arrival in Spain, compared to the fun-loving extrovert I had married six years earlier. I was reminded of the sun when it is temporarily covered by dark clouds; you can no longer see its glow but you know, or at least hope, it is still there. However, the longer the clouds remain the harder it is to believe. Maybe it was my fault. Maybe he was upset because I spent less time with him and so much time with Tanya. Perhaps some special time alone, just the two of us, would help. Then, while watching

Maria, our housekeeper, talking with Tanya in the courtyard, I had what I thought was a good idea.

'Hadi, why don't we get Maria to look after Tanya one night while we go out?'

'Where do you want to go?'

'We might be able to find a concert or something.'

'I haven't heard of anything like that in Malaga and doubt that there is such a thing.'

'Well, if that is not possible we could find a nice little restaurant and have a romantic dinner, like we used to.'

'Why would we want to do that? You know I love your cooking and we could get food poisoning or something. In any case, Tanya is too young to leave with a stranger.'

'Maria is not a stranger. She is a responsible woman, has raised five children of her own and adores Tanya. In any case Tanya would be in bed.'

'Why would you want to be running around at night? You are a mother now.'

'I just thought it would be nice for us to go out for a change.'

'You are talking like a stupid single girl. We have a child now and responsibilities. There will be plenty of time when Tanya is older.'

With my 'good idea' shot down in flames I had no desire to create an argument so let the matter drop. But I couldn't help wondering why I was so lonely and unhappy when continually being told I had everything and was very lucky. After living in Spain for over a year the only people I knew were the few people Hadi had met and introduced me to while we lived in Marbella. They were really only acquaintances and after we moved to Malaga they were too far away to see, except on our visits every few weeks to the coast.

There was one older English woman with whom we did maintain a closer association. Hadi met Edith soon after our arrival in

Marbella. She was a widow and lived in an apartment one block away from ours and took pleasure in seeing Tanya develop. After our move to Malaga, meetings with Edith were infrequent but I always tried to see her when we visited Marbella. After one particular incident, even those rare meetings virtually ceased.

On this visit, we drove Edith to Puerto Banus, the nearby marina, for a pleasant afternoon stroll among the luxurious yachts moored within its protective harbour walls. Towards the end of the afternoon Tanya was getting irritable so we bought her an ice-cream and decided it was time to move on and drive back to Marbella. I strapped Tanya into her baby seat in the back of the car next to Edith. She was tired and miserable and had missed her afternoon nap. Edith tried to pacify Tanya but she was out of her routine and creating a fuss. Even the ice-cream didn't improve her mood. She whinged and whined in her tired little voice as she wriggled within the constraints of her baby seat. Nothing Edith or I said made any difference and as the ice-cream slowly melted over her tiny podgy fingers she cried tears of frustration. Suddenly Hadi stopped the car on the side of the road, got out, opened the back door and screamed and shouted at Tanya. She was just over one year old at the time. Tanya's little face and big wide eyes registered a stunned expression before she burst into sobbing tears.

The overflowing well of anger and fury that accompanied Hadi's outburst was without warning and so violent that Edith and I froze in our seats. After shouting again at Tanya he flung the door closed, stormed back to the front of the car, got in, slammed his door, crashed through the gears and took off at great speed. I was so upset and so embarrassed I could not look at Edith. But as I turned to try and console Tanya, I saw Edith's eyes fill with tears and her frown of anguish. I also saw her blood boiling with wrath, but her stiffened body hugged the side of the car and she was afraid to say anything. The heat of the afternoon, the sickly sweet smell of ice-cream and the hurt in Tanya's eyes only added to my distress and the nauseous feeling in my stomach. I had witnessed these scenes before but it was poor Edith's first time. It was obvious she was both horrified and terrified. We hardly ever saw Edith again.

Hadi's whole facial expression changed when these outbursts occurred and his body seemed to take on a frightening strength and power. His voice would rise to decibel-breaking levels, his face blackened, his green eyes became dark slits and his manner was so threatening that I was almost scared to breathe. What held him back from striking people when in this state was always a mystery to me, and I dreaded that that day might soon come. A scene of this nature could last just a few seconds or several minutes, but in the heat of the moment time became suspended and the episode seemed more like hours. The aftermath was deathly silence. When it happened at home, I would tremble, fearful of doing or saying anything that would elicit another outburst. I would escape to another part of the house as soon as possible. This timid reaction was the only way I knew how to cope.

As a child I was chronically shy and always felt I was the odd one out. By my twenties, I had learned to camouflage this awkwardness – which I considered a shortcoming – and softly tiptoed through social gatherings with false ease. However, the pain of feeling different from everyone else and feeling alone persisted as an undercurrent of my being. Now with only superficial contact with the outside world the pain was reasserting itself, intensifying with every day. My insecurities were creeping back silently like a slow-growing cancer and taking over my entire personality without me realising it. The empty hole in the pit of my stomach never went away. I felt as though I was stumbling through life with a lantern, taking only a few steps at a time, unable to see a clear path ahead.

Gloom surrounded me and I was stalked by an unknown fear that shadowed my outwardly perfect life.

But one day there was a ray of light. Hadi came home from his morning visit to town and announced he had found some friends for me. While sipping his morning coffee in one of Malaga's small bars he heard distinctive antipodean accents coming from a table nearby. Introducing himself to the two women – Dorothea and Clare – he told them his wife was Australian and perhaps we should meet. They exchanged telephone numbers and to my delight our friendships began. At the time I was sure these introductions by Hadi were instigated to make me happy, but on reflection they were probably to control the friendships I made, or to confine me to the house and not allow me on the streets. Maybe it was so I would be grateful to him. The only people I ever met were through Hadi, as I never went out alone.

It seemed that having friends to the house was fine but going out to meet them was unacceptable. On their first visit to our home, I learned that Dorothea was from New Zealand, of my age, married to a Spaniard, Modesto, had two daughters, and lived a few minutes' drive from us. Clare was an adventurous, mature Australian woman who had retired to Malaga several years before. Although our backgrounds were different, our common nationality was a bond from the start.

The highlight of my week was when Clare and Dorothea came to our house to practise yoga. The ancient Hindu art had been part of my life since I was fourteen and I was always anxious to practise with friends at any opportunity. It was one of the few things that helped me retain my sanity during all those lonely years. Clare also had an excellent knowledge of yoga and it gave the two of us great pleasure to see Dorothea make good progress.

In addition to our yoga mornings there were also the many lovely surprise visits. The doorbell would ring – Hadi always answered the door, which he felt was his right as head of the household – then I would hear Dorothea's cheerful voice, 'Hello my dear. Just popped in to get that mousse recipe you told me about the other day.'

'It's lovely to see you. Will you have a coffee while I write it down for you?'

On other occasions, it would be Clare.

'I was just passing and wondered if you could lend me your copy of *The White Nile*? I've run out of reading material.'

They were my only visitors and these welcome diversions, whether they were for the purpose of borrowing something, returning something or just popping in for a cup of tea, brightened up my day and were a great joy in the long, lonely weeks. Along with my yoga, the friendship and sense of humour of these two women kept me sane.

In spite of my isolation, I somehow managed to keep myself busy – playing with and looking after Tanya, making most of her clothes and smocking pretty dresses. Cooking was something else I could explore and over the months, in addition to baking, I added pickling and preserves to my repertoire. Seville orange trees lined our neighbourhood streets and instead of letting the fruit rot on the path, I learned how to make marmalade.

By this time, Hadi was withdrawn and our conversations were reduced to topics concerning household routines or Tanya's latest antic. It was difficult for Hadi to make friends because men of his age worked during the day and were at home with their families at night. When I suggested that he sign up for lessons in drawing or painting, his only hobbies, he informed me that classes were stupid, they wouldn't teach him anything, and he was not interested. I tried to think of things that might engage him and allow him to meet people with similar interests. Apart from his trips to town each morning, he sat around the house all day with nothing to do.

When Tanya was almost two and more independent, I decided it was time for me to do something serious about learning Spanish. The two years we had been in Spain and trying to learn from books was all very well but I needed the discipline and expertise of a classroom and lessons. It wasn't too difficult to find the name of a school specialising in teaching foreigners and, luckily, it was only a couple of bus stops from where we lived. The classes took place in the mornings and I could be home in time for a late lunch.

Although Hadi was less than enthusiastic about my attendance and couldn't seem to understand why I was so anxious to learn Spanish, he reluctantly agreed to look after Tanya for the couple of hours I was away.

The first couple of days my excitement at being away from the house and finally at Spanish school blinded me to any negative reactions on Hadi's part. He insisted on driving me to the school each morning and collecting me at the end of the sessions. After several days at the school, he asked why I was so late leaving the class even though I arrived on time. If I left the building with a male student, he would ask me to whom I was talking. He complained about lunch being late, despite the fact I made sure it was prepared in the morning before I left for school and only required heating when I returned. When I tried to study in the afternoon or evening he complained that I should be playing with Tanya as I had deserted her all morning, or that I should be attending to some menial task in the house. After he complained about everything possible, he would then sulk and not talk at all. If I queried why he ignored me or why he was upset he would then go into a tantrum and tell me I was stupid, that I was exaggerating and creating problems. I tried to ignore his complaints and continue with the lessons but finally, when he insisted that he was no longer able to look after Tanya in the mornings, I realised that if I wanted any harmony at all in my life I needed to abandon the lessons. He had made such a fuss and created such an unpleasant atmosphere in the house that I had no other choice. Although I knew speaking Spanish was a crucial part of my living in the country, the lessons weren't worth the arguments and tension that followed.

Apart from those random visits from Dorothea and Clare, I was isolated in a big rambling house. Even though Hadi was at home most of the time, I was lonely. In fact I never went anywhere without Hadi; he even accompanied me when I went to my local hairdresser, two blocks away. Any outing without Hadi by my side just did not happen – he made sure of that.

Still unable to speak Spanish, even a casual friendship over the fence with the woman next door was out of the question. I only saw her on rare occasions because walls and hedges hid our house and I was inside most of the time. She had four school-age children and was perpetually rushing so even if I had been able to speak Spanish I doubted we would have had long conversations. There was always a warm smile and an 'Oolah', but nothing more. Why would she want to even bother trying to communicate with someone she had absolutely nothing in common with and no doubt thought was a bit strange anyway – an Australian woman so far away from home, married to an Arab, living in an established, traditional Spanish suburb and not able to speak the language?

She would never know how I held on to those 'Oolahs' for so long and wished one day they would lead to something more. She was approximately my age, attractive, vibrant and a mother, and I didn't even know her name. Spanish people love children so she would always make a fuss of Tanya if she saw us together but inevitably it was a brief interlude in what appeared to be her busy life. If only I could converse in some small way other than body language.

One day while playing with Tanya in the front garden I noticed a shiny black cat slink through the high hedge that lined our fence. He was a most handsome cat and Tanya's squeals of delight did not deter his curiosity. 'Cat', as we christened him, became a regular visitor, in spite of the way Tanya chased him from one corner of the garden to the other, and the awkward way she picked him up, leaving him dangling from her arms like a tangled net. Every time 'Cat' visited I wondered where he came from, what kind of life he led, the other people he had seen. How I wished he could give me news or details of the world around me.

There must be something wrong with me. Why was I so ungrateful for the bounteous good fortune that life had bestowed on me? Here I was with what I had always believed to be everything – a husband who loved me, a beautiful healthy daughter and a comfortable home. Hadi had given me beautiful jewellery, I wore designer clothes, we lived in the wealthiest area of Malaga, and every time we went out in our latest Mercedes coupé people stopped and turned their heads in our direction.

What was I looking for? Seemingly I had everything but I was desperately unhappy. Would I ever find the missing component and how would I look for it? How could I ever admit or explain such a shortcoming in my character? When we drove past the poorer areas of the city and through the villages of the less fortunate in the rural outskirts of Malaga, I noticed that although the people had so little they were always happy and laughing. What magic ingredient did they have that I didn't? I felt I was viewing life from inside a goldfish bowl, looking out at real life from within – and the confines of those shiny glass walls were suffocating.

Hadi's bouts of anger were becoming more and more frequent. I never knew what would spark his ire and frequently I could see no reason for it at all. On a good day he would scream and shout then disappear in a rage to another area of the house. At other times his whole body seemed to expand and shake, his face would blacken, and he would take on the power and fury of a raging storm. These outbursts were terrifying, and when displayed outside the house I feared he didn't know what he was doing. The happy, carefree man I loved was less and less apparent. The bouts of fury were seldom directed at me, but sometimes were directed towards Tanya. He would scream and shout at her until her terrified little body would shake and her sobbing tears flowed uncontrollably. This concerned me more than anything else.

The weeks continued to drag by. It was after Tanya's second birthday that my mother arrived from Australia to spend six weeks with us during the European summer. She missed both Tanya and me terribly and was overjoyed with the amount of time she could now devote to the two of us. Soon after she arrived, she asked why the gate that led from the street into the garden at the front of our house was locked and chained. I explained that Hadi had put this in place to ensure Tanya couldn't get out onto the street.

'But there are two heavy six-foot metal gates and a solid lock. Tanya could never open those,' Mummy said in bewilderment.

'I know, but he just wants to be sure,' I replied defensively.

I refrained from telling her that this was the latest in a series of locks which had previously been placed on the front door, the back door and rear garden gates.

We spent happy days together at the beach, at the parks, and generally showing Mummy around Malaga and the Costa del Sol. One evening as we were having dinner the telephone rang. Hadi returned from the call to say his sister Aminah, her husband, Ibrahim, and their three daughters were arriving in a few days to spend a week or two with us. After the revolution in Libya, they had moved to France and had visited us the previous year for a couple of days when we were still living on the coast in Marbella. Our apartment there was not large enough to accommodate them, but now in our six-bedroom, two-storeyed house there was plenty of room.

Aminah, blonde, fashionable and the youngest of Hadi's siblings, was without any doubt his favourite. They were close in age and, because of the gap between them and the other three siblings, had much more in common. I had always found Aminah's husband, Ibrahim, charming. Although he was a successful businessman of considerable wealth, he had a very down-to-earth attitude and a lovely sense of humour. He adored his wife and daughters and had always shown me great respect and hospitality. I was fond of them all and knew Tanya would be delighted to have three young cousins to play with. Mummy had not met any of Hadi's family so I was particularly pleased that she was to have this opportunity to get to know them.

The planning for their visit began almost immediately and by the time they reached our home there was great excitement. The day after their arrival we went to a local beach, where it gave me great satisfaction to see Tanya happily playing in the sand with her cousins, finally having the opportunity to mix with other children. It was a very active day for them and that evening we bathed all our girls and put them to bed early. It was then the adults' turn to relax over dinner, which had been prepared well in advance, and enjoy a glass of wine.

We had finished dessert and I was just thinking of clearing the table. The delicate perfume of jasmine and the sounds of crickets drifted through the dining-room window. I had used our best Swiss-embroidered linen, Limoges china and Christofle silverware but it was now all in disarray. The yellow candles had burned down and even the white bougainvillea from our garden was wilting. Aminah and my mother were engaged in warm conversation but paused when the Arabic conversation between Hadi and Ibrahim escalated to a much higher pitch. We watched as their expressions hardened and before long their voices were at screaming point. The shouting and yelling continued unabated. After a number of minutes, Aminah started yelling at Ibrahim and Hadi in what I assumed was an attempt to have them stop.

Mummy, who was opposite me at the table, sat with her mouth open and her eyes stretched in amazement like bubbles on the point of bursting. I could see she was shocked by this behaviour and, like me, had no idea what was going on. The arguing continued, and I noticed Mummy cowering in her chair. Just as I was wondering if our neighbours could hear this frightening tirade, Hadi brought his fist down on the mahogany tabletop, and the china, cutlery and crystal glasses all danced in unison. Ibrahim jumped up from his chair, red in the face, and still shouting. Next thing Hadi and Aminah were also on their feet, both shouting together. Aminah rushed to Ibrahim and forcibly led him from the room. Hadi soon followed, while Mummy and I remained seated at the table, shaking in stunned silence, having no idea what had caused the altercation. All I could do was wonder what she must have been thinking. Here were two grown men almost coming to physical blows over the dining table, the likes of which I was certain she had never witnessed before.

The fact that this incident happened in front of my mother shot my anxiety for her peace of mind to a new level. I knew her concern for my health and happiness, like any mother, was always foremost in her mind. She would think that if Hadi could behave like this in public, what would I, as his wife, have to suffer in private? Was this scene she had just witnessed a glimpse of the reign of terror under which I lived? The episode frightened me because for the first time I fleetingly wondered if I was denying the truth and trying to avoid the reality of my situation. Was I trying to shield Hadi's behaviour from the world? Was I embarrassed that I had made a mistake in this marriage? For my mother, all the generous things that Hadi had done during her visit would fade into the background – the horror of this scene was what she would remember when she was back in Australia and it would stab at her mind.

We waited a long time, slowly whispering to each other in confusion, before we cleared the dishes from the dining room to the kitchen. As everything was now very quiet with no sign of Hadi, Aminah or Ibrahim anywhere, we decided to go to bed.

The following morning when I got up and went out into our courtyard, I asked Hadi where the children were. In a matter-of-fact way he told me that Aminah and Ibrahim had packed, departed and wouldn't be returning. This was all before eight o'clock in the morning!

I couldn't believe this had happened. When I asked why he and Ibrahim had argued, all I was told was that Ibrahim was stupid, he always made trouble, and Hadi would never speak to him again. Mummy and I were still on tenterhooks as a result of the incident and, being uncertain as to Hadi's frame of mind, moved around very gingerly for the rest of the day. For the remainder of Mummy's visit I could tell she was uncomfortable. I could sense her fear that she might do or say something that would elicit another outburst.

After my mother left, I felt the emptiness of my life more than ever. We had no real plan for our future, we were not making any inroads into local life, Tanya was growing up cocooned in an unnatural environment, and there seemed no purpose to anything. Talking to Hadi about my concerns or trying to make him see reason was impossible. His reply would be either that I was exaggerating or I was stupid. Whether it was about our future, about some business idea he had, or how he saw Tanya's future, it was always the same; either I didn't know anything about it or I had no idea what I was talking about. In fact being told I was stupid was a regular response to many things I said.

In my isolation, I sought comfort in reading, especially at night while Hadi watched Spanish television. I had a number of books in my own library that had come with us from Libya and I knew I could always rely on Clare to supplement my supply. But even reading elicited scorn. Hadi informed me that books were rubbish and only filled my head with nonsense. Ultimately it was easier to conform than to create tension and arguments. His constant undermining of my actions and his continual psychological abuse were coming close to making me believe some of the things he was saying.

The only things Hadi talked about on a regular basis were his ideas for new business ventures. They ranged from building a hospital in Spain specialising in medical treatments exclusively for Arabs, manufacturing jeans in a nearby suburb, designing fancy frames for sunglasses, opening a coffee shop and tea house, and importing furniture from the Far East. He talked endlessly about each idea as it arose and on occasions travelled to Madrid or Barcelona to try and find someone who was interested in a joint venture. Envelopes containing reams of papers and brochures would arrive in the mail after these business trips, most of which were never opened. Telephone calls from people he met were not followed up.

The one highlight of my day was at noon, tuning the radio in to the BBC for the world news. An update given by reporters from the current hot spots in various countries around the world followed the news. All those familiar English voices with the latest details on life on the outside were wonderful company in those empty rooms. Although most of the stories were depressing and about the latest catastrophe, they made me feel connected and grateful for everything I had.

I was so lonely and ached for the intimacy that did not exist in my life. When I first arrived in Spain as a wife and mother, over three years earlier, I had not been daunted by the prospect of being a foreigner, unable to communicate with the local people, because I had excitedly looked forward to learning the language and experiencing a new way of life. It would be the start of a new adventure. I never dreamed the adventure would turn into a nightmare.

Hadi's possessiveness became more evident and more obsessive every day. He would not let me drive our Mercedes, claiming it was too big and powerful, even though I had previously driven sports cars and big American vehicles. As well as being denied the opportunity to learn Spanish, and not being allowed to walk outside the garden walls by myself, our house was kept under lock and key. Trapped as a prisoner in my own home, with no communication with the world outside, my sense of isolation escalated.

Hadi insidiously assumed control of every aspect of my life: I had little or no say in what we ate as he did the shopping; I had little input into what we purchased as he would see things he liked, then take me to see them before he bought them; I had no involvement in where we went as he made the plans or arrangements; I could not choose friends or acquaintances without his approval; and he controlled our love life, which virtually became non-existent. It was as though he had placed me in a rarefied chamber like a prize possession.

I was certainly not permitted to have anything to do with the financial running of the house or our financial affairs. Even though I had handled millions of dollars when working for Occidental, and was responsible for the ship's cash when working aboard a round-the-world cruise liner, I now didn't even have an allowance. If I was out with Hadi and I needed to buy a postcard or a sheet of tracing paper I had to ask for money. The only source of financial independence I had was my bank account in London, set up when I first arrived in 1966 and retained through my working days in Libya.

Hadi became obsessed with secrecy and security. As my mother had noticed, our house was like a fortress, with locks and bolts on the doors and chains on the gates. On one occasion, while away on a business trip for several days, Hadi took with him all the keys to the house and the keys to the locks and chains on the gates. Tanya and I could go into the garden or the inner courtyard of the house but if we had wanted to get into the street we would have had to climb a four-foot hedge and fence. On his return when I questioned him about this I was made to feel that I was the one being absurd; it was done for our own safety.

Any mail that arrived was immediately collected and squirrelled away, unless it was marked to me personally from someone Hadi knew. As far as I could see there was nothing important and it was mainly bills, but when I asked what he'd received I was told it didn't concern me and I shouldn't worry about such things. He did not even trust our housekeeper, who had been with us since our move to Malaga. After telling me not to be so friendly with Maria, he also told me to watch when she was cleaning because he was sure she was searching through his papers. What papers? There was nothing secret that I knew of and they were in such a terrible state of disarray I doubted anyone could make sense of them. He was so suspicious of everyone and so secretive I sometimes wondered if he was hiding something from me.

This abnormal behaviour and paranoia just seemed to intensify. Some days he would be in such a black mood he would stay in his pyjamas the entire day, either watching television or sketching and painting. This inertia, together with his violent and furious outbursts, made me wonder if he had become unhinged.

Another winter passed and we were experiencing a warm tranquil spring before the intense summer heat. We had been in Spain over two years when one bright spot appeared on my horizon. My dear surrogate mum, Alice, was coming to visit us from England and I anxiously looked forward to seeing her.

I had invited her to come and stay with us for a holiday as Pop had passed away earlier in the year, and I knew she would be lonely and need some nurturing. She and Pop had been so good to me when I had arrived in London all those years ago. After my year as a Golden Girl finished, when I had travelled the length and breadth of the United Kingdom, I took a public relations job with the International Wool Secretariat in London. This made it easier to keep in contact with Pop and Alice and we could see each other more frequently.

There was much excitement in 1967 when they had to come to London for Pop to receive his Order of the British Empire from the Queen at Buckingham Palace. I asked them to stay overnight at my small but comfortable bed-sitter. This not only allowed me to see them but also to repay some of the hospitality I had received. After the excitement of the day, the three of us shared a wonderful, jovial evening. Now, ten years later, I was married, had a baby daughter and lived in Malaga.

Hadi and I collected Alice from the airport. She was now in her eighties and seemed even smaller than her mere one hundred and fifty-two centimetres. She still had the same short, tightly permed grey hair and granny glasses. I was relieved to see her small frame still bounced along at great speed. But when she emerged from the customs hall I was somewhat shocked at her dismissive greeting and her urgent need to get out of the terminal as quickly as possible. While silently walking to the car I was afraid that Pop's death might have had more effect than I realised, that perhaps she had undergone a slight personality change. Hopefully the holiday would help. Once safely in the car and out of the airport, Alice's laughter filled the car.

'Thank goodness. Now that I am clear of customs, I can relax.'

'What do you mean?'

'Well my dear, my suitcase is half full of cigarettes and alcohol,' Alice announced with a chuckle.

Absolutely shocked at this news, but highly relieved there was a reason for her uncharacteristic behaviour, I chastised her.

'Alice, do you know what would have happened if you were caught?'

'Don't be silly, my dear – they never bother about little grey-haired old ladies.'

Thank goodness they hadn't. Alice's wicked sense of fun had certainly not diminished and this was the same Alice I knew and loved. I was so excited and looked forward to the ensuing two weeks.

The time flew by. Our happy days swimming in the clear blue Mediterranean Sea outside our apartment in Marbella, walking and laughing our way along the sandy beach, and the fun of shopping for souvenirs, were over all too soon. Hadi, Tanya, Alice and I had done everything together, both in Malaga and Marbella, so I was a little disappointed that I had not had the opportunity to spend any time alone with Alice. Nevertheless, I enjoyed more laughs in those two weeks than I had done for ages.

On the eve of her departure I was terribly sad at the thought of her leaving and did not want her to go. After dinner when Tanya was in bed, Alice came and asked me to help her with the last of her packing. I knocked on her door. Hurriedly she pulled me into the room, closed the door and sat me on the bed. Her luggage was closed, locked and neatly lined up by the wall. I was confused. I thought she wanted me to help her pack. In her very matter-of-fact way she waved her index finger at me, as though scolding a youngster, and said,

'You know you have to leave, don't you?'

I was speechless. As far as I was aware, there had been no really bad outbursts from Hadi during her stay. To my relief he had been an attentive, charming host and his friendly, amusing former self. I did not think he had shown any of his controlling, manipulative traits. Clearly my efforts to conceal any tension had not worked.

Alice's next statement took my breath away.

'Even if you have to leave the child behind, you have to go.'

I could not believe my ears. This loving grandmother was speaking words I could not comprehend. Then there was a knock on the door and Hadi's voice came through the locked entrance to the room.

'Do you girls need any help?'

Fortunately Alice reacted quickly and replied that we had finished. She opened the door, but not before glaring at me and forcefully whispering, 'You do understand, don't you?'

The only thing I could think of in those few seconds was whether Hadi had heard our conversation. Maybe Alice suspected that he was listening all along. The following morning as we said our final farewells at the airport, Alice hugged me tightly and whispered, 'Promise you won't forget what I told you last night.'

Then she was gone. Her words continued to haunt me as I struggled through the endless unhappy months that followed. I was always expecting a storm, living my life without a weather report and never certain when a hurricane might strike.

One morning, as I was playing with Tanya in the garden, my spirits were boosted when Hadi called me to the telephone. Telephone calls for me were like moon landings. They came infrequently. It was a dear friend from Australia, Barry, to say he was visiting London and could he come to Malaga to see us? When I was in my early teens, Barry was rumoured to be my first boyfriend. We had remained very close over the years, and he had become part of my Australian family. During my absence, he remained constantly in touch with my mother and father and I relied on him to give me any 'bad' news from which my parents thought I should be protected.

Hadi had met him, and his present partner, John, several times during our visits to Sydney and, I thought, enjoyed Barry's engaging and amusing company.

The excitement of having an old friend from home visit us in Malaga was intoxicating and I spent days planning an itinerary as well as all the exotic meals I would prepare. Two days before Barry was due to arrive, Hadi, while in one of his rages, announced that Barry was not to come. My disbelief was so intense I continued with my preparations for his arrival. It wasn't until Hadi stood over me at the telephone and forced me to call Barry in London and tell him not to come that I accepted the reality. I cried bitterly and wallowed in my sorrow and loneliness. Hadi never gave a reason. Was it that in our teens Barry was regarded as my boyfriend, or was it that he was gay? Try as hard as I could to get Hadi to discuss his reasons, it was a closed subject, as was everything that was not to his liking.

I knew my personality was being dramatically suppressed. At the same time, my concern for Tanya's future also grew. Here she was, detached from relatives and friends, a foreigner whose parents – especially her mother – were not part of the community. In addition to this, my fear for her physical wellbeing emerged. There was no doubt that Hadi was a devoted father but on a few recent occasions, while in the depths of an outburst of rage, he had come close to hitting her. He had certainly shaken her once or twice and this frightened me. I was afraid that in a fit of rage he would unintentionally hurt her.

All these thoughts rushed around in my head, making me wonder if this was what dear Alice had meant on that fateful last night of her visit to us in Malaga. In fact, I now realise it was after Alice's visit that the wheels of my brain slowly went into motion.

I was facing an agonising dilemma. In Muslim culture the male is revered and is always right. From birth they are treated as special and can do no wrong. Paternal possession is their birthright. But I had thought Hadi was different. He had spent his adult life with Westerners. He had married and loved a Western woman who worked for the first four years of their marriage. I told myself that Hadi was basically a good person. Yes, he had become very erratic, but I still clung to the hope that this behaviour would pass.

Hadi had assured me he was very happy but I suspected that he found it difficult living in Spain away from his family and country. He had walked away from his businesses and now had nothing to fill his days. But his change in personality was something I couldn't deal with. I reasoned that if I could spend some time in Australia I would have the opportunity to think, to clear my brain. If I was able to talk to my family and friends I would be able to form a plan and find help. When I tried to discuss my concerns about Hadi's peculiar behaviour with Dorothea and Clare in Malaga they simply replied that Hadi was either mad or psychotic and there was nothing I could do to change him. But I hoped that with time and the love of my family I would find a way to solve the problems and regain the man I loved.

Hadi, of course, would have denied there was anything wrong. Therefore, I never raised the issue for fear of how he would react – undoubtedly with indignant and bitter resentment before flying into a frightening rage. He would have somehow punished me for suggesting there was a problem.

Thus it was that my plan of escape evolved over the next eighteen months following Alice's visit. I would have to wait until Hadi disappeared on one of his periodic business trips. As long as he was away for more than twenty-four hours there would be enough time to pack Tanya's toys and belongings and my own clothes, buy an airline ticket and leave the country. The minor details could be worked out on the day. In the meantime I could not utter a word about this plan to a single soul. Every time these thoughts came into my head I knew I was embarking on very dangerous territory and beads of perspiration would form on my forehead. If Hadi ever read my mind, heaven knew what the consequences would be, so I could only think about these plans when he was not around.

The opportunity for escape finally presented itself when Hadi announced he was going away on business. Once he had departed I contacted a transport company in Malaga that delivered overnight freight to England, arranging for them to collect the bulky items I could not take on the plane. In England it would be easy to organise their onward freight to Australia. After buying the air tickets, the day before Tanya and I left, I told Dorothea what I was doing and asked if she would drive us to the airport. The whole plan was carried out as clandestinely as possible; I wanted to ensure that we left without anyone seeing us.

Outside 1977

LONDON
Abduction: December 1977

When I realised it was Hadi standing at the front door of Elm Road, I found myself frozen to the spot. How on earth did he find us? What should I do – slam the door, scream, or move outside the door to prevent him from entering? The noise of my pounding heart was so overwhelming that my thought processes ceased functioning.

In the minutes that passed during my shocked silence, the figure on the doorstep, instead of resorting to the violent rage I had expected, pleaded forgiveness and only wanted to talk. There seemed no civilised alternative but to allow him inside. At first Tanya would have nothing to do with him. Maybe, like me, she didn't recognise him in his new English garb. But eventually she went to him and seemed genuinely pleased at his presence.

Hadi pledged his love for Tanya and me – something I had never questioned – and implored me to return home to Malaga. He talked, he even cried, and to my relief he did not once become hostile.

I explained why Tanya and I were at Maureen's house, that it was still too soon for Tanya to be allowed to fly but thankfully she was much better than she had been. When finally I asked him how he had found us, he said he had gone to Occidental, told them Maureen was an old friend, and had been given her address. Knowing the company's privacy policy, and my own experience only days earlier when I had been unable to get this information myself, his explanation seemed highly unlikely. To this day neither Maureen nor I know how Hadi managed to persuade the staff to bend the rules. However, I had witnessed Hadi's powers of persuasion on many occasions over the years, his ability to convince people that something was in fact the opposite to what it really was. His charming and silver-tongued manners could work wonders and I had watched in amazement when he had put on these performances.

At the end of the afternoon Hadi asked if he could come again the following day. There was no way I wanted him to come, but with this broken man in front of me I felt powerless to refuse.

That night I barely slept. My desertion from our marriage continually played on my mind and I kept going back over our life in Spain – the good things and the not-so-good things. Among the happy memories were the occasional weekends spent with Dorothea and Modesto, and their daughters Emma and Beatriz, who were five and seven years of age. Tanya loved playing with these girls, who were always very gentle and patient with her. Perhaps her greatest joy was when they wore their little tutus and practised ballet for her – she simply sat mesmerised. How she loved dancing, of any description, and would sit in front of the television for hours whenever a program featured some form of dance.

It wasn't until I was in London, after leaving Malaga, that Dorothea told me that she and Clare had made a long-term pact that one of them would physically check on me every day, as they were both fearful for my safety. Hadi's terrible rages were very frightening but I had never been worried that I was in any danger and it came as an enormous shock to discover that my two friends were obviously so concerned. I recalled all those impromptu visits with great affection and how I had sincerely believed they were what they purported to be: dropping off a book, borrowing a kitchen implement, getting a recipe, or simply just popping in for a cup of tea.

Then I remembered the time when I raised the question with Hadi of living in Australia. My reasoning was that it would give us a high standard of living, allow Hadi – if he wished – to do business in a relaxed atmosphere, but most importantly Tanya would grow up surrounded by some family. Hadi refused to discuss the matter claiming he was 'European', Australia was too remote, he did not want to be so far away from his own country (which he could not visit), and in any case it was a wife's duty to follow her husband and go where he wanted or needed to live.

During the next couple of days Hadi's demeanour did not change and he almost resembled the man I had met nine years earlier. He was willing to make any promise if I would agree to return to Malaga and not once did he threaten or become hysterical.

All this was very hard. But something in my soul whispered to me that life would only get worse if I returned. Hadi's jealousy, control, and verbal abuse, together with my isolation, had driven me to this desperate course of action. It had taken me many months of soul-searching and planning to leave the once carefree, fun-loving man I had married eight years before. But when I had made my decision I knew instinctively it was the right thing to do.

As I was financially reliant on Hadi there was nowhere else

I could go except home to Australia where I would depend on the support of my family. There was no way I could remain alone in Spain. Without the language I could not work and in any case Tanya was too young to go to school. Catholic Spain was still very conservative, divorce was unheard of and, to my knowledge, single parenting did not exist. In fact, the law at that time stipulated a woman was not permitted to leave or desert the family home; penalties were imposed for any such behaviour. In Spain, irrespective of Hadi's treatment of me, he had the law on his side.

The memory of the oppression I had endured in Malaga strengthened my resolve. I knew I had done the right thing to maintain my sanity and ensure my survival. I also now felt a real sense of fear emerge for my safety during those few days of Hadi's visits. His mild manner was comforting but I was frightened that beneath the passive exterior a more sinister person was lurking. I was constantly wary that any second a tiny spark might ignite Hadi's fuse.

It was now well into the second week since Tanya and I had fled from Malaga, and after a number of Hadi's daily visits to Claygate, I realised that although the house was still groaning with food, Tanya's medication was running seriously low. Hadi was still on his best behaviour so I welcomed the opportunity to escape the confines of those small rooms and go to the local pharmacy, leaving Tanya in his care. The village was about fifteen minutes' walk but I enjoyed the exercise and at a fast pace could do it in much less time.

I returned to Elm Road, entered the house and was struck by the silence. I could not hear a sound and the house seemed very still. This was strange, because it was not time for Tanya's afternoon nap. I rushed through the house, racing up the stairs to the bedrooms but there was no trace of Hadi or Tanya. I felt numb. Maybe it was one of Hadi's silly tricks that he had played many times in the past. Once, years before, he had written a note saying he had left me when, in fact, he was hiding in our bedroom behind the heavy, cream brocade curtains. Could this be another of his tricks? Tanya's clothes were still there and Lambie, which never left her side, was draped forlornly across the chair.

In total confusion I clutched the lambskin to my chest. It was perfumed with Tanya's gentle baby scent and its soft warm feel reminded me of her beautiful skin. Surely he would not have taken her anywhere without her security blanket. My mind immediately jumped to her passport. My heart was now pounding like a generator as I ran to the green canvas bag holding all our papers of importance. Her passport was still there. Nevertheless, my panic heightened as I searched the house again, calling Tanya's name. After this I ran out into the street and walked up and down numerous times. Nothing. The fear in the pit of my stomach was impossible to contain. I returned to the house, sat on the sofa and tried to think where they could be, and how far they could have gone. By what means had they left? Had Hadi hired a car? I did not know of any friends he had in England who were not also my friends. Would he have sought help from his friend the Libyan ambassador in London? How would he cope with Tanya's meals and what about her medication? A closer inspection had revealed that he had taken a few of her clothes so maybe in a day or two he planned to reappear.

As I paced the floor I kept wondering where he could go with her. It would have to be a hotel. He would probably phone me any minute to say where he was. Should I really be concerned? I found it difficult to believe he would actually take her. He loved Tanya and loved me. He wouldn't want to harm Tanya and he must know keeping her from her mother would be traumatic for her. What could I do? Should I ring the police? What if he was just playing a trick? But what if he was not? No, I kept telling myself, he would never do something as terrible as that. Although Hadi had a vivid imagination and a somewhat conspiring nature, this was the welfare of his only child that was at stake, the child he loved and cared for. He might try to get to his sister Aminah, but she was in France. But they could fly to Geneva and be over the border at Aminah's home in just a few hours. No, he could not do that, he did not have Tanya's passport.

Was that a knock at the door? The gush of cold air that greeted me confirmed it was my imagination. It would be getting dark soon and it was already cold. Were they safely inside and warm or were they roaming the streets somewhere? My thoughts raced around in circles. Finally, I telephoned the local police, who arrived at the house within minutes.

By now I was trembling so much I could barely open the door. Trying to give the necessary information through my uncontrollable sobbing was agonising. My mind was racing in a hundred different directions and I couldn't think coherently. To my dismay, after much questioning, the two policemen advised me there was nothing they could do. If Hadi had taken Tanya, he was her father, so this was a personal problem, not a criminal one.

On hearing this statement I thought I must have been imagining things. A child is kidnapped but as long as the kidnapping is by one of the parents it is perfectly okay! It only becomes a crime when the child is not your own. Who would make such a senseless law? I tuned back into what the police were saying. Their advice was to try and have her made a Ward of Court as soon as possible, and for this I would need the services of a lawyer.

Never having had the need for a lawyer, I was at a loss as to where to start. Again I turned for help from a close friend. Susan was another colleague from my days at Occidental in Libya and she, Maureen and I had been a close trio. After a brief time Susan called me back.

'Margaret, I have spoken with a colleague and he has suggested a law firm in London that he thinks can help. Do you have a pen and paper?'

'Yes, just a minute.'

'These are the details. Please let me know how you get on and if you hear anything of Hadi and Tanya.'

'Yes, of course. Thank you. I'll try and telephone right away.'

I telephoned immediately but it was after five-thirty in the afternoon and there was no response. I would have to wait until morning.

How had I let this happen? Why, oh why, did I leave Tanya alone with Hadi? Had someone else suggested he do this? Perhaps one of his coffee cronies whom he had befriended in a bar? No, Hadi couldn't be told anything; he was always the one telling others what they should do. I knew he was a good person, generous, kind and loving. He was Tanya's father and would only want the very best for her. How could he take her outside in the cold when he knew she was not well? This was only a ploy to get me back to Malaga.

After desperately trying to think of something practical to do, I sat by the telephone with both the local and London directories next to me. First I called the local taxi company to see if they had collected anyone from Elm Road. My next calls were to the local hotels in the Claygate area, of which there were few, and then I started on the London ones. The insipid November light had long disappeared and I was enguled in an eerie darkness. As I kept hearing the same negative response over and over and over again I began to wonder if Hadi was using a false name. On and on I dialled, halfway through the night, but to no avail.

Completely drained, I sat in the brown velvet wingback chair in the small sitting room visualising Tanya, only the day before, lying on the new carpet watching her favourite cartoons. Where was she, and what would she be doing now? Tanya had never been away from me for more than an hour or so since she was born. This was just not happening, I continually thought. Hadi couldn't go very far without her passport so it would only be a matter of time before he contacted me. My gaze was fixed on a small chip at the edge of one of the green floral tiles that surrounded the Victorian fireplace. Mindlessly I wondered if the workmen had done it when they were laying the new carpet. As I sat staring at the chip, tears streamed down my face, feelings of nausea welled in my stomach and I must have slipped into an exhausted sleep. The telephone ringing next to the chair brought me back to reality. I grabbed the handpiece thinking it would be news of Tanya.

'Margaret, have you heard anything?' It was Susan.

The tears started to roll down my cheeks again in an ever-increasing stream.

'No. I have not heard anything. It was too late to speak to the lawyers but I hope to see them tomorrow.'

After hanging up the phone I was overcome with lassitude and fell into bed.

I made sure I was in central London the next morning by nine o'clock, telephoned the law office and was lucky enough to make an appointment for that day. The solicitor agreed with the advice given to me by the local police that obtaining a Ward of Court order should be my first step. He outlined the necessary procedure and advised this would entail my going to court. In order to obtain the document I would have to convince the judge that I was resident in the jurisdiction and planned to remain so, together with Tanya, for at least one year. I would have agreed to anything if it meant getting Tanya back. With my consent the law firm would act as quickly as possible. The following day saw me at the Old Bailey.

I had paid special attention to my appearance that morning. Luckily in my luggage I had a tailored beige dress and matching topcoat, which I thought would be appropriate for a courtroom. However, much more time was given to gathering papers I thought might be useful. There was Tanya's birth certificate, her passport, and my passport – what else would be helpful? I took an early commuter train from Claygate to London and, envying my fellow travellers, wished I were going to the comfort of a familiar office rather than the cold atmosphere of a London court. I made my way to the lawyers' office, where I signed documents and made a payment by cheque, before we left for the Old Bailey.

This was the first time I had been in a working court with a judge, tipstaffs, barristers, solicitors, court recorders and so on, all in all many more people than I had ever imagined. The seriousness of the Old Bailey – with the judge in his crimson robes and curly horsehair wig, and everyone with purposeful movements and manners – was very intimidating and a stark contrast to the courtrooms at home where I had grown up.

Sitting on the hard wooden bench I was consumed with nervousness and felt totally inadequate. The solicitor by my side was whispering instructions, telling me who my barrister was, what he would be doing, and informing me that we would be next. Afterwards my memory of taking the oath and getting to the witness box was just a blur and I certainly cannot remember the judge's questioning. But I do remember that my solicitor was quite cross with me because the judge was apparently hand-feeding the questions and I took longer than necessary to give the 'correct' answers. Prior to the hearing I was told we were very lucky because we had drawn a sympathetic judge, for which my barrister appeared pleased. This seemed to indicate some form of collusion but I never discovered if this was the case.

Finally I was out of the witness box and out of the courtroom into the lofty corridors. The judge had agreed to make Tanya a Ward of Court in my custody and she was not to be removed from the jurisdiction. This meant a stop would be issued to all ports – air and sea – so that she could not be taken out of the United Kingdom. British Airways and Iberia Airlines, the two airlines servicing Spain, would be informed directly. What a relief. It would surely only be a matter of time before Tanya was discovered at an airport or seaport and returned to me. The best thing I could do was to go home and wait by the telephone. It was now in the hands of the authorities. Of course there was much paperwork to be done by the lawyers but this did not involve me, except for the handsome payment of bills, which I was soon to learn would be an ongoing and ever-increasing burden.

At Elm Road I sat transfixed, watching the telephone and willing it to ring. The hours seemed like days and from time to time I lifted the receiver to make sure it was still working. As I agonised about what I could possibly do, I berated myself again and again for being so stupid as to trust Hadi alone with Tanya.

But somehow in my confused mind the love I still felt for Hadi automatically embraced trust as well. To me the two things were synonymous. This belief was no doubt instilled into my subconscious as a child by my loving parents. Now all it had achieved was a disaster for which I was not equipped.

I told myself that I had to keep busy. It was time to make a cup of tea. In the kitchen I cursed that the teabags had run out and I had to use loose tea and a pot. Why was everything so complicated?

As time passed I still believed Hadi would return. Although he had changed from the person I married and thought I knew, surely he was still an honourable and caring man. If he wanted to inflict pain on me there was no logic in inflicting it on Tanya in the process. But that was the whole point; he wasn't logical. I had struggled to understand this aspect of his personality for a long time, wondering why he did not share the same thought processes as my own. Maybe he didn't see that what he was doing was wrong, or that it might harm Tanya.

I recalled the many times Hadi had insisted that Tanya was his child. I was merely the warehouse where she had been housed for nine months – she really belonged to him. He always advanced this point of view whenever we disagreed on anything to do with Tanya's wellbeing or future. He was adamant on the matter and refused to listen regardless of how hard I argued against him or what biological facts I put forward to refute his position. As I remembered those arguments a chill of fear that he might not return overwhelmed me but I tried to regain my composure.

I went upstairs to the bedroom to check once again what Hadi had taken and to look at what he had left behind, trying to find a clue that might enlighten me as to his intentions. I picked up one of Tanya's dresses and held it to my cheek, her soft smell filling my nostrils, wracking me with pain. If I hadn't left Tanya alone with Hadi this wouldn't have happened. How did our love go so wrong? Where did I go so wrong? Was I the selfish one? Could I return to Malaga and continue living as before? No. I knew my sanity would be at stake, but worse, Hadi would never trust me again. His possessiveness and controlling ways would increase. And now I could no longer trust him – I would feel threatened and would live in fear. I had not considered myself in danger before but this now loomed as a harsh reality.

Should I therefore fear for Tanya? No, he truly loved her. She was *his* child. He would not do anything that he thought would harm her. But here was yet another area of contention between us. I did not necessarily agree with what he thought was perfectly normal. One of my main concerns was that he would leave her with someone while he went off to make arrangements or perform some chore. This might last several days. How would Tanya cope, left with strangers, with no-one she knew or trusted to comfort her?

The days following my appearance at the Old Bailey slowly stretched into weeks. Previously, each morning when I awoke I had automatically gone to Tanya's bed to get her up and dressed for the day. But now there was no routine, no splashing of water and laughing as I washed her hands and face and played with a toothbrush pretending to clean her teeth. No preparing breakfast together, holding back my frustration when, with Tanya's help, more milk went on the tablecloth than into her cereal bowl. Certainly no squeals of delight, as in Malaga, when the shiny black cat would visit from next door. The rhythm of my days had changed from a polka to a funeral march; time had no meaning and all was just darkness.

I tried everything I could possibly think of to get some idea where Tanya might be. One by one I telephoned all our friends in England, Spain and France, former neighbours, as well as business contacts in several countries. They all echoed the same shock and horror on hearing what had happened but no one had any news of either Hadi or Tanya.

Scotland Yard was first on my list of places to visit. This was a wasted journey as I was given the same response that I had received from the local police in Claygate. Not to be put off by the lack of cooperation from local authorities, I paid a visit to Interpol. There for the third time I received exactly the same message – this was a personal matter, not a criminal one, and they could not help.

How could nobody be interested in taking this matter seriously? Did they not care about a kidnapped child, or in helping me? There must be someone or somewhere I could go to get help. I wished I had a saviour, someone I could turn to in this mire. But I had no-one. I just had to proceed on my own by following any possible lead that came to mind.

The Libyan Embassy, suitably located in Princes Gate, was my next stop. The ambassador was an old school friend of Hadi's – as were the ambassadors in Paris and Madrid, two other places where Hadi might go for help. These friends whom I had never met but knew Hadi was in contact with and visited whenever he was in London, Paris or Madrid, would be useful allies for him. They could arrange secret accommodation or transport in or out of a country. My worst fear was that one of them would arrange for Tanya to be included on Hadi's passport, thus giving him a right of passage to take her anywhere. My only hope was that if the ambassador were not involved, maybe he would help me? I knew I was clutching at straws but I had to try.

I never did see the ambassador on that or any of my numerous visits to the Libyan Embassy; he had always been mysteriously spirited away. Nor did I ever receive a response to any of my letters. The consul, however, was always patient and courteous and assured me everything possible would be done to locate Hadi and Tanya.

The silence of the empty London house rang in my ears. Where were the yells of 'Mummy, Mummy'; the clunk of crashing blocks on our terracotta floor in Malaga, when Tanya's latest building experiment had come to grief; the strange Spanish sounds of 'Heidi', a Japanese cartoon character who filled our television screen each afternoon? Instead of these endearing sounds I now heard the children arrive each morning at the school opposite. The yelling and noisy chatter evoked images of happy, carefree lives. What a contrast to the terrible predicament in which I had placed my own daughter. Would she ever be happy and free? Could her father's possessive mentality allow her to enjoy a normal childhood?

My visit to the Spanish Embassy to see if there was any way

Hadi or Tanya could be traced should they return to Spain was also a waste of time. As none of the involved parties was Spanish, the embassy officials were not interested. This prompted the realisation that Tanya's plight might provoke some sympathetic reaction from the Australian Embassy. Again, the visit proved to be another dead end and proffered a similar response. Despite mother and daughter being Australian, my situation was a personal matter and the embassy could not get involved. It was at this time the phrase 'possession is nine-tenths of the law' started to fall on my ears. These words were to haunt me for many years to come.

The only other avenue I could think of was the press. Off I went to Fleet Street full of hope. The first thing they asked for was a picture of Tanya. The only photograph I had was her passport photo that had been taken when she was six weeks old; all the others were with our personal belongings that I had placed in storage, awaiting transport to Australia. No photo, no story, was basically the rebuff. In my despair I forgot all about the image of that sad little figure sitting on Santa's knee, taken several weeks earlier. I had never been back to claim it and would not think about recovering it until almost a year later.

After exhausting all other contacts I could think of, I telephoned Aminah in France. When she said she had not seen or heard from Hadi I was somewhat sceptical, but her apparent shock, gasps of horror, and expressions of disbelief seemed genuine and convincing. I now knew of nowhere else to go.

Once diagnosed with viral polyneuritis, Maureen was soon discharged from hospital and had gone to convalesce with family for a few weeks. I was alone at Elm Road. Night-time was always the worst. During the day I could struggle and pretend to find something to do. It was not possible to telephone friends after a certain hour and I lacked the concentration to read. In the dark silent nights there were only nightmares to haunt me. The hushed quiet made time stand still, encouraging my mind to venture into obscure places where insidious thoughts crawled into my head. I would feel the perspiration slide down my back as I wrestled with the nightmare that had become my world. Outside the damp acrid smell of wet leaves wafted through the open window, filling my nostrils and turning my stomach. Would morning never come?

Maureen finally returned home to Claygate with instructions to recuperate for six months. At least I was able to care for her in those early days of her convalescence and I had the comfort and compassion of a close friend. I was still at Elm Road as Christmas and New Year passed.

At some point during this time, in my haze of confusion, I flew back to Malaga but our house was deserted. I had neglected to take keys to the house, gates and chains when I left Spain, so was unable to get into my own home. I visited or made contact with every possible person I could think of in Malaga and Marbella but nobody had seen or heard anything of Hadi or Tanya. The one thing I did do in Marbella at this time was appoint a lawyer, Señor Fonseca, to make enquiries about Hadi's whereabouts. He was to set up a regular system of enquiry and advise me if he located Hadi or found anyone who had seen him.

Going up and down to London was not getting me anywhere and my small savings were slowly being eroded. My friends in England were all suggesting I should look for a job as at least it would keep my mind occupied and would help financially. Finding work in England had always proved easy for me and in no time I had answered an advertisement in the *Evening Standard* for a live-in housekeeping position in Belgravia, for a member of parliament and his wife.

This was a totally new work environment for me but one I felt would allow me the flexibility I needed. Settling in with Anthony and Jane was easy and once I was fully employed the days passed a little more quickly. However, the nights were long and lonely and I longed to know where Tanya was.

Now the telephone became my greatest ally. While I waited for lawyers to languidly work through the legal systems, I constantly telephoned anyone I could possibly think of who might have seen or heard from Hadi – his family, friends, acquaintances, and neighbours in Malaga. Because of the different time zones in London, Europe, the Middle East and Australia, calls could range from early morning to late at night seven days a week. These calls always ended unproductively but at least I felt I was doing something.

It was a cold winter's night towards the end of February and none of my enquiries had elicited any hint of Hadi or Tanya's whereabouts. I was tucked up on the cosy chintz sofa watching television. Anthony and Jane had gone to the theatre and I was thinking of the work I needed to complete the following day. The shrieking ring of the telephone interrupted me from my trance. I left the warm red glow and comforting crackle of the open fire to go to the hall where, surrounded by exotic objets d'art collected in Africa, the phone resided on a long wooden table.

When I heard Hadi's voice on the other end of the line I nearly dropped the receiver. How on earth did he find me? How did he get this number? Gathering myself together, I asked him where he was and if Tanya was with him. He didn't hesitate in telling me that he was in London. Not wanting to upset or anger him I kept my voice controlled and our conversation at first was quite civilised, but as usual it did not take long for him to start playing tricks and tormenting me. He told me he had placed Tanya in a school in France and he was staying nearby. I desperately clung to every word he uttered trying to get some clue as to his whereabouts, even straining to pick up background noises. After spending time and energy searching for the writing pad that was normally by the telephone, in desperation I scribbled tiny notes straight onto the wall. During the course of the conversation he again said he was in London then confided he was in Morocco. This dialogue was leading nowhere, but when I started to raise my voice, trying to force him see reason, he screamed his ultimate threat. If ever I tried to see or contact Tanya he would kill me. Visions of high drama flashed through my brain. Would he carry out this threat himself or contract someone else?

After the conversation was over I was no further enlightened as to Tanya's whereabouts, but was left with the knowledge that Hadi knew my telephone number. Did he also have my address? He had told me various stories, that he was in several different countries, that Tanya was with him, was not with him, and that certainly I would never see her again. My grief, always at the forefront of my mind, now erupted and I collapsed in a sobbing mess.

I have no idea how much time passed on that cold wet night before I looked up and saw Jane and Anthony standing over me trying to understand what had transpired. For a moment I thought Jane was an apparition – she appeared somewhat surreal in a full-length, arctic-fox coat – but then she hastily removed it and bent down to try to comfort me.

Tanya

LONDON – MADRID – LONDON
'You will never know where she is': 1978

It was less than six weeks since I had joined the employ of Anthony and Jane and they were due to go on their annual two-week skiing holiday to Kloisters in Switzerland, which would leave me in London with plenty of time on my hands. During my vigil of telephone calls to mutual friends and acquaintances, Michelle, who had recently moved from Paris to Madrid and was a business acquaintance of Hadi's, told me he had contacted her, and she felt he and Tanya might be in Madrid. He had visited her to collect a Persian rug we had left in her care while visiting France prior to our departure from Tripoli in 1973.

The rug was a valuable silk and wool Nain carpet that Hadi had given me as a gift after our marriage, and we had wanted to make sure it was safely away from Libya. Nain rugs are especially fine, with a minimum of four hundred and fifty knots per square inch, and are regarded among the best in the world, hailing from a small village of the same name in central Iran, some one hundred and fifty kilometres east of Isfahan. The tiny place in the middle of the Iranian desert, comprising crude dwellings of baked sand, only began producing rugs after World War II. This one, I thought, was particularly attractive with its cream background and curvilinear pattern in muted hues of light and dark blues and maroon.

Overjoyed that I had found someone who had actually seen Hadi, I timidly approached Anthony and Jane to request a few days off to visit Madrid while they were in Switzerland. During my initial interview I had told them of my personal situation, even though I knew this could jeopardise my chances of employment. To their lasting credit they were sympathetic and showed great compassion, employing me in spite of my plight. On receiving their good wishes, all I had to do was make flight reservations, book a hotel and patiently wait for the next couple of days to pass.

A few days earlier I had had a telephone conversation with Blair Cook, forlornly going over my hopeless situation. As none of my other pursuits had divulged any clue to Tanya's whereabouts, Blair suggested I visit a clairvoyant, Anne Leith Walker, whom she highly recommended. This suggestion seemed astonishing to me and coming from Blair – the sophisticated businesswoman – I was even more flabbergasted. She went on to say that Anne had been reading for her for many years, and her predictions about the most outlandish and unexpected occurrences had always been totally accurate, not only for herself but for her husband, Geoffrey, as well. She told me about a number of these intimate incidents while I listened in total surprise, completely nonplussed.

To satisfy my own curiosity I made an appointment with Anne

Leith Walker the evening before I flew to Madrid. When Anne greeted me I received another surprise – she was a grey-haired, seventy-year-old woman. I was further astounded when she told me before I left that she had had a similar experience to mine with her own daughter many years before.

At the beginning of my reading she explained Hadi's personality and temperament perfectly and was also extremely accurate in what she said about me. Her forecast that I would be travelling over water within twenty-four hours was correct but she got the destination wrong. According to her, I was going to stay in a corner room of a large stone building – probably a hotel – overlooking beautiful gardens that swept down to an ink-blue sea. However, I was booked to fly to Madrid, situated in the centre of Spain and surrounded by desert-like landscape!

'Oh well,' I thought, 'I suppose she can't get everything right.'

I was distressed to hear that she believed Tanya could be six or seven years old before I found her and, even more horrifying to contemplate, that she could be as old as sixteen or seventeen! Anne, I thought, must be having a bad day, as there was no way I could conceive of another three years elapsing before I found Tanya, let alone thirteen or fourteen. I consoled myself with the thought that time is always the most difficult thing for clairvoyants to predict.

It transpired that Anne was an artist as well as a fortune-teller. At the end of my session we discussed her many paintings – some were still works in progress, sitting on easels – and I couldn't help but surprised by the odd juxtaposition of her skills; she was not only a serious clairvoyant but an accomplished portrait artist as well.

The following day, which also happened to be the first day of British Summer Time when the clocks are adjusted by one hour, I made my way to Gatwick Airport. My ticket clearly stated my departure time as two o'clock in the afternoon. When I checked in at the Iberia counter just before one o'clock I was told that I was too late and had missed my flight. I looked at my watch in disbelief.

'But it's only one o'clock and the flight doesn't leave until two,' I pleaded.

The uninterested attendant then informed me that the flight in fact left at one o'clock, the gates were closed and nothing could be done. If my travel agent had put the incorrect time on my ticket it was not his problem. Frantically I explained that I had to be in Madrid the following morning for a ten o'clock meeting. Finally, after further remonstrations of despair, the young man serving me showed a little concern and said although Iberia had no more flights to Madrid that day he would check with British Airways. After returning from making these enquiries, his despondent look warned me that this was not an option either. There were no other flights from Gatwick to Madrid that day.

As my shoulders sank even further and my spirits plummeted, the young man, perhaps sensing my utter desperation, surprised me by suggesting I take their four o'clock flight to Barcelona and then the first flight to Madrid the next morning, which would enable me to keep my appointment. This was quickly organised with Iberia, who also arranged overnight accommodation for me. When I reached Barcelona and arrived at the hotel, I was astonished to find it an imposing stone building and, more incredibly, I had been given a corner room overlooking large gardens that led down to the Mediterranean Sea. The entire scene was identical to that described in Anne Leith Walker's prediction! Early the following morning I was on my way to Madrid.

Before leaving London I had contacted my solicitors to enquire if they knew any legal people in the Spanish capital. This time I was in luck. Brian Lewis, an Englishman, had been working in Spain as a lawyer for some years, spoke fluent Spanish, and knew the city well. I checked into the Gran Versalles Hotel, in a quiet area of Madrid but within walking distance of Calle Goya (where Brian Lewis's office was located) and Calle Serrano, two streets I was familiar with in the commercial district. My immediate task was to telephone Michelle.

Michelle, the tall, glamorous business associate of Hadi's, had been a guest in our home in Tripoli and, when she had lived in Paris, we had visited her with my mother when Tanya was twelve months old. Michelle, a successful career woman, also had a seven-year-old son whom she adored. Her job, exporting French couture fashion such as Dior, Leonard and other famous fashion-house brands to Argentina and Brazil, involved heavy travel commitments, which meant she was often separated from her son for short periods of time. She could understand and sympathise with my predicament.

Michelle gave me precise directions and I made my way to her new home. We diligently scoured the telephone book looking for boarding schools that would take children below the normal school age and Michelle, who spoke Spanish, started calling. After a couple of hours we had to admit we were not on the right track.

Thanking Michelle for her efforts, I telephoned Brian Lewis's office and made an appointment to see him that afternoon. Once in his office I relayed my predicament. Although advising me that in his opinion I was facing an impossible task, he was very sympathetic and agreed to help in whatever way he could. I returned to the hotel, not quite as exuberant as I had been on my arrival.

The following morning I set off for the Australian Embassy and was received by the consul, Douglas Quail. At last this was somewhere where I felt comfortable. Everyone spoke English and they were my own people. They would surely have the answer. Once again I described my predicament and again I was assured of all possible assistance. However, it was a personal matter and as such the embassy could not intervene. But surely in the case of a missing Australian national the embassy could make enquiries? Mr Quail advised that he would have to seek permission from Canberra to make enquiries on my behalf and, if permission were granted, it would be a very lengthy process. Knowing all too well the snail's pace at which diplomatic channels work I nevertheless accepted the offer. But I asked if the embassy could approach the Spanish education department for a list of schools willing to accommodate a three-year-old. They would try, I was assured.

The Libyan Embassy was my next stop. As usual they were polite but when they informed me they knew nothing of Hadi or Tanya, I had the overwhelming feeling I was being shunned.

I then visited the Director General de Seguridad, the Department of Extranjeros at Police Headquarters, the Spanish–Arab Chamber of Commerce and the Spanish Arab Bank – the latter two being places where I knew Hadi had contacts – but to no avail. No-one admitted to having any knowledge of Hadi or my daughter. I made several further visits to Brian Lewis, who was most generous with his time and sympathy.

Over a typical French breakfast of hot croissants and coffee I relayed all these events to Michelle. I also told her what I had already established in London, that the police, Interpol, and the Libyan and Australian embassies were of no help and preferred to distance themselves from what they regarded as a personal problem.

With no help forthcoming from the authorities, we decided there was only one avenue left. If Hadi or Tanya were in Madrid, I would have to resort to employing a private investigator to find them. We turned to the telephone book once again and Michelle started telephoning. Either they did not speak English, which was one of my requirements, or they were not interested in my case. Finally, when we were nearing the bottom of the list of possibilities, we struck it lucky with a Señor Martinez, who said he would meet me that afternoon.

Michelle had prior commitments and could not accompany me, but as Señor Martinez spoke a little English I went off armed with my Ward of Court document and all other relevant papers, quite excited that at last someone was willing to help. Señor Martinez's office building was on the other side of Madrid. Its appearance was nondescript, quite the opposite of the impressive buildings occupied by the numerous lawyers I had already seen. Leaving the lift on the third floor I walked along the corridor in search of his suite number. Somewhat disconcerted, I found Señor Martinez occupied a small room that looked as though it could be a bookmaker's office, with frosted glass panelling all the way around the top part of the walls. The desk and several side tables were untidily stacked with bulging files and well-worn books. A large overflowing ashtray explained the heavy odour in the room.

He listened carefully to every detail as I explained what had happened and my attempts, to date, to locate Tanya. After a number of questions and discussing some points in detail, he finally said that he was sorry but could not take the case – there were insufficient clues and no leads to pursue. He advised me to be extremely careful of anyone who did agree to take my case as I would end up paying a lot of money for what, he believed, was an insurmountable task.

Crestfallen, I made my way back to the hotel. I was so overwhelmed by tears and a sense of helplessness that I didn't even search the face of every passing child, something I had become accustomed to doing in the hope that I might see Tanya. There didn't appear to be anything further I could achieve in Madrid, but as I was in Spain I decided to fly down to Malaga again to see if I could discover any clues near our old home. It had been eight weeks since I was last there and maybe something had changed in that time. During my brief farewell to Michelle she promised to let me know if she heard anything further.

It was now Saturday. My first stop after leaving Malaga airport was Hadi's lawyer's office but, as expected, he said he had no idea of Hadi's whereabouts. He told me he hadn't seen him for many weeks. I took the opportunity to show him the Ward of Court papers from London, pleading with him to let me know if he knew anything. I tried my best to imply that to do otherwise would be dishonourable but eventually I left feeling the meeting had been a waste of time. Not far from his offices was the Hotel Residencia, and knowing it to be a modest establishment I was grateful to find they had a single room available.

To try and revive my momentum I formulated a basic plan of action. After numerous calls and finally one to a neighbour in Malaga, there was a ray of hope. Teresa and her husband, a judge, lived opposite our house and Teresa spoke excellent English, a great advantage when trying to explain my impossible predicament. My instinct that she and her husband were shielding Hadi proved correct when she eventually confided that they had seen him occasionally as he passed by to collect mail. Tanya was never with him. Finally she said she thought they may be living in Madrid and agreed to try to organise a meeting.

On the Sunday evening Teresa called to say she had arranged for me to meet Hadi at the Hotel Aitana in Madrid at noon the following day. At last I had something concrete. Hadi respected Teresa and her husband and if he had agreed to an arrangement with Teresa he was sure to keep it. Although I had mixed emotions about seeing Hadi, I reasoned that it should be safe enough because the meeting was in a public place. Excited at the prospect of arriving at the end of my search I slept fitfully.

The following morning I was lucky enough to get a seat on an early flight to Madrid, which seemed an excellent omen. I arrived at the Hotel Aitana just before eleven o'clock and chose a seat in the foyer that was conspicuous to anyone coming or going. I picked up a magazine, turning the pages perfunctorily, not seeing a single word and looking up at the first sign of movement or noise of any kind, hoping to see Hadi arrive. Noon came and went. One o'clock, two o'clock. Could he really be doing this to me? Various members of the hotel staff were very suspicious and several times asked if they could be of any assistance. If only they knew. At six o'clock I picked up my overnight bag and headed for the airport. Drained and heartbroken yet again by the torment of a wasted journey, the prospect of returning to the familiarity of London and the warmth and compassion of my friends seemed to offer some comfort.

One of the first things I did on my arrival back in London was to telephone Blair, not only to tell her about my fruitless efforts to track Hadi and Tanya down in Spain, but more specifically what had transpired during my trip to Madrid. I recounted my extraordinary session with Anne Leith Walker, how her prediction of me going to the seaside was uncannily accurate but how I was extremely concerned about her forecast on the time it would take to find Tanya.

In April, just nine weeks after I had started working for Anthony and Jane, I received a wonderful surprise. Barry, my friend from Australia, was to pay a visit to London. His company was sending him to Amsterdam on business for a week and he could spend three days in London before returning home. Hadi had prevented him visiting us in Malaga so to see him now would be marvellous. Tears of joy filled my lifeless eyes as I anticipated the comfort this reunion would bring me. We had experienced so many happy times during our twenty-year friendship. His warm nature, spontaneous laughter and sense of the ridiculous were a tonic at any time and I happily counted off the hours to his arrival. I could talk to Barry about anything and anxiously awaited his truthful opinion of how my mother was coping with the situation.

My job allowed me some freedom in the middle of the day so I planned to collect him when he arrived at Heathrow airport. Barry, like many gay men, was often surrounded by glamorous women and I wanted to look my best for him. It wasn't until I started to dress for the occasion that I realised my problem. I hadn't worn my beige dress since the day at the Old Bailey. It had a long zipper from the neck down the back to the middle of my hips but when I tried to pull the zipper up it would not budge beyond my waist. Without realising it, the weight had been piling on. Comfort eating had shaped my life once before, when I first left Australia as a young woman and found myself alone in London. At that time my normal sixty-one kilogram frame had enlarged by two dress sizes and now it was doing it again. My days as a size ten had vanished along with my heart. The extra helpings of bread and potatoes, not to mention the chocolate bars and biscuits, were doing their job. Reluctantly I stepped out of my figure-hugging beige dress and settled for something more comfortable. I was to remain a size fourteen for many years until I slowly returned to a ten, but the battle against comfort eating was an ongoing one. It's lucky I am so tall.

Barry and I were so delighted to see each other again, it really didn't matter what I looked like. The following couple of days were nourishment for my broken soul: walking through St James Park and feeling heady with the intoxicating perfume of early spring flowers, calling into Harrods to buy some Brussels sprouts for Anthony and Jane, and buying an Indian takeaway to share on our way to the theatre. We laughed about driving my employers' Rolls Royce to buy potatoes, and how I secretly referred to recipe books for simple fare yet could prepare exotic recipes by heart for the household. This fun and silliness provided temporary relief from my daily despair.

It was only two weeks later, when I was busily trying to finish part of my afternoon's work before Anthony and Jane arrived home from an official luncheon at the Houses of Parliament, that I had a second telephone call from Hadi. I recognised his voice immediately.

'Hadi, where are you?' I cried.

'I'm in Zurich, staying in the Savoy, just around the corner from UBS.' His tone was as normal as if he were discussing the weather.

'Where is Tanya?' I screamed.

'I have arranged for her to go into a school here in Switzerland.' His voice was still maintaining a level pitch.

'What kind of school? For how long? Why Switzerland? She's only three.'

Ignoring my questions he continued in the same matter-of-fact manner.

'Well no, actually I'm in Spain. I have been talking to my friend the manager at Banco Espanol in Madrid and I have got a very good job for you.'

'I don't want a job in Madrid. Where is Tanya?'

'Look, if you come home, I agree that you can go to work, and now there is a really good job I have arranged for you.'

'Hadi, please just let me know where Tanya is?'

'You will never know where she is. I am taking her to Libya. You will never see her again.'

Now my fear escalated to a new level. I knew if this were true, if he did take her to Libya, I would never see her again.

'All right,' I coyly replied, 'I will do whatever you want. Just let me know where you and Tanya are.'

The tone of Hadi's voice now hardened and in my mind's eye I could see the black shadow falling across his face. I knew nothing was going to be achieved from this conversation. His final words were cold and threatening.

'You will never know where she is and if you ever try to find her I will kill you.'

The line went dead. Immediately I started calling all the people who might have had contact with Hadi. I phoned everyone I could think of in Spain who may have seen or heard of him or Tanya. I called his bank manager at UBS in Switzerland. I called Aminah. Nobody had seen or heard from him. I then phoned the Swiss Embassy and they kindly agreed to post me a list of boarding schools in Switzerland that would accept a child of three years of age. With the usual Swiss efficiency the list arrived the following day. It was not a very long list so I rang each school. Thankfully I was able to converse with all of them in English, but not one delivered the response I longed for.

I repeated the telephone conversations I had had the previous day over and over in my head, especially the one with Aminah. She was a mother; she would surely understand and help if she could. But she was also Hadi's sister and as the old saying goes, blood is thicker than water. I sadly recalled the last time I had seen her, almost eighteen months earlier, when she and her family were visiting us in Spain at the same time as my mother.

I had absolutely no idea where Tanya was or even if she was with her father. How on earth would I ever find her? Now my own life was being threatened – not that that would deter me for one second from trying to find my daughter, but maybe I would need to be a little more careful.

My real fear was Hadi's erratic behaviour. Why bother phoning me if he would not tell me where he was or where I could join them?

What could he achieve by misleading me about their whereabouts, telling me they were in one place and then suggesting they were in another? Maybe he was just around the corner and wanted to come and catch me in floods of tears. Where was Tanya and why wouldn't he let me talk to her? I remembered something I had once read, some words of Indian philosophy: 'The things we perceive as real are actually an illusion concealing the reality that lies behind appearances.'

There was no doubt that Hadi loved Tanya, so I didn't think that he would harm her, not physically anyway. But I could imagine him leaving her with someone or in a school if he needed to, or if it suited him. One way he showed his affection would be to buy her sweets or ice-cream, but cuddles would be in short supply. Brief bear hugs were more his style. If he did leave her in someone's care, how would they treat her? Certainly not with the same love and affection as a parent. Would Tanya be afraid? She would certainly miss her mother and father and her familiar surroundings. Would this person speak English, Tanya's only language? Would Tanya be eating healthy food or would she be so upset that she wouldn't eat at all? These questions and many more plagued my mind every waking minute.

Tanya & "Cat"

SPAIN
Schools in Barcelona: May 1978

I continued my work in London. After another two months of enquiries, the feedback I started to receive from my numerous telephone calls to friends and acquaintances in Spain suggested that Hadi and Tanya were in Barcelona. There was no specific information but I had to follow every possible clue. Again Anthony and Jane agreed that I could take a few days' leave.

Aware of my dwindling finances I had to look for ways to reduce my travel expenses. It was May and not yet the tourist season so luckily I was able to purchase a reasonably priced ticket to Barcelona with the budget airline Dan Air. However, as with all the new charter airlines, I had to commit to definite departure and return dates. This would only present a financial disadvantage if something unexpected happened and I had to forfeit the return ticket. But if I found Tanya I wouldn't be coming straight back in any case, and like Scarlett O'Hara, would face that problem another day.

On arrival in Barcelona, armed with a list of hotels I had received from the Spanish Embassy in London, I made my way to a small *residencia* in the centre of town. Hotel Monegal was on the fourth floor of a corner building overlooking the traffic-filled Plaza Cataluña, right in the heart of the city. This location had the advantage of being very central, and was conveniently opposite the main telephone exchange, which I was to use constantly, but it was also very noisy. The lift was old and shaky, with temperamental metal doors that had to be perfectly closed before the ancient structure would jolt into action. The room was sparsely furnished with a narrow single bed, rickety bedside table and a wooden dining chair. The bathroom was even smaller, with a shower, tiny basin, toilet and no window. However, what these lodgings lacked in style they made up for in cleanliness, which was the most important thing.

My first call was to the American school. I didn't believe for one minute that Tanya would be there but I could at least speak to them in my own language and hoped it would be a good stepping-stone, which it was. They gave me a list of names and numbers to start my search. As I made calls, additional numbers I was given along the way also gave me hope. They included an English school, an English vicar, and finally someone who suggested I go to the central bureau, where a record of all schools was kept. This seemed like a real breakthrough, particularly as the familiar Yellow Pages telephone directory I was accustomed to in London didn't seem to exist in Barcelona, or if it did no-one I asked seemed to know of it. Very few of these people spoke English so maybe it was my almost non-existent Spanish that let me down.

The central bureau was located in a narrow alleyway in the

Gothic section of Barcelona and the tall slim buildings all seemed to lean inwards, creating an atmosphere that was dark, mysterious and intimidating. I found it hard to imagine that any good was going to come from this place. But this was where I had been told I could obtain a list of all the junior schools in Barcelona.

When I came to the address I was looking for, it was not the imposing official building I had expected, but a small structure situated in the middle of the alleyway at a three-way junction. The dome-shaped entranceway was oversized, with strange doors and passageways leading off in several directions. Everyone was engrossed in their own particular task and no-one took any notice of me.

All I wanted was a list of schools and their addresses. I was sure I would find Tanya enrolled at one of them. But where to start and how to explain my quest to one of these people? Just then, a rather academic-looking woman carrying a large bundle of folders passed in front of me. I had to start somewhere. After I excused myself and tried to explain what I was looking for she quickly fobbed me off onto a colleague. This started a chain of discussion with several employees who couldn't seem to understand what I wanted or what I was doing there in the first place.

After what seemed like hours of tedious frustration I was handed a messy list of two pages. It was all in Spanish, there was no uniformity in the presentation of the list and no headings; in fact, there seemed to be no order to it at all. As I quickly looked at the two sheets of paper, while profusely thanking the clerk, I could see that very few school names included telephone numbers and the addresses in many cases were incomplete, making their location especially hard to find for a stranger in the city. There were also other details, in abbreviated Spanish, which meant nothing to me. Nevertheless I felt grateful to have something in my hands at last.

In the privacy of my hotel room I tried to make some sense of the list but the type was faded and difficult to read. The typing was inaccurate in places and abbreviations had been used frequently. Together with my Spanish dictionary and map of Barcelona I tried to locate the areas where the schools were situated. Once this was accomplished I devised a schedule that would enable me to see each school. It was now mid-afternoon but I decided I must make a start.

The school I chose to visit first was listed as being in Montgat and the hotel manager suggested I could catch a bus two blocks away that would take me to the area. When I found the school, I was overcome with anticipation and my adrenalin was racing. All that was visible was a long, single-storey, whitewashed wall protecting the buildings from the road. They looked more like an old row of workmen's cottages than a school. The entrance was hidden on a side street and I found my way to the office. Armed with all my papers, I explained in broken Spanish who I was and who I was looking for. The teacher was dismissive, telling me they only had children over five years of age. He didn't know any school that took children of three years. I was made to feel very foolish by this man but despite being despondent I was not going to let his ridicule defeat me. After safely putting the papers away I made my way back to the hotel.

I patiently worked my way through the list, visiting the various schools one after the other. My first disappointing experience was repeated many times during the ensuing days. With the tatty list of schools and the help and advice I received from some of the teachers along the way I continued my search. My feet hurt and the heat made me feel more tired than I had anticipated. My thirst was a daily aggravation, and the language barrier a constant frustration. After five days I had visited a total of thirty-two schools. I was met with politeness at each one and many were helpful, giving me names and addresses of other schools to try, but none of them harboured Tanya.

On the second-last night in my hotel room I was deeply depressed. Lying there alone and vulnerable, suddenly I was sure I saw the handle of the door turn. By myself, in this secluded hotel, well hidden in the dark recess of an old building, I was afraid no-one would hear a cry for help. This was a journey I had undertaken independently, and if Hadi's death threats were carried out, who would know where I was? And how long would it take for anyone to realise I was missing?

I had heard Hadi make threats to all and sundry in the past but I had always doubted that he would ever follow them through. Yes, he was very volatile and could be a frightening foe when in a rage but I could not believe he would carry out a death threat in cold blood. But then I had an alarming thought. Hadi was used to ordering people around and having everything done for him so he wouldn't carry out such an act himself – he would hire a hit man. As this new realisation dawned I broke out in a cold sweat.

I lay completely still, not game to breathe, hoping the would-be intruder would go away. In an effort to control my fear I tried to be rational about my situation. Even though Hadi's love for me – which years before I knew to be real – had now turned to hate, I couldn't believe he would kill the mother of his only child. Assuring myself that the door handle was no longer turning, and that someone had simply come to the wrong room by mistake, I eventually dropped into a fitful sleep, knowing this stage of my search was coming to an end.

The last school to visit was in the mountains behind Barcelona and a rickety old train was my only means of getting there. It was a long journey full of anticipation and, when I finally arrived, I found the school was run by nuns. The ancient, stone two-storeyed building was completely closed to the outside world by high walls that ran all the way around it. This fortress-like structure was surely where

Tanya was hidden. For a long time I tried to gain entrance through one of the locked metal gates set in the high wall, or at least attract someone's attention. Finally I saw a gardener on the other side of the wall and shouted to him. He slowly walked to where I was standing on tiptoe, peering over a dip in the wall. After agonising attempts to explain myself I was able to convince him to bring someone to whom I could speak.

When I saw an elderly nun approaching, covered from head to foot by her long black habit, I was briefly reminded of Arab women from the Middle East, but the great difference here was that this woman would never have had children – she would never have been a mother. Would she truly understand my plight? Not being a Catholic or sure of the protocol in such situations I felt intimidated. She stood very stiffly on the other side of the iron-barred gate and looked impatiently around while I explained my quest. At first she wasn't even going to let me in, which immediately led me to suspect that this was where I would find Tanya; the days and days of searching had at last paid off. However, after ushering me inside the building, struggling with my Spanish and listening to further details of my story, the nun was most convincing in her denial of any knowledge of Tanya.

I returned to Barcelona and sat in the hotel room listening to the noise of the world outside, the traffic and the people going about their normal everyday lives, and I wondered where I could possibly go from here. I felt the physical and emotional toll of the past few days roll over me like a huge boulder. I cried hysterically and clung to the pillow for support. My stomach was churning like a washing machine on spin and my mind was racing with incoherent thoughts. Why couldn't I find anyone to help me? Why didn't I know how and where to find my daughter? The only thing that encouraged me to carry on was the prospect of having Tanya in my arms again.

The following day I reluctantly flew back to London.

Malaga.

SPAIN
Gaol in Malaga: June 1978

My enquiries in London continued to lead nowhere and I knew I had to do something more specific. There had been one or two brief sightings of Hadi in Marbella but never of Tanya. Our principal Spanish bank account was in Marbella, as well as four investment properties, so I assumed Hadi had been there to collect rents and attend to banking matters. My visit to Marbella earlier in the year had been unsuccessful but I had appointed the lawyer Señor Fonseca to make enquiries on my behalf. To date he had come up with nothing so I decided it was time to pay a further visit.

I made an appointment with Señor Fonseca and flew to Spain. It was a Thursday. When I arrived at his office for our meeting I was informed by his secretary that he was out of town on urgent business, but would see me on his return the following Monday. I was incensed by this lack of consideration and it took some time for me to overcome my anger. He had not had the courtesy to give me any prior warning that he would not be there even though I had flown from London to keep the appointment and taken time off from my work, not to mention the inconvenience and additional cost for me to remain in Spain for the extra days. Even worse, I was unable to establish what progress he had made. It did not occur to me to do anything except await his return.

At least I was in a familiar environment, the place where Hadi and I had come to live when Tanya was six weeks old. On Friday afternoon, while waiting in the travel agency for confirmation of my return flight to London, it dawned on me that I only had a three-day visa. At that time Australian passport holders required a visa for Spain and as I had planned a quick visit, I had only been given a three-day visa by the embassy in London. I frantically interrupted one of the travel agents and asked if the relevant authorities granting visas were open the next day. At last one bit of good news – yes, they were open until lunchtime on Saturday but I would have to go to Malaga.

The following morning, in order to have plenty of time, I caught an early bus from Marbella and settled down for the hour-long journey. The municipality building where I was told visas were issued was a long way from where I alighted the bus but I had been given good directions and set a determined pace. It was now mid-morning and I envied the many holidaymakers I passed in their shorts, T-shirts and sandals. Because I had come on what I thought was to be a brief business trip, my limited wardrobe did not include such comfortable attire. I looked totally out of place in my tailored linen suit and high-heeled shoes on this relaxed Saturday morning.

Inside the large imposing municipality building I discovered a long, enclosed counter and, at each cubicle, metal grilles similar to those installed for tellers in Australian banks. Spanish authorities were always far more formal than I was used to elsewhere. The many queues were long and slow and I joined what I thought was the shortest, hoping it was the correct one, as obviously there were many other things being dealt with here besides tourists wanting to extend their visas.

When finally I reached the stern official, I handed him my passport and in halting Spanish requested an extension to my visa. He busied himself by looking at books and lists and after some minutes, without any communication, left his cubicle clutching my passport. Curious as to the reason, I hoped I wouldn't have to answer any difficult questions in Spanish. He spoke to several colleagues and then disappeared into a closed office. Some minutes passed then to my relief I saw him returning to his station. However, I didn't realise that as he approached two armed guards were shadowing him on the outside of the counter. I then became aware of the two guards standing on either side of me. I was ordered by the official to accompany them and, in front of curious stares by onlookers, not to mention my own consternation, the guards signalled me to follow.

I don't remember the journey through the building until our arrival at a row of cells at the rear. There were four or five cells and as I furtively glanced at the occupants I was alarmed to see an array of dark, threatening, undesirable men. A third guard appeared and instead of holding a rifle, he held a bunch of keys. The door of an empty cell at the end of the row was opened and I was motioned inside and locked in.

Why on earth was I here? What had happened? What would I do? As these questions were racing through my mind a man in a suit appeared. Through the bars and in meagre English he apologised that I was in the cell. He explained that as it was a Saturday the courts were not open, so I would have to wait until Monday.

But wait for what? Eventually I understood him to be telling me that a case had been brought against me and I would have to appear before a judge.

Who could be bringing a case against me, and why? I asked myself. Surely it wasn't the immigration department; my visa did not expire until the next day. Sunday! Oh my goodness, I thought, if I had to wait until Monday I would be in Spain illegally! No, surely the charge could not be related to my visa request. It had to be Hadi, but what could he be charging me with? I soon realised that trying to think of answers to these questions was pointless and that it would be better to concentrate on how to address my situation.

As I sat in the small cell I couldn't imagine how I would pass the next day and a half. I convinced myself the tiny space only looked dirty – it had obviously been a long time since the whitewashed walls were last painted and their peeling surface was less than attractive. The cement floor did look as though it had been swept. The only 'furniture' comprised two wooden benches, one along each side wall, and full-length bars ran across the front. How had I ended up in this predicament? More importantly, how was I going to get out of it? My lawyer in Marbella, for what he was worth, was out of town. I couldn't think of anyone else who could help me.

I sat there for what seemed like ages, my mind in a whirl, trying to think of a way out of my situation. Finally I thought of Teresa, our neighbour in Malaga. Her husband, Jorge, was a senior judge. They had lived opposite us with their teenage children for nearly three years. Although Jorge was not a close friend, we enjoyed a convivial association. Surely he would help me and explain what was happening. At least we could communicate in English. I would call him. Having made a decision I returned to the reality of my surroundings. Apart from the row of cells and the incarcerated occupants, the place seemed totally abandoned. There was nobody to call and no-one whose attention I could attract. Outside the cells was a covered area then some open space beyond which was a set of double metal gates. At least the open area allowed us fresh air but it could not eliminate the stale smell of humanity and cigarettes.

A horrendous thought entered my head. What if they brought someone to share my cell? Surely not! But then at least I could request a phone call. No, I couldn't believe they would put someone else in with me. But what if nobody came until Monday morning?

Preoccupied with this appalling thought, the rattle of keys alerted me. Another victim was being led in and put in an adjoining cell with one of the men. When the guard had locked the door I called to him and tried to explain that I wanted to phone a friend who was a judge. Although he listened I wasn't sure he understood and he departed without a word. Some minutes later a more senior-looking official appeared.

In broken English he said, 'You know one judge?'

I was not allowed out of the cell but I wrote Jorge's name and telephone number on a piece of paper, praying that someone would call him and praying that there would be someone at home to answer the phone.

Within ten minutes I was taken from the cell, ushered to the rear of the municipality building and led to a police car parked outside. Two policemen got into the front of the car and a third climbed into the back beside me. They were not impolite, simply very official. However, as I was getting into the back behind the driver I was horrified when I stumbled over the butt of a rifle, which had been placed upright between the two front seats. The policemen paid no attention to my clumsiness but made it obvious that they were anxious to proceed with the job at hand. I felt uncomfortable and apprehensive but anything was better than the cell where I had recently been confined. Hopefully my pleadings to telephone my ex-neighbour, the judge, had brought about this change of circumstance.

It was only a short time before we arrived at the court building. It was not particularly impressive and once inside it became quite eerie as we passed the deserted offices, their interiors dark behind the closed window shutters. The heavy shoes of my police escorts clanked on the terrazzo floor, sending hollow echoes along the wood-panelled corridors. Air-conditioning had not reached the south of Spain and the thick musty air, impregnated with the smell of stale cigarettes, increased my feelings of nausea.

Entering what I assumed was the courtroom, I was asked to wait. How different this was to the Old Bailey. However, it was presumably an emergency court being opened for my 'convenience'. It was a smallish room on what appeared to be two levels, with the customary distinction between the judge's elevated domain and the public area. There was no plush furniture here, simply utilitarian fixtures. In the quietness of the room and as its only occupant, I hoped that Jorge's familiar face would magically manifest itself in front of me. At last a man in a suit entered the room and approached me. He said the judge would arrive shortly and I should stand when he entered the room. Then he disappeared.

Being well aware that Napoleonic Law was still enforced in Spain, meaning that one was guilty until proven innocent, I wondered how this would apply in my case, whatever that might be. The sounds of muffled voices and shuffling footsteps permeated into the court from a side door. When it opened, the same man in the suit who had spoken to me earlier returned, along with a second larger man, also in a suit. As they entered the room the man who had previously addressed me gestured for me to rise.

After I had performed the perfunctory swearing on the Bible, the judge, now behind his bench, advised me in English that I had been denounced in Malaga by one Hadi Senussi, for abandoning the marital home. This was a crime in Spain, but I had no idea of the punishment. No other information from the *denuncia* – the formal document, lodged by Hadi, denouncing me as a criminal – was given and the judge proceeded to ask why I had committed this illegal act.

As I told my story and, in particular, when I explained why I was currently in Spain, the judge seemed confused. He continued his questioning and showed surprise to learn that Hadi was an Arab, obviously thinking, like most people, that Hadi was Italian, which he frequently claimed. The judge then made reference to Jorge and I explained our association. The questioning did not last much longer and the judge turned to the suited man, spoke in Spanish, closed his folder and walked out. The man in the suit then advised me the case had been dismissed and the policemen would take me back to the municipality to adjust my visa for my requested extended stay in Spain.

Still somewhat shaken by my first ever scrape with the criminal justice system, I was grateful for the slow bus trip back to Marbella, as it gave me a little time to gather my thoughts. Although all I wanted now was to get back to the safety of England, I couldn't help but think of the happy times that we had had in this sunny country, despite its occasionally confusing and frustrating customs.

There was the joy of watching Tanya develop and flourish: her first tooth, her first step, her first Christmas, and her growth into a happy chatterbox who would dance at any given opportunity. The warm friendship of Clare and Dorothea had given me many hours of fun and amusement. The occasional picnics Hadi, Tanya and I took into the countryside, especially in spring, gave me great pleasure. And, of course, the happy times spent when my mother came from Australia to visit were very special. But these events, when critically observed, were thinly spread over nearly four years.

I was left to contemplate yet again all the restrictions placed on my life during our marriage. If only I could have persuaded Hadi to give me more freedom, allow me to choose my own friends, visit Clare and Dorothea without him, or even go to an English film or the theatre with them occasionally. He had not wanted me to study Spanish; in the same way he had never wanted me to learn Arabic when we lived in Libya.

What if I had stayed on and not run away? Tanya was at an age where she would soon be going to school; when that happened, my days would have been completely empty. Maybe Hadi and I would have then done things together, but what things? He wasn't interested in sport or in taking part in anything. When I thought about the situation rationally I could see that it was impossible. The price of my actions was enormous but surely it was only temporary. I consoled myself with the thought that it wouldn't be much longer before I had Tanya back in my arms.

I was suddenly aware that I was the only person left on the bus. I was back in Marbella, still with another day to wait before seeing my lawyer.

The meeting with Señor Fonseca was a non-event and I wondered why I had bothered to come. Despite his many words, the message was that there was nothing to report. According to him, he had contacted numerous people but he could discover no trail. Hadi had visited Marbella but nobody could remember when, how long he stayed or precisely whom he saw. The only thing they were definite about was that Tanya was not with him.

At this point I had not contemplated the possibility that Señor Fonseca was lying to me. Growing up in the environment of the courts, I believed anyone connected with the law was honest, especially a lawyer, and I had no reason to believe otherwise. It wasn't until much later that I became suspicious, even to the point where I considered it possible that Señor Fonseca was in touch with Hadi.

Dejectedly I made my way to the airport and back to London. I had now made numerous trips to Europe, believing Tanya's location would be revealed. So many times it seemed that my search would be successful, but then the trail would mysteriously run cold.

My shoulders felt very heavy with the weight of all this failure and my body was almost too tired to move. Whenever my emotions surged to the surface while I was in public I tried to push them away. I had become expert at finding private spaces at any given moment that would allow me time to control my grief. I sought refuge in bathrooms, toilets, or simply an empty room; failing that, I would pretend to look for something I'd dropped on the floor, stare into shop windows, dash into alleyways or stand between parked buses and trucks. All these ploys were used to camouflage outbreaks of heartbreak and devastation.

DUBAL
Dinner

DUBAI
Lowest ebb: 1978

At my initial meeting with Anne Leith Walker earlier in the year, she made it very clear she would not give a further reading before a minimum of six months had passed as it was unlikely anything new in my long-term future would materialise in that time. I understood her ethical stand on this issue but I couldn't suppress my urge to see her again, even though it was only three months since my previous reading when she had so accurately predicted my unplanned trip to Barcelona. In those three months Hadi and Tanya might have moved; or wherever they were, Hadi might have put her in the care of some-one else, therefore making it easier for Anne to ascertain a location. After much persuasion Anne agreed to a further meeting.

On this occasion she told me nothing new about Hadi or Tanya, but said that I was going to leave England to live in a place with a very hot climate. She described small, whitewashed houses, palm trees, beautiful blue sea and sandy beaches. This sounded remarkably like Spain, a place to which I had no intention whatsoever of returning on a permanent basis. In fact, at that time, I had no intention of leaving London, so all this sounded ridiculous.

Anne went on to tell me that I would be working for an important company. It would comprise a large single-storey structure and numerous rectangular-shaped buildings. The company product, which she could not quite fathom, would be energy-intensive and based on state-of-the-art technology. Along with the physical aspects of the company's location, she finished by declaring that my office would be in a completely different area. In fact I would be in a very tall building with a large ornamental fountain at its entrance, and a semicircular drive.

My dejection on leaving that reading was enormous. Not only did I have no intention of moving from England but I was also content in my job with Anthony and Jane and had no thought of changing it.

It was now seven months since Tanya had been taken and having spent all my money on lawyers, plane travel, hotels and other expenses, I knew I would have to continue to earn as much money as possible to continue my search. By this time, with no real leads, my mental state was also deteriorating rapidly.

During the week Anthony's personal assistant, Barbara, worked in the house. I was able to use her small office when she was absent, especially in the evenings and on weekends. Barbara, a petite blonde with a bubbly personality, had been secretary to Edward Heath before coming to work for Anthony and she had a fund of amusing stories from her time in the prime minister's employ. She was a great deal of fun and gave me a lot of strength in those dark days. I had shared my desperate plight with her and she was sympathetic to my needs. One morning when I joined her in the office an open copy of *The Times* was on the desk with an advertisement, circled in thick red ink, prominently displayed. A position was advertised for an executive assistant to the CEO of a new international company set up by the ruler of Dubai, Sheikh Rashid, and offered a handsome salary. In spite of my opposition and having no desire to return to the Middle East, Barbara insisted I sit down and write a letter of application. Little did I know that three hundred and forty other people would also apply! The interview process continued for some weeks until I was finally offered the position with the Dubai Aluminium Company (DUBAL). It then took several more weeks before my work permit was issued.

When Barbara and I shared a farewell drink in a local pub in Chelsea, I had no idea I would spend the next fifteen years in this then little-known desert town perched on the shore of the Persian Gulf, or that I would grow to love the country, the people and every minute of my time there. If I had known this, I would not have been so adamant about signing only a two-year contract. The company was insistent that I sign for a minimum of three years, arguing this was essential because of the amount of money they were investing in me, and the need for continuity. This was a real sticking point. We finally agreed on the two-year period and my initial caution was a great source of laughter fifteen years later in the country that had by then become very much my home. I not only became immensely proud of the company, but my work colleagues also became, in many ways, my surrogate family.

Before I left for Dubai and while I was going through the lengthy business of obtaining a work permit, I decided to visit Hadi's sister in France. Of all the people I could think of, I believed Aminah – always his favourite sibling – was the most likely person he would contact. She also had a young family.

This would be the first time I had seen Aminah since Tanya's abduction. In fact I hadn't seen her since the fateful visit to our home in Malaga several years earlier when Hadi and Ibrahim had argued so fiercely. She had been warm and sympathetic during our many telephone conversations in the past months but I was not sure what reception I would receive in person, so naturally I was apprehensive. She had consistently claimed to know nothing of the whereabouts of Hadi or Tanya, but I couldn't help thinking that she wouldn't tell me even if she did know something. I found it very hard to believe that Hadi would not be in contact with her.

Aminah and her family lived in France, near the Swiss border, so I flew to Geneva. On my arrival at their home, the ritual Arab hospitality of a cold refreshment followed by a hot drink and sweetmeats took place, for which I was grateful. However, it was difficult to gauge if this was a genuine welcome or just a formality. We talked for a while then discussed other members of Hadi's family, and I learned of their surprise, shock and sadness at what had happened. Slowly I relaxed a little but I found Aminah a difficult person to read in this situation. Her natural warmth and friendliness were evident but I was still a little hesitant to believe I was truly welcome and being told the truth.

Both Aminah and Ibrahim were very European in their manner and way of life but I couldn't be certain about the extent of their Islamic beliefs. I knew Aminah to be religious, despite her totally Western appearance – her blonde hair, gentle round face, slim figure and stylish dress. Before the revolution, when the entire family lived in Libya, they had sent their eldest daughter at the age of seven to boarding school in France, but this wasn't proof that deep down their Islamic beliefs still didn't prevail. Did they think Hadi, according to sharia law, had a right as a Muslim father to sole custody of Tanya without further contact with me?

Aminah insisted I stay with them overnight. This invitation was totally unexpected and I politely declined, but Aminah wouldn't hear of it and was adamant I stay. As we sat in the small sitting room going over and over where Hadi could be and ways in which we could locate him I heard the front door open. Thinking it was the maid, I was surprised when Ibrahim walked into the room – I had assumed, for some reason, he was away on one of his regular trips to Tripoli. Without hesitation he threw his arms around me, said how sorry he was about what had happened, and how good it was to see me.

Much of my previous conversation with Aminah was repeated and shared with Ibrahim. He was very clear in his criticism of Hadi's despicable conduct and implied that it had sullied the entire family's reputation. Without any consultation with Aminah, Ibrahim assumed I would stay with them and refused to accept my protestations to the contrary.

The hours passed rapidly and during the course of the afternoon their three oldest girls, now fifteen, twelve and eight, came to the sitting room from time to time, while the baby of seven months gurgled happily in her pram. The girls were absolutely delighted to hear that I was staying overnight and immediately began to argue among themselves as to whose bedroom I would share!

The following day when I left to fly back to London there were tears, much hugging and promises on both sides to stay in touch. My emotions were catapulting all over the place during that journey: desperation at another unsuccessful trip because I had learned nothing new about Tanya's whereabouts; appreciation for the hospitality of Aminah and Ibrahim; uncertainty about their claims of knowing nothing of Hadi or Tanya; and apprehension at the prospect of living in yet another Arab country.

Three weeks later my work permit was granted and arrangements were made for my departure to the Middle East.

It was 14 August 1978, and as the plane circled over Dubai anyone lucky enough to have a window seat was afforded a majestic view of the area. The city, on the eastern edge of the inky blue Persian Gulf, was divided in two by its famous natural harbour, the Creek. The landscape was as flat as a tabletop, with the desert stretching as far as the eye could see. This city of approximately three hundred and fifty thousand people was much smaller than I had imagined, and from ten thousand feet looked motionless and quiet.

The British Airways plane came to a halt outside a modern, white single-storey, Arab-style terminal building and when finally the forward door opened, the rush of humid heat invaded the aisles. It was the middle of August and the month of Ramadan – the Islamic holy month, when fasting from sunrise to sundown is demanded. I had been warned before leaving London that under no circumstances should I eat or drink in public during daylight hours at this time and, of course, that I should follow the ever-present conservative dress code. There was no need to cover one's head but some sleeve should be present and a skirt of respectable length was expected.

I reached the top stair of the gantry and it was reminiscent of walking fully clothed into a sauna. The temperature was over forty degrees centigrade and the humidity in the high eighties, which was normal for this time of the year. Sometimes, the heat and the humidity could be worse!

Before I had taken my first step I was struck blind. The condensation on my sunglasses had totally blocked my sight. Quickly removing the offending article only marginally helped as the fiery brightness of the sun physically hurt my eyes.

Once at the foot of the stairs I was approached by a young Pakistani man in a short-sleeved white shirt and beige cotton trousers.

'Miss Margaret?'

After four years in Libya I was used to this formal greeting. Mohamed was employed by DUBAL as a driver, but his role was also to ease the passage of official visitors and company employees through immigration and customs.

While standing in the comfort of the air-conditioned arrivals hall waiting for my luggage, I noticed that the number of women in this large cavernous area could be counted on less than one hand, and although I was very conspicuous, I did not feel the undercurrent of hostility that I remembered being so omnipresent in Libya.

The number of Indians and Pakistanis surprised me, as did the absence of Arabs in their long white robes. I later learned that men from the Indian subcontinent made up the largest number of employees in Dubai, doing every kind of job from labouring and shopkeeping to working in government departments and professional positions.

The drive from the airport to the Hilton hotel was comfortable and short. The hotel was to be my home until the block of apartments where I would eventually be housed was completed. We passed a clock tower, a traditional fixture in most Arab cities, then drove across the Maktoum Bridge spanning the creek.

Dubai Creek had been a safe haven for seafarers for over three thousand years and it had played a major role in the escapades of pirates and smugglers. As the scene of constant commercial activity, the settlement was fondly named 'City of Merchants'. The angular wooden dhows that plied their trade mainly between Dubai, Iran, India and Pakistan lined both sides of the creek and softened the flat, stark-white walls of Arab houses behind the sandy shores.

From the bridge I could look back at the commercial centre already boasting a number of new buildings of seven or eight storeys. The centre was one of the few areas that had the luxury of pavements and some shelter from the searing sun. The opulence of oil wealth was already evident in isolated areas of this developing metropolis. Then the Sheraton hotel came into view. This newly constructed edifice standing majestically on the edge of the creek, with its lofty glass roof and geometrical shapes, was one of the most modernistic I had ever seen. The only people we saw were in the other cars that filled the roads – no doubt due to the combination of summer heat and Ramadan.

The Hilton, my first 'home' in Dubai, was a square, four-storeyed cream building, and although new, of no particular architectural merit. It stood adjacent to the Dubai World Trade Centre with over thirty storeys, which, when completed, would not only be the home to DUBAL's headquarters and my office, but the tallest building in the Middle East.

As I would later experience, Dubai became famous for many 'firsts' over the years, mainly due to the incredible foresight of its illustrious ruler, Sheikh Rashid bin Saeed Al Maktoum, indirectly my new boss. Sheikh Rashid was responsible, with Sheikh Zayed of Abu Dhabi, for forming the United Arab Emirates when British rule of the Trucial States ended in 1971. Changing this small desert community that had relied on the pearling industry and the importing then 're-exporting' of numerous commodities – such as gold, which went to India where the taxes were much higher – into the international city it has become was due to this much-loved ruler's imagination and vision. In 1959, even before the discovery of oil, he appointed a town planner to lay the foundations for the developing city, thereby allowing for Dubai's housing and industrial growth to progress in an organised and systematic fashion.

At seven o'clock the following morning Mohamed collected me from the Hilton and drove me to DUBAL's temporary office in the Bank of Oman building in the centre of town. The company's aluminium smelter, its power station and desalination plant were still holes in the desert, where seven thousand labourers toiled each day to bring the project to life. DUBAL's general office complex, to be situated at the smelter, was also still under construction, as was the city building that would include my future apartment. This was a good start, I thought! However, these proved to be minor problems compared with the financing arrangements still to be made and the political undercurrents.

Driving through the morning traffic on that first day I couldn't help but think, here I am again, living a lie once more. This lie was reminiscent of the one Hadi and I had perpetrated on our return to Libya, which involved keeping our marriage secret. Now, some eight years later, I was doing the same thing again, pretending to be someone I wasn't.

My employment with DUBAL was on the basis of being a single woman. During the job interviews I never said I was single. Nor did I say I was married with a missing child. This was not so much out of deceit but for reasons of self-preservation. For the last ten months or so in London I had been surrounded by friends and colleagues who asked continually about the latest developments in my search. With sincere compassion and in good faith they meant well, little realising the increased level of pain I felt every time the subject was raised. It was the need to avoid these questions that convinced me to masquerade as a single woman in my new home and workplace. And in effect I was a single woman. By now I had no thoughts of being reunited with my husband and, my greatest tragedy, I had no idea of the whereabouts of my darling daughter.

This job promised to be a very busy one – a complicated start-up project in a foreign environment. Because I had experienced start-up situations before, such as Occidental Oil in Libya, I was aware of the confusion, hassle and workload involved.

When I arrived at the open-plan office I was greeted by the secretary. Greta, an English girl, had been hired locally as she was in Dubai with her husband, who worked for an engineering company. Ian, my boss, although expecting me, was on a protracted long-distance telephone call so Greta showed me my office, where piles of papers were already stacked up, and started introducing me to the other staff. There was only a handful, all male and all English except for the Indian tea boy, a mail boy and a driver. As I was desperately trying to remember the new names and faces, Ian appeared and ushered me into his office. We had met a couple of times in London during the interviewing stage but I felt far from comfortable with this high-powered, highly respected man who, I had been informed, was equally well-known in the Arab world as he was in the upper echelons of British industry.

He quickly told me that many new employees would be arriving during the coming months and things would be busy. There was a terrible shortage of housing; he and his wife, Kate, had been lucky and had recently moved into a new villa. Hopefully I would meet Kate in the near future but initially she would be spending a lot of time in England. The new apartment building where I was to live, although behind in its construction schedule, should be completed in a few weeks and meanwhile I would remain at the Hilton. I should waste no time in buying myself a car as there was no public transport and, if I needed it, a bank loan could be arranged.

An important telephone call interrupted us and I left to try to make sense of my office. The room, which was directly next to Ian's, was small and spartan. There were only the essentials – several telephones, an electric typewriter and a filing cabinet. During my short time in Ian's office the paper piles had grown considerably larger. It didn't take long to realise that although Ian was facing an enormous task with this multi-faceted, billion-dollar project, he was a workaholic – one would have to be to undertake such a job.

My own mental state had reached a worryingly low ebb and I knew my only salvation would be to immerse myself fully in the task at hand. So far the position as Ian's executive assistant promised all the requisite hallmarks of a high-level and demanding workload. As it turned out, the madness of those initial months was surreal.

I threw myself into the job. I wasn't interested in socialising, which was helped by the fact that I didn't know anyone except my work colleagues – of these, the men were all married and the only other woman, Greta, was also married. I was lacking in confidence but I somehow hid my low self-esteem behind a facade of frantic work activity. It was as though I was skimming across the surface of real life. I knew if I delved down and entered the real world of personal relationships I might not survive. I was cocooned – like the air-conditioned bubble that engulfed the city in which I lived. In Dubai every place was air-conditioned and, if one ventured outside, the one-hundred-and-forty-degree heat and 90 per cent plus humidity could kill you. It was much safer to remain inside. My bubble was psychological and its fortress-like covering protected me on all sides – from any kind of familiarity. The momentous pace of my life, fuelled by work and long hours, prevented anyone or anything joining me on the treadmill. I felt that if I kept running at this pace I would be safe in my solitude.

The new and strange environment that surrounded me was dazzling. There was construction taking place in every direction and area I visited and scores of huge cranes stretched like sentinels across the horizon. It was just like 'Lego land'. During my first venture beyond the hotel, and our temporary office in the heart of the commercial district, I was amazed at the network of new four-lane roads running through the desert, seemingly going nowhere. Years later, when the desert was no longer visible from the city centre, these roadworks had become the modern suburbs and new industrial areas. When I first arrived, there was also an enormous chunk being dug out of the desert on the edge of the coastal fringe, twenty-eight kilometres from town. This massive hole would later be lined with rocks and cement to become Jebel Ali Port, rivalling Rotterdam in size and developing into one of the most successful free-trade zones in the world.

I was living in one of the most sensuous areas imaginable. Surrounding me was the icy smoothness of marble floors, the textured yellow granules of desert sand, the vibrant colours and rich coarse weave of tribal rugs, the clear blue expanses of azure skies and the green-fringed branches of exotic palms. Along with the sights, the aromas were also overwhelming and diverse. Particularly noticeable was the strongly scented eau de Cologne favoured by Arab men in their bright white dish-dashes. Joining them in a lift – frequently as the only woman present – the men's perfume was sometimes overpowering, and far more rich and evocative than my own. Outside, hot spicy curries were available on every corner. If you went to the local markets the spices could transport you to any country of the world, the sickly sweetness of exotic fruits ripened by the sun could be enticing, but the odour of a cranky camel would soon jolt you back to reality. It was a wonderful kaleidoscope of sights and sounds and scents but nothing soothed my pain.

Those first few months in Dubai passed in a hapless haze. However, I did receive one significant telephone call, just days after my arrival, from the secretary to the president of Dubai Petroleum, inviting me to dinner. Ann, who had only been in Dubai a couple of months, had heard there was a new single girl in town, hence her invitation. We were the same age, the same towering height and, as it transpired, shared many of the same interests. Belfast was Ann's family home but she had lived and worked for many years in London and travelled extensively before arriving in Dubai.

December, with its cooler temperatures, is an excellent time to visit Dubai and that first Christmas, in 1978, saw Ann's parents and younger brother visit for two weeks. Ann, most graciously, included me in all their family Christmas celebrations and I found it humbling to be made part of a family unit. The Irish fun and laughter that filled those happy hours over Christmas lunch would have been a tonic for anyone. In the ensuing years Ann and I were to embark on a life-long friendship, experiencing many happy times together both in Dubai and during numerous trips abroad. However, that was in the future.

The joy of Christmas passed and I returned to the isolation of my apartment. A few days later I found myself confronting the second New Year's Eve since Tanya had been taken. I had been in Dubai for four and a half months and had not developed a close friendship with anyone. Most of the expatriate population was married and to my knowledge I was one of only four single Western young women in town. Invitations were generously offered and on this occasion I had been invited to a party given by one of our senior managers, a Canadian and his wife.

It was late afternoon and I lay in my bed in the apartment that had recently become my new home. The pressure of work had prevented me from giving it any attention. The important elements had been covered – among other things, the washing machine was connected and there were curtains on the windows – but there were still cartons and crates of my belongings waiting to be unpacked. My bedroom was reasonably well organised, particularly my clothes, as I had to dress appropriately each day for the office and look the part. But the rest of the rooms were in chaos.

As I lay under the bedcovers reflecting on the past twelve months, my life appeared to be just as shambolic as my flat. The pressure of working seven days a week, including taking work home when I left the office, usually at nine or ten o'clock at night, was starting to take its toll. This full work schedule was one of the main reasons why I had wanted the job. It allowed me little time to reflect on my personal situation. But now, on New Year's Eve, I stopped to brood on the past.

Tanya's whereabouts was still a mystery to me and I didn't have any leads. Every time my hopes were raised they were cruelly shattered. Insurmountable obstacles appeared in my path every step of the way. I felt myself caught in a downhill spiral and the longer I lay there thinking, the more morose I became and the lower I sank.

I knew it was time to start getting ready for the party but that thought made me even more depressed. I had never liked New Year's Eve with its forced fun and contrived joviality, and on this occasion I knew it would be impossible to muster my emotions and pretend to be happy. How could I possibly join families having fun, laughing, joking and anticipating the joys of a new year ahead when mine was looking so empty and bleak?

The longer I lay there the blacker my whole situation became. Until now I had managed to remain optimistic. Somehow, I had struggled through my difficult times and pulled myself back from the crevasse of despair. But this time was different. The heaviness of my burden seemed overpowering and I could see no faint glimmer of light from the dark depths to which I had fallen. This time there seemed no hope left, and worse, there was not even any desire to continue the search. Every avenue I had pursued had ended in failure. No official authority wanted to know about or listen to my problem, insisting it was a personal matter, not a criminal one. Here I was in a very foreign environment thousands of miles from my family and friends. I had purposely woven a web of secrecy around my private life, but now everything seemed so futile. I would never find Tanya. I could not carry this burden any longer, life without Tanya was not worthwhile and my life was not worth living.

I thought if this were the case, why not end it now? Get rid of the pain permanently. Escape from the fear of facing another day, of always putting on a facade. But how best to do it? I thought of the sleeping tablets in the bathroom cupboard. That would be the easiest method. Then I would not have to find my way out of this empty black hole or face any tomorrows ever again. Tears streamed uncontrollably and swept me further into the depths of gloom.

My crying must have completely exhausted me because when I woke it was just before midnight. New Year was about to dawn. Inexplicably, the thought of a new day somehow gave me a little encouragement. If I could just make it through for another hour or so I might be able to find the strength to continue.

My thoughts turned to my mother. How could I burden her with a further loss after all she had suffered? Mummy was a beautiful lady, both physically and personally, and certainly had not been without admirers until she met the love of her life and married. An idyllic life followed until Daddy was taken by his fatal heart attack at fifty-five years of age, leaving her a widow at forty-eight. The fact that her adored eldest daughter was living and working overseas when it happened didn't help. I had always been very special to my mother and I don't think she ever fully recovered from the loss when I left home. Now years later when her only grandchild had been cruelly taken, she not only suffered her own loss, but I knew she bore mine as well. The only time she had seen Tanya was for six weeks after she was born, a month when she visited us for Tanya's first birthday, and for another six weeks during her stay with us in Malaga. I knew Mummy's one wish was to hold her granddaughter again. It was unthinkable that I should add to all this sorrow. Such a selfish action as suicide would only increase her suffering. No, for her sake alone, I somehow had to use every ounce of strength to pull myself back from this abyss.

The following day, after offering my apologies for my non-attendance at the New Year's Eve party, I dragged myself back to my office and the mountainous workload. There was always a multitude of things happening at once. Now arriving on a daily basis were new employees, who not only needed desks, chairs and consumables for the office but also required accommodation, so houses and furniture had to be obtained. The employees to run such departments as Housing, Personnel, Accounts, Purchasing and so on were only then in the course of being hired, so anybody who was already on board had to do a bit of everything. There was no such thing as prioritising in those days. You just tackled the next disaster! Construction of the smelter and our power station was continuing at a whirlwind pace with the seven thousand labourers on site every day. In addition to this, the completion of our desalination plant was imminent, and Queen Elizabeth II was scheduled to officially open it during her visit in February.

Although the British Embassy was officially responsible for the Queen's visit, there were many dignitaries and VIPs arriving for our inauguration ceremony for whom DUBAL was directly responsible. Several lords, a number of knights of the realm, heads of international banks – the list seemed endless. As well as my daily workload it was my responsibility to arrange accommodation, official functions, cars, drivers and more for all these people. I remember that one of my favourite visitors, a senior banker, arrived without a dinner suit and pleaded with me to sort out the problem. As Billy was well over one hundred and eighty-five centimetres tall and there was no such thing as a local Moss Brothers in Dubai, it was one of the more tricky tasks! However, I did manage to borrow a well-fitting dinner suit from one of our engineers and all was fine on the night. I also recall a very senior gentleman coming to my desk one morning looking very sheepish and holding a pair of trousers, wondering if I had a needle and thread he could borrow to repair a faulty zipper. These episodes were some of the bizarre things that managed to get me through those desperately manic days.

DUBAI
An affair of the heart: 1979–1982

By mid-1979 my life in Dubai had started to return to a slightly more normal pattern. Working hours were still, and would remain, excruciatingly long but my personal life was in better shape. While making a tour of the aluminium smelter, which was due to commence production at the end of October, I suddenly realised its layout was exactly as Anne Leith Walker had described in her reading. Also, I had now moved from my temporary office in the Bank of Oman building to my permanent office on the thirty-third floor of the newly completed World Trade Centre. The entrance to this building had a semicircular drive and a large fountain and was located twenty-six kilometres from the smelter.

My friend Ann, still with Dubai Petroleum, was one of the reasons for the improvement in my existence. Her working hours were also lengthy but we managed to spend a great deal of our leisure time together. Dubai Petroleum had a number of young Dubaians on its staff, which in those days was most unusual – at DUBAL we had been unable to find any locals to employ as the local population was so small. These young men had recently returned from their Dubai Petroleum-sponsored studies in the United States and found it very difficult to settle into the expected confines of life in Dubai after the freedom they had obviously enjoyed in America. There were few people they felt they could relate to: most of the older male Dubaians had not had the luxury of a foreign education; the only local women they were permitted to associate with were the older women in their immediate families; and the expatriate community was made up mainly of older members and family units. Ann and I seemed to fit in with these strays!

In her warm, mothering way Ann befriended the young locals and we spent many happy and often hilarious hours in their company. They showed us parts of the country that other expatriates would unfortunately never enjoy. We visited and stayed at 'farms' owned by their families or relatives. These farms were not the normal working farms I had been accustomed to in Australia, but were luxurious, multistorey buildings with vast, air-conditioned rooms, and indoor swimming pools! The concept of a farm was somewhat different in the desert. There was very little evidence of farming other than perhaps a small vegetable garden or a couple of goats. The entire complex comprised little more than a house in the desert.

One of the greatest privileges that resulted from these friendships was an introduction to the local female population, something not experienced by most foreigners. It was not long before we found ourselves included in a family celebration. A wedding was to take place and Ann and I were generously invited. As neither of us spoke

Arabic we were somewhat apprehensive about being thrust into the insulated environment of a harem.

Ann telephoned me the afternoon of our adventure.

'What are you going to wear?' she asked.

'I think that dark blue floral dress with the white peter pan collar. It is very conservative, comes well below my knees and the sleeves come to my elbows.'

'That sounds great. I'll wear something similar. I wonder what it will be like?'

'I don't know. I just hope that as honoured guests we are not expected to eat the eye of the sheep!'

'Honoured guests! We'll be lucky if anyone takes any notice of us at all.'

'I hope you are right. I'll collect you at seven.'

Following Mustafa, from whom the invitation emanated, we drove a little way out of town to the house where the festivities were to take place. Turning onto a dirt road we continued further until, seemingly in the middle of nowhere, a modest house appeared. Mustafa jumped out of his car while we parked. He quickly announced our arrival to someone behind a slightly open door and Ann and I were whisked inside. A friendly, veiled woman led us into a central courtyard, around which most traditional Arab houses are built. The earthen floor bore a single gnarled acacia tree that was almost bereft of leaves. The pungent, sticky aroma of Arab incense scattered on burning coals filled the air. Noisy children were running in and out having a wonderful time and seated on the ground elderly women, covered by their black abayas and berkas, were smoking hookahs. There was much chatter and laughter in every corner but Ann and I felt uncomfortably conspicuous in this alien world.

As we slowly tried to digest this new experience our arms were tugged and we were ushered back inside, out of the heat of the courtyard. The plaster walls were unadorned and there was no sign of Western furniture. Long, cotton-covered mattresses and cushions were laid at the base of the walls and light mats were scattered on the floor. In a small adjoining room a group of women was seated on the floor and we were encouraged to join them. Ann and I, both being taller than most and not used to sitting on the floor in dresses, awkwardly sat facing each other on opposite sides of a very large tablecloth, while the surrounding women tried to engage us in their incomprehensible conversation. There was much laughing and all Ann and I could do was smile and look bemused. Arabic was beyond us and English was not part of their vocabulary.

Here were women who did not spend hours in beauty salons, worry about their expanded figures, or concern themselves with the latest fashions. They were comfortable in their traditional brightly coloured full-length dresses that covered long trousers – all normally hidden beneath their abayas. That all-encompassing black cover was discarded in the safety of the house. There was no sign of oppression here. These women bore children, loved, nurtured and protected their families, and seemed genuinely happy with their lot.

In later years when we met local women who did speak English they could not imagine why Ann and I were happy to live alone and go to work each day. The idea of being independent in this tribal environment was unthinkable. Surely we would be much happier with a husband who would provide for us!

As Ann and I sat uncomfortably in the midst of this gathering, several women literally dumped a huge platter of rice adorned by hunks of lamb in the centre of the tablecloth. We were encouraged to start. Not used to eating with our fingers, without a plate, and trying to be polite, we each took a small piece of lamb and started to chew. Without any warning a beefy arm flew across my chest thrusting the largest lamb bone in front of my nose. I knew enough Arabic to understand my companion was saying 'Eat, eat'. This was Arabic hospitality at its very best. Ann and I struggled to satisfy the women's insistence that we eat more and more but we only added to their amusement by demonstrating our difficulty in managing rice with our fingers and gnawing meat off the huge bones.

Thankfully the women's attention was suddenly directed to events outside and we were rushed back to the courtyard. The bride, in white Western bridal gown and veil, had appeared and was seated on what resembled a love seat. From outside the high walls came the sounds of shotgun fire and the beating of drums, while inside the women were emitting their high-pitched trilling squeals reserved for special occasions. The groom was about to arrive. The women somehow had miraculously all hidden behind their abayas because of the imminent arrival of the men.

The high, metal double gates on the far side of the courtyard were thrown open and the groom, surrounded by a bevy of men, was brought in and seated next to the bride. As soon as he was securely in place all the other men retreated through the gates and outside the walls. The marriage had taken place and the dancing began – under sharia law the two fathers sign the documents and exchange the dowry well in advance of the party.

Over the years I was lucky enough to be invited to many local weddings, but as Dubai became more sophisticated so did its traditions. The weddings I attended in later years were extremely lavish affairs either in five-star hotels or occasionally in one of the palaces and I was no longer one of only two foreigners present. At these events the women wore long glamorous designer gowns, the latest make-up and hairstyles, and jewellery the likes of which I had only seen in various collections of Crown jewels. The bridal gowns were so elaborately beaded that small ball bearings were sewn into the hemlines and trains to enable the bride to walk and bear the weight of the dress. The men meanwhile were elsewhere at their own party. These 'modern' celebrations certainly lacked the spontaneity and fun of those earlier days.

Some of the best times with our young Dubai Petroleum friends were spent camping on the beach at the east coast, where white sand ran down to the clear blue water of the Gulf of Oman, at the north-western reaches of the Arabian Sea. This was a two to three hour trip through the desert from Dubai, preferably in a four-wheel-drive vehicle if you wanted to arrive without too much trouble on the way. We pitched our tents on the sand and collected driftwood for a fire. There was no sign of other human life in this area except on the rare occasions when local fishermen would sail by. At night it was incredibly quiet and still and the stars were so brilliant you almost felt you could reach up and touch them.

On one occasion I went off to explore by myself. I stopped at a small oasis, bordered by a village that I mistook for an uninhabited ghost town. As I rounded the corner of one of the high-walled, white-washed houses I stumbled on a small group of boys of about nine or ten years of age, all huddled in a circle on the sand playing with some small stones. They were dressed in their little dish-dashes, in varying degrees of white – some still spotless, others covered with red dust from the day's play. There was no one else in sight but as I slowed my pace I could hear the high-pitched chatter of the women from behind the lofty walls and solid metal gates. The boys looked up in unison at this unusual foreign intruder. No one spoke and none of them moved. They just looked – their little round faces surrounded by dark tangled hair and their large black eyes staring at me. We were all surprised.

As I looked at this little cluster of male unity I was struck, as I had been on previous occasions, by the similarities and differences between various cultures. Here were innocent children, happily playing in the dirt, as you might find in any number of places throughout the world. However, one of the main differences in Arab culture, compared to Western tradition, is that the male child is treated like a god. He is given anything he wants and every whim is granted. The patriarchal right of possession is instilled in him from birth. Whereas Western society promotes individualism and admires those who go against the mainstream to succeed and prosper, Arab culture encourages conformity.

On our return to Dubai after this particular overnight adventure, Ann and I had a coffee and laughed about the general chaos and disorganisation of these trips. At times Arab men don't seem to have the same form of Western logic. These young inexperienced men had no idea about planning or order. They were completely spontaneous. If they forgot to bring some necessary items, such as mattresses or lamps, we simply detoured and purchased them from a little stall on the side of the road en route. On one occasion we bought foam mattresses on the way, used them overnight and took them back the next day for a refund!

The conversation slid into a discussion about men in general and Ann commented on the wonderful characteristics that these young Arab men displayed and how enriching such traits would be to a relationship. Before I knew it, the conversation had become deeper and more searching about relationships, marriage and children – as is frequently the case in discussions between single females. Ann was now my very close friend and confidant and I realised to honour that friendship I could not continue to lie about my status. Without a thought to the repercussions, I blurted out my story and why I was really in Dubai. Ann, with enormous grace and compassion, sat quietly and listened. We talked at length about the various details of my past few years. Finally I drove home exhausted from the experience, relieved that I had confided in Ann, but guilty that

I had weighed her down with my burden.

The comfort that my confession to Ann gave me in those early years in Dubai was amazingly therapeutic. Now I had someone to confide in, someone with whom I could talk, whether I was facing an unfathomable decision in Dubai or sleuthing overseas. In the latter case, it was incredibly reassuring to have someone to report to each day, someone who either knew I was safe or would raise an alarm if she lost contact with me.

What a contrast to those first six months in Dubai. In addition to the relaxed, carefree days in the desert with our local friends, there was no end of formal socialising. Smart cocktail parties given by major companies and banks ran almost non-stop from September to April, the cooler and less humid part of the year. Glamorous balls to celebrate Poppy Day, the national days of various countries, as well as those hosted by the various sporting clubs, were prominent features on our annual calendar. Endless dinner parties were given for visiting business associates, visiting friends, anyone's birthday, in fact, any reason at all.

I indulged myself in this social whirl with great gusto. When I wasn't at work, I was either attending or planning a dinner, a cocktail party, or a leisure activity with friends. This was my escape from the heartache and helplessness that surfaced when I was alone. By filling every minute there was little time to think.

Everyone had houseboys to help with the mammoth amount of entertaining and one very enterprising Englishwoman set up a business called The Party People. Through Jane you could order a three- or four-course meal for any number of people. This would arrive at your home in her old ambulance, which no doubt had been picked up very cheaply for the purpose. Out of the ambulance all the essentials would materialise, together with a chef to complete the preparations and oversee the cooking, as well as waiters to make sure the food arrived at the table looking perfect and on time. I felt very uncomfortable having an ambulance in front of my home when guests arrived and, to Jane's surprise, always asked her to park around the corner. Jane's Party People saved my reputation as a hostess on many an occasion when time just didn't allow the necessary thinking process to arrange a formal dinner party, even though my houseboy was there to undertake the work. Phoning through my selection from her menu list was much easier.

The one disguise I knew I had to wear, day in and day out, was my persona as a single woman. This prevented me having to answer painful questions, protected my privacy from curious and prying eyes, and allowed me to pretend for most of my day that everything in my life was normal. Dubai's expatriate community was small and, like all tiny communities, pounced on any behaviour that slightly deviated from the norm. Any such action immediately became the subject of the latest gossip and stories were inevitably exaggerated and enhanced as they progressed along the line from one person to the next. My story would spread like released mercury on glass and would be the talk of the town. This in itself would be unbearable, but I also feared that the more people who knew about my circumstances the greater chance Hadi would have of finding me. The extent of his network in the Arab world was an unknown factor.

'How do you manage as a single woman in an Arab country?' was always the first question I was asked when away from Dubai. It was the thing that fascinated people most. It wasn't until a year or so after my arrival in the country that I started to realise the irony inherent in the question. It was not the Arab men I had to fear.

In my early days at DUBAL I learned that the majority of our small number of employees had followed Ian to Dubai from his previous company. They were loyal, hardworking colleagues who had worked for him for some years. One of them, Stephen, had worked with him for eight years and was now his assistant. Knowing Ian so well, Stephen was a great help to me while I was treading gently in my new role. During those first months I felt very uncertain in the strange environment but when Stephen told me I was brilliant, being able to juggle so many balls in the air at once, I felt much better and a little more confident. After several more months it was Stephen who assured me that Ian was delighted with my work and thought I was doing a great job.

Tall, dark, green-eyed, amusing and entertaining, Stephen was one of those people who always had a story to tell. His public relations background had trained him to get the best out of people. When he was in a room the atmosphere always seemed brighter. In those first six or eight months there was not a lot of socialising among the staff but when there was, Stephen was usually the centre of attention, telling jokes, relating anecdotes and hinting at interesting gossip.

One night quite late, while Ian was away on a business trip, Stephen had used his office to meet with two journalists. The rest of the staff had left hours earlier, the incessant ringing of the telephones had quietened, and I was trying to finish my daily load. After ushering the journalists to the door Stephen returned to my office, sitting, as he usually did, back to front on the chair, and said I should pack up for the day. He slowly leaned the back of the chair closer and in a hushed voice said he wanted to talk to me.

Did I know that because my car was frequently parked outside Ian's house late at night and on weekends, I should be careful? Dubai was a small place and people would gossip. He didn't want me to become a victim.

I slammed shut the file I was working on so hard that a bundle of papers fell from the corner of my desk to the floor. My eyes must have been like slits and my jaw clenched in disbelief.

I shouted at him, 'You, of all people, know how hard I work and the long hours that are necessary to keep this job under control. Not to mention the need to accommodate Ian's availability when he is in Dubai and that means being available at all hours.'

Stephen backed away from me.

'Oh, I know that perfectly well. It's just that —'

Before he had a chance to continue, I shouted at him again.

'I really don't care what people think. The people who really matter, Ian, Kate and I, know the truth. If people are so small-minded and vicious, with nothing better to do, I want nothing to do with them.'

'But, I just meant, if it got to the wrong people —'

'If the authorities want to throw me out for improprieties then let them prove it.'

Sharia law does not permit cohabiting with the opposite sex unless you are related or married. Similarly, any form of sexual promiscuity or indiscriminate behaviour is strictly forbidden.

The air-conditioning was not able to cope with the furious heat exuding from me and I was vaguely aware that my body odour was filling the air. Stephen, clearly surprised by my reaction, stood up and while apologising for upsetting me, backed out of the room. It was almost ten o'clock. I was tired, hungry and overwhelmed by the amount of work still to be tackled, but worst of all wounded that my honour had been called into question. Who were these people talking such nonsense? Very few things make me really angry but questioning my integrity is one of them. Who could I talk to about such a sensitive issue? There was not a soul in the company I was close enough to or with whom I could discuss such a horrible accusation. A good night's sleep, another pile of problems to be solved the following morning, and my knowledge that Stephen's insinuation was totally unfounded helped to put the unpleasant conversation at the back of my mind, but it never completely went away.

By mid-1979, Ian, a couple of other employees and I had moved into the newly completed World Trade Centre overlooking the spread of Dubai. The rest of the staff, including Stephen, had moved to the new offices at the smelter, outside the city.

After some twelve months in Dubai I was comfortable and confident in my job. I was also aware that the Arab people I came to deal with on a daily basis at the ruler's office and the various ministries held me in high regard. My dealings with them were not only easy but also friendly and relaxed. They knew I would do what I promised, they knew I would tell them the truth, they knew I would honour their confidences, and they knew I would help them sort through any problem. Arab men respect and protect their women and I felt they always treated me honourably and with due deference. Rather than presenting a hazard, being a woman was an advantage.

Ian had given me more and more responsibility. He took me completely into his confidence about every detail of our business, which helped me work more effectively. It wasn't long before I knew more confidential information than most others in the company. Soon I was the only conduit between the government bodies and my boss during his frequent absences from Dubai. The Arab officials knew I would track him down wherever he might be in the world and get a response for them as quickly as I could.

Towards the end of the year – possibly early in 1980 – I became aware that Stephen was treating me very differently. I was slow to detect it at first but then wondered why it had not been obvious to me sooner. Also it was clear he was withholding information that I needed to work efficiently and make correct, informed decisions. He was even telling me things that I believed were incorrect. If

I spoke of facts given to me by Ian that Stephen was unaware of he became very agitated.

Ultimately Stephen's overt hostility reached a pitch I could no longer ignore. One morning he arrived from the smelter for an appointment with Ian. Looking morose, he walked up and down, waiting his turn to go in. This I thought, as brief as it might be, was my opportunity. I called him to my desk and asked him to sit down. Without any preamble or niceties I asked straight out, 'Stephen, what have I done to offend or upset you?'

His face went blank, he wriggled in his chair and casting his eyes downwards, denied that I had done anything or that there was a problem. Pressing the issue, I named several incidents I knew he couldn't deny. This was the first time I had ever seen him flustered or lost for words. He had started to mumble some incomprehensible excuse when the door to Ian's office opened as he farewelled his visitor. Stephen lost no time in jumping up out of the chair and almost ran into Ian's office.

A short time later, once the smelter had finished its start-up period and reached full production, a number of staff members, as is always the case, were made redundant. Stephen was among them.

Unfortunately this was not my only experience with Western men who felt threatened or who were jealous of my position in the company and the close contact I had with our many associates worldwide. However, after that first experience I was more aware of the problem, quicker to recognise it and better able to deal with the challenge it presented.

By 1980, some eighteen months after meeting Ann, I had also become friendly with several other single women with whom I socialised. Most were English secretaries employed by the large international companies. We were all used to being invited to formal dinner parties to 'make up the number'. There was always a constant stream of visiting businessmen to be entertained, as well as a few professional male expatriates employed on 'single' status, while their wives and families remained in their home country. Filling the odd seat was almost a professional fait accompli.

It was March and on my one-day 'weekends' – Friday in a Muslim country – as well as water-skiing at the local ski club, I had started learning golf. After a few lessons, Shirley, who was kindly teaching me, invited me to her home for dinner. I had not met her husband before, nor did I know any of their assembled guests. After a period of small talk and convivial conversation over drinks we were led to the table and I tried to figure out who was the visiting 'fireman' – as they were commonly called among the expatriate community. It was not difficult to recognise the married couples in the group and the only stray person, besides me, was a handsome Englishman about my age, sitting opposite me. Conversation flowed freely at dinner and although Crispin and I didn't have too much direct conversation, I found him attractive and slightly mysterious. It seemed that he lived in Dubai and ran his own business. At the end of the evening several guests left together and once outside, Crispin offered to walk me to my car.

My heart jumped when I heard his deep voice on the office telephone the following morning – my adrenalin picked up speed and I felt beads of perspiration appearing on my forehead. He invited me to dinner that evening. This was the start of a passionate affair but, more than that, I had met the love of my life. After the first evening we saw each other as often as possible, making every effort to manoeuvre around the constraints of work and business. As an Aquarian, and loving anything related to water, I was thrilled to learn Crispin had his own yacht moored at the local marina.

Escaping the city to sail on this small craft, swimming on deserted beaches and enjoying barbecues and picnics was how we spent most of our Fridays. During the week, whenever we could, it was dinner at his place or mine.

I had seen a photograph of four small children on a side table in his sitting room but foolishly didn't enquire any further, firmly believing that if Crispin had been married and these were his children, it might be too painful for him to talk about them when they were thousands of miles away. He would enlighten me when he was ready.

Three months later I was enlightened. The 'single' man I thought I had been seeing informed me he was still married and his wife, Amanda, was in England. Although their children were in boarding school she felt the need to be close by. Mortified at this news, I asked him to leave my house immediately. The shock and abhorrence of learning I had been having an affair with a married man initially stalled the pain and heartbreak that soon followed. How could this man, whom I loved unconditionally, have done this to me?

A stream of phone calls, visits and letters to my home followed – all of which I ignored. My apartment, after daily deliveries of plants and flowers, was beginning to look like a florist shop. Four days later, after dinner at the Country Club with Ann, I arrived home to find Crispin waiting on my doorstep. Hours later, after much talking and crying by both of us, the lights were extinguished, but not on our affair. Without further discussion the liaison continued.

Our affair was torrid and the relationship escalated at a rapid rate. I had never felt so contented and so connected to anyone in my entire life. Crispin seemed to know every facet of me – the good and the bad – and for once I was comfortable with this. But of course there was still one thing he didn't know about – Tanya.

It was a Friday night after a long day on the water. We had sailed up the coast from Dubai, cutting through the deep blue sea of the

Persian Gulf. We manoeuvred the boat to catch every slight breeze, seeking some welcome relief from the heat of the sun on our exposed bodies. From time to time we stopped and dived into the cool sapphire water and swam in the buoyant, salty openness. Within minutes of returning to the boat, sparkling salt crystals formed on our bronze bodies and in our tangled hair. There was the smell of wet rope in the salt-laden breeze, and suntan oil tickled my nose. Occasionally we saw the glint of a large turtle skimming the surface of the water before disappearing to its mysterious habitat below.

The galley was my domain and a picnic of smoked salmon, barbecued chicken, a large salad and a warm French breadstick nourished our tide of happiness. Crispin maintained our fluid intake by creating cold, delicious quantities of gin, tonic and fresh lime. Hearing the sound of waves gently lapping on the side of the boat, I imagined all the tiny sea creatures knocking, trying to get in and join our bliss.

That night I lit the candles on my dining table and the soft strains of Frank Sinatra's 'Summer Wind' played in the background as I put the finishing touches to our light supper. It had been such a magic day I wanted it to go on forever. We were both relaxed and lazy after the heat of the sun. The laughter and merriment took a sharp turn when Crispin started to talk about our future. I knew I couldn't keep my secret any longer. If I was to tell this man the truth, it had to be now. There was a long lull in the conversation as I collected my thoughts. The guilt that thus far I had lied, the fear that once he knew the truth he might want nothing more to do with me, filled me with apprehension. I was very nervous about the response this news might engender, but most of all I was terrified I might lose him.

As always, when I told anyone what had happened there was stunned silence. Crispin did not move, did not say anything. My heart raced and the cheese-based dish I had recently consumed churned in my stomach. Conditioned by Hadi to expect screaming, shouting and abuse if I had done something he didn't approve of I found myself cowering, waiting for a threatening reaction.

Without a word, Crispin stood up and walked around to my side of the table. He knelt down by the side of my chair, put his arms around me, and his head against the side of my neck.

'I cannot imagine what you have been through. This can be resolved. I know you are strong and resourceful and I love you more for it.'

He continued to hold me close as he absorbed the news.

Later that night we were both exhausted by my emotional outpouring and it was not long before Crispin had drifted into a sound sleep. Although physically tired my mind was still racing after the relief of unburdening my secret to someone who had listened, without passing any judgement on my actions. He had been sympathetic, understanding and, I believed, as a father could fully comprehend my despair.

I lay admiring the nape of his neck that I so loved; it was so strong and muscular yet slim and refined. I felt safe and secure. With the support of this man, I could do anything. Now that he knew my dark secret, nothing else would faze him. Crispin still loved me even knowing of my failure. For so long I had borne the guilt of losing Tanya. I had always felt that I had been irresponsible, leaving her with Hadi. The failure of my marriage had indirectly led to the terrible predicament in which Tanya had been placed. Now, I felt the comfort of unconditional love. The feeling of confidence this gave me was new and overwhelming and I felt I could achieve the impossible.

Towards the end of July, Crispin was due to go back to England on annual leave. This I knew was going to be an extremely difficult period for both of us, and as he planned to speak to his wife about a separation it would be a very anxious time. On the eve of his departure we had dinner at our favourite French restaurant at the Intercontinental hotel. At the end of the evening he gently placed a small box in my hand, saying that it represented the past, the present and our future. Then he slipped a perfectly fitting Cartier Russian wedding ring onto my finger.

He was to be away for six weeks, and during that time I did not hear a single word. When he was due to arrive back in Dubai I contacted a friend in the travel business and was able to check the manifest so I knew he was on his scheduled flight. I sat by the telephone and waited. No call. No letter. Nothing.

Six days later, beside myself with confusion and despair, I looked up while walking through the local supermarket to see Crispin approaching from the opposite direction. He saw me, smiled, nodded hello and just kept walking – as though I was someone he had been introduced to at a function the evening before. Trembling with emotion I dropped the shopping basket and ran outside to my car. As I was driving out of the car park I realised my stupidity. Surely I had a right to know what was happening in his life, and mine. Backing up, I positioned my car behind Crispin's, blocking his exit. He gingerly walked towards my open window and made some inane comment and excuse as to why he hadn't contacted me. Hurt and angry I sped off, driving home in floods of tears.

As I walked through my front door the telephone was ringing and when I lifted the receiver I heard his voice. He gave me an account of the conversations he had had with his wife during the holiday, the obvious concern he had for making his children a priority, and finished by saying Amanda was arriving in Dubai the following day.

The weeks and months that followed were a blur. I would arrive somewhere after driving for half an hour and couldn't remember how I got there. I made small, stupid mistakes in my work. Worst of all I berated myself for confiding in Crispin about Tanya. Dubai being a small community and the expatriate social scene so active, it was predictable our paths would cross. In the early months when this happened I would simply leave, or if I saw Crispin before I entered a function or a club I would not even go inside. As time went on his presence became easier to deal with and I would merely keep my distance, but the pain of lost love remained.

A couple of years later the inevitable happened. It was a Thursday night and we were both present at a small dinner party, where the hosts had no idea that we knew each other. I arrived unaware that Crispin would be there. As soon as I saw him I could feel the blood rush to my face. Was my blushing due to the embarrassment that our love might be exposed, guilt at our past relationship, or just sheer panic about how Crispin would react? I could feel my legs shaking and my heart pounding. My brain seemed completely numb, leaving me without any idea of what to say or do. The hostess introduced me to a couple of guests I did not know, then to Crispin. We shook hands and he gently squeezed my fingers. I was acutely aware that he held my hand a few more seconds than is considered polite, looked me straight in the eye and beamed a familiar smile. After just a few more minutes I realised we were the only two 'single' guests present.

During dinner and general conversation, Crispin announced to the assembled table that he and a couple of his friends were going on an excursion the following day. They would be heading off in their four-wheel-drive vehicles to the uncharted mountains of Oman, approximately one hundred and seventy kilometres from Dubai, and would I like to join them? Caught completely off guard by this public invitation – and secretly desperate to visit the mysterious area – I could not immediately think of a valid reason to decline.

The following night, after our return from the Musandam Peninsula and as we sat sharing an intimate dinner in my apartment,
Crispin admitted he had issued the invitation knowing I would be
unable to resist such an adventurous journey to unknown territory.

Amanda was on one her frequent long absences from Dubai and
it was all too easy to slip back into old habits and familiar happiness.
As pathetic as it sounds, there were a number of these interludes
over the ensuing years. Although I was aware of the rashness of my
actions and that I was exposing myself to further heartache, I lived
in hope that each time it might be forever. The happiness I experienced in those periods was worthwhile. But, of course, Amanda
always returned.

Over the years, in spite of my deep feelings, I ultimately realised there was no long-term future for me and somehow I found
the strength to avoid any further assignations. Meanwhile, my
job demanded I travel more frequently to Europe and other Gulf
countries and, aided by the significant increase in the expatriate
community in Dubai, our paths crossed less and less.

Coincidentally, almost fourteen years after our initial meeting
Crispin and I both left Dubai at the same time, fortunately to the
safety of different countries.

Dinner at Ann's

DUBAI – AUSTRALIA – DUBAI
Keeping one step ahead: 1978–1982

In December 1978, while enjoying Ann's family visit, I had learned that a lawyer of Hadi's in Malaga, Señor Gavaldon, was trying to obtain a copy of Tanya's birth certificate, as well as a copy of our marriage certificate. This immediately started my pulse racing and my stomach churning because with a birth certificate Hadi would be able to apply for an Australian passport for Tanya. The passport I held for her was only valid for five years and was due to expire in seven months. If Hadi succeeded in acquiring a new passport, and being well aware of his powers of persuasion I knew this was a possibility, the world would be open to them. While they were still in Europe, as I assumed, at least my search area was somewhat contained.

Immediately I sent off a letter to Señor Gavaldon reminding him of all the details of the case, which I had already done in several previous letters over the past year. Again I stressed that with a passport for Tanya Hadi could take her – illegally, because of the Ward of Court document – to any country in the world. I also enclosed a personal letter to Hadi asking him that we at least talk and reconsider our situations. I requested the lawyer deliver this but if he did there was no response.

In the same month I received a letter from Doug Quail, who was still the Australian Consul in Madrid, advising that there had been no response from Canberra regarding the request that the embassy in Madrid be given permission to make enquiries on my behalf.

Then, in early February 1979, an unexpected letter arrived from the embassy. With great excitement I tore open the envelope only to find a letter addressed to someone else! I returned the offending letter to Doug Quail by the next post with a request for a copy of the letter I should have received and waited anxiously. Finally at the end of February I received a photocopy of a letter dated 13 January, advising me that the embassy had been asked by Señor Ricardo Aguilar, another lawyer acting on behalf of Hadi, how he could obtain copies of an Australian birth certificate and a marriage certificate for his client. Doug Quail had told Señor Aguilar to apply to the Registrar General in Sydney for the certificates and had given him the postal address!

Immediately I rushed off a letter to the Chief Registrar of Births Deaths and Marriages in Sydney, setting out the details of my case and requesting them not to issue a birth certificate for Tanya – if they had not done so already. At the same time I sent a letter to my lawyer in Marbella, Señor Fonseca, giving details of the events so far, with the request that he translate it into Spanish and send it to Señor Aguilar. In the middle of March I received a response from the Chief Registrar in Sydney, refusing to cooperate. I wrote a further letter to him with more details and copies of all the relevant documents, but this time I received no reply.

At the same time I put my own wheels in motion. The passport I held for Tanya, issued when she was six weeks old, was due to expire in July. This date had been on my mind for some time and, knowing I would need an up-to-date photo to renew the passport, I had been in touch the previous October with the photographer from Whiteleys. Luck was on my side and he still had the negative of Tanya with Santa Claus. I purchased a print, hoping that the issuing passport officer would accept that she looked like a five-year-old. An application form, the photograph and her old passport were dispatched to the Australian Consul in Athens and I waited.

As Hadi was obviously trying to obtain papers for Tanya I decided to make a quick trip to Spain. At a meeting with Señor Fonseca he advised me that he now believed it would be best for me to apply for custody of Tanya in Spain, explaining that while the case was going through the courts Tanya could not be removed from the country. However, in order to initiate these legal processes I would need to be officially separated.

Willing to try anything, I agreed to commence proceedings for a separation and asked Señor Fonseca to go ahead with this new course of action. He would now need an additional power of attorney to the ones he already held, to enable him to act on my behalf in the court and to seek police cooperation in locating Hadi. Unfortunately the document was not prepared prior to my departure from Marbella. Following my return to Dubai there were many faxes, letters and telephone calls to Señor Fonseca requesting the document. First it had not been sent, then it was supposedly lost in the post. In desperation I had him telex me the content and had the document prepared by the Spanish Embassy. On 3 May, three months after

I had instructed Señor Fonseca to commence court proceedings in Spain, I was able to swear and formalise the necessary power of attorney in the Spanish Embassy in Abu Dhabi, a four-hour return trip from Dubai.

On my return from Marbella I had instructed my solicitor in Sydney, Tony Houen, now used to getting a variety of requests from me from numerous countries around the world, to file for my divorce. This, Tony assured me, because we did not know Hadi's whereabouts, would be tricky, lengthy and expensive – if, in fact, it was possible at all! Nevertheless, proceed we would. Tony appointed a lawyer in Madrid to act on our behalf. We subsequently learned that Señor Gavaldon in Malaga no longer acted for Hadi, nor did a number of his other former lawyers who were contacted. The Libyan Embassy in Madrid said they had no knowledge of him. In order to make any progress with the divorce proceedings it was necessary to convince the court that Hadi could not be traced, so the next step was to place advertisements in all the local Spanish newspapers. Eventually after two years, in March 1981, our divorce was complete, without Hadi ever knowing.

In fact that was only one thing he didn't know. Another surprising letter that arrived on my desk was from Aminah. Apart from very close friends, everyone thought my home address was in Australia. This caused a slight delay with mail but at least it kept my presence in Dubai a secret from Hadi. Since his death threats my fear of what he might do was always at the back of my mind. The letter from Aminah, via Australia, was to advise me of the death of their mother, Om Saad. Once again, Aminah told me she did not know of Hadi's whereabouts. She gave me her new address in France, invited me to visit at any time, and enclosed recent photographs of her girls. As always Aminah's tone was warm and friendly and a pang of guilt struck me for lying to her about my whereabouts.

The news of Om Saad's death filled me with great sadness, more so because Aminah's letter also suggested that Hadi didn't even know about it. At least I was able to express my sadness to my good friend Ann.

During this time another of my prime concerns was the number of bombings carried out throughout Spain by the terrorist group ETA, a Basque nationalist movement that was campaigning for an independent Basque state. The Basques, with their own language and distinct culture, had lived since the Stone Age in the mountainous regions in the north of Spain and south-west France. If Hadi and Tanya were living in Spain they could easily be caught up at any time in one of these terrorist acts.

The ETA threat was bad enough but then my fear escalated to a much greater degree when I read a chilling headline in a London newspaper. Colonel Gaddafi's henchmen in Italy had assassinated a Libyan national. Such reports became a regular feature in national newspapers and international magazines such as *The Economist* and *Newsweek* as Libyans were killed in Rome, London and Bonn. There was obviously a systematic plan in place to kill all Libyans living outside the country who had any connection with the previous regime or who were in any way critical of Gaddafi's government. In fact Colonel Gaddafi publicly announced that all Libyan expatriates should return to Libya or be 'eliminated'!

Libya had a very small population and in the early 1980s it was highly unusual for Libyan nationals to live outside the country, mainly because of the severe currency restrictions disallowing the transfer of funds abroad. It had only been fortuitous that nearly all members of the royal family, the previous government, and a number of the educated elite were elsewhere at the time of the revolution, or had managed to leave, and were now living outside Libya.

Hadi, whose family had had a long history in politics, and who was a distant member of the royal family, was an obvious target. If anything happened to him, what would become of Tanya? How would I find her? Nobody would know where she was or who she was, or if they did, they would not know whom to contact.

After all this time, Tanya's birth certificate and her passport, now renewed, were the only tangible things I had left. I kept them in a special brown leather wallet, which was never far from my side. The two documents made me feel I still had some small important parts of her to cling to. Although her father had managed to get her out of the United Kingdom without these, I wondered how much further he could really travel?

The next piece of information reached me from a contact in Malaga. I was told that Hadi was in touch with a Spanish man in Sydney who, on his behalf, was yet again endeavouring to obtain a birth certificate for Tanya. The urgency now was to try to impede this misappropriation of documents from an Australian government body. Immediately I penned another detailed letter to the Department of Births, Deaths and Marriages in Sydney explaining the situation. To my great relief, this time I received a comforting response advising that without both parents' identification and consent, the obtaining of a birth certificate for a minor would be impossible. Although this should have satisfied me, I had been let down before by government and official bodies. Rules and regulations are one thing but slick-talking people of ill intent, and in some cases the passing of money, have a mysterious way of bending or breaking the rules. With the letter in my possession I made plans to visit Sydney and seek out the Spanish accomplice, whom Hadi had apparently met on a flight in Europe.

I flew to Australia. Finding someone through a Sydney telephone directory is very easy, but as my knowledge of the suburbs was vague at best I enlisted the help of my mother's friend John. Armed with an address for the Spaniard, John drove me to the house, which was not a great distance from where my mother lived. I assumed this person would work during the day so planned our surprise visit after dark. Although I was apprehensive of what might take place after I introduced myself to this stranger, I knew I had the support of John, who I had asked to wait in the car.

Although confused, the man who answered the front door asked me inside. As simply and concisely as I could I told my story to the man and his wife. After I had shown this apparently innocent couple the Ward of Court documents and various other papers to verify what I had told them, they were clearly distressed. Once again Hadi's power of persuasion had convinced them, through a colourful tale, to help him with his plight. They were now clearly embarrassed and assured me that in no way would they get involved with Hadi again.

My visits to Australia every year were both challenging and nurturing. All my friends knew of my predicament and were naturally full of questions and curious to know if there were any new developments; my mother, on the other hand, simply showered me with love, warmth and affection.

My sister Kim was rarely around or even in Sydney. She was now in her twenties and like me had spread her wings, albeit in Australia. She was usually either in the ski fields or working at a beachside resort. This absence during my visits was upsetting and I wondered if her intense dislike of Hadi had influenced her feelings towards me.

After our marriage, following the sudden death of my father, Hadi had seen his role as the new head of the family, and as such felt the necessity to control a spirited teenager who openly resented him and regarded him as an intruder. Poor Mummy, never comfortable with underlying tensions, wanted to avoid any friction and tried to be a mediator, but was not very successful. I well remember the pouting looks and scowl on Kim's face as she flung thunderous looks at Hadi across the dining table when he told her what to wear or what *not* to wear, what time to be home, and questioned her endlessly about her friends. For the entire duration of our visits to Sydney – before the birth of Tanya – Mummy would be on tenterhooks trying to maintain as little acrimony between Kim and Hadi as was possible.

Could that be why Kim was avoiding me?

In spite of Mummy's intense fear of flying, she visited me each year in Dubai. She loved meeting and being entertained by my generous friends and witnessing my busy lifestyle first-hand. I will never forget the alarmed expression on her face the first time we put her on a camel; her awe at the modern architecture of the ever-increasing number of high-rise buildings and spectacular hotels; her disgust when she first tasted hummus; and her delight and laughter while in the company of our mischievous local Dubaian friends. However, while Mummy loved her visits to Dubai and looked forward to the next time, I failed in persuading Kim to join her.

After my visit to Sydney and my meeting with the Spanish couple, I was relieved that for the moment I appeared to be one step ahead of Hadi's attempts to obtain a birth certificate for Tanya.

On return to Dubai I received a call from Eleanor, a friend I had met originally at a small yoga class some years before. Her half-Malaysian, half-English background was the origin of her exotic beauty – highlighted by her high cheekbones, dark hair and laughing eyes. Her slim figure was always wrapped in slightly sexy but elegant clothes. We had shared skiing holidays together and her love of adventure and fun were intoxicating but, more importantly, she was a kind and generous friend.

Eleanor told me of a course she was about to commence. It was starting at the end of the week and she asked whether I would like to join her. The lectures were to be given by an American woman, who was flying in to conduct the course. I had never heard of Silva mind control, started by Jose Silva in the late 1960s in Texas, and thought it sounded somewhat fanciful. However, secretly I also thought it might aid me in some small way in my search for Tanya and was prepared to try anything.

Mind control, I was told, teaches you how to go into your inner consciousness, how to change yourself, to solve problems and help others, and learn to harness the power of your mind.

The course was run from a small room in the company offices of an earlier 'graduate'. The room was set up like a theatre with four or five chairs on either side of a central aisle. We were cocooned in this small space somewhat reminiscent of a tiny aircraft, and affording equally limited escape opportunities! There was a slight tension in the room among the approximately forty male and female strangers, covering a broad age group and numerous nationalities, as no-one was quite sure what to expect.

After a brief outline of the course we were launched straight into the basis of the Silva method – going to alpha level – where the brain operates at a much slower rate and where the creative right hemisphere is specifically enhanced. Relaxation encourages this enhancement. Because of our yoga experience, Eleanor and I found going to alpha level relatively easy but we were aware that other members of the class found it difficult to totally relax.

During the eight-night course, we were promised we would be instilled with great confidence to determine our life and future. At the finish and armed with these new tools, I sent my wish into the universe, 'To know of Tanya's whereabouts'. At that time I was only vaguely aware of the expression 'Be careful what you ask for', and was later to regret I had not been more careful and more precise when making my wish.

Tanya Senussi
1982

BARCELONA
Anonymous letter: January 1983

After what seemed like countless trips to Europe, which always culminated in a dead end, one night a telephone call interrupted a dinner party at my home in Dubai. It was a call from my mother in Sydney, who had received an unmarked letter from Spain addressed to me. On asking Mummy to open the envelope, she discovered inside a small white piece of paper with Tanya's name and the name and address of a school in Barcelona printed in black biro. My overwhelming surprise and joy were immediate. After a long period of crying and trying to control my emotions, I asked my mother to forward the envelope and note to me by express mail. After replacing the telephone receiver I continued to cry uncontrollably. The years of heartache and sadness seemed to all flood out at once.

Several days passed while I waited for this mysterious missive. Every time a mail delivery was put on my desk I stopped whatever I was doing to see if my mother's handwritten envelope had arrived. It finally came.

Until that moment, only two people in Dubai, Ann and Crispin, knew my story. Due to important commercial developments in the company, Ian had asked me to cancel a long-planned skiing holiday I had arranged with a group of friends later that month. How could I explain my sudden desire to run off to Europe? Now my hand was being forced. The only thing to do was to confide in Ian and admit that – although now divorced – I was not the single person he thought he had employed. I had been living a lie and deceived him. How would I face this honourable man who had trusted me and been so generous?

The following morning in Ian's office I felt sick to the pit of my stomach as I clumsily attempted to explain the reality of my personal situation. Ian sat quietly for what seemed like an eternity and eventually, very calmly, said we would have to do everything possible, as quickly as possible, to retrieve Tanya, and if I thought there was anything he could do, I must just ask. This was an indication of the magnanimous nature of the man I worked for and who became a treasured friend.

Five years earlier, after an introduction from Brian Lewis, I had engaged the services of a lawyer in Barcelona, Señor Morales. He was the next person I contacted, quickly bringing him up to date on the latest developments. He suggested that in order to make use of the few days prior to my arrival, we should employ a private investigator to find out as much as we could about Hadi and his present circumstances. I readily agreed.

The plane trip to Spain seemed the longest journey I had ever made. Who would I encounter at the other end? Where would I start?

What would I say? How would I cope without speaking the language? Could I prove my story? Yes, of course I could – with my marriage certificate, birth certificates for Tanya and me, and the passport I still had for Tanya. Surely this would be sufficient evidence.

I had booked into the modest Hotel Monegal, where I had stayed five years before when I visited all those schools, thinking Tanya would be at one of them. This time I arrived feeling far more confident. Despite a tiring overnight journey from Dubai via Frankfurt to reach Barcelona, I was frantic with anticipation, believing my long search for Tanya would soon be over. Further confirmation that my luck had definitely changed was the presence of an antiquated telephone sitting on the bedside table. Rooms with this modern facility were limited but my request, made at the time of booking, had paid off.

I wasted no time in meeting with Señor Morales. It transpired that in the few days prior to my arrival, he and the private investigator had been able to establish that Hadi lived with a Spanish woman and her three teenage children. They lived in an apartment she owned not far from the school that was listed on my mysterious note. She also owned and ran a dry-cleaning business in the centre of town. Our car was still registered in Hadi's name. The silver Mercedes coupé was readily recognisable among the small and economical European cars that dominated Spanish roads. However, there didn't seem to be any official record of Tanya anywhere.

At the end of our meeting Señor Morales advised me he had to leave the following day for a pre-arranged one-day appointment in Madrid, but agreed he would meet me the morning after his return and we would go together to the school. He begged me, in the meantime, not to make contact with Tanya, Hadi or the school.

I made my way back to the hotel, knowing there was no way I could just sit and wait for Señor Morales to return. I hailed a taxi and the driver nodded his acknowledgement of the school's where-abouts from the address I showed him – I had transcribed it onto a flimsy piece of notepaper. Before I had time to think more about it I was outside the school, not quite knowing what I was going to do. It was just before the children were due to leave for the day so I waited patiently. Noisily the children started to file out of the school. I searched every little girl's face, looking for Tanya. The children continued to walk out of the school while my eyes darted from one to the other. It was now over five years since I had last seen my precious bundle of joy, so would I even recognise her?

My breathing suddenly stopped and my heart pounded as the familiar long silver Mercedes glided to a slow stop directly in front of the school gate. The car reminded me of the predacious and vicious barracudas I had seen and been frightened by many times when scuba diving. I did not see Tanya but because the passenger door opened and closed before the car slid away, I knew she had been collected. The car had come from behind me so I didn't get a good view of Hadi but I saw enough to know it was him.

Many minutes must have passed while I sat foolishly in the back of the taxi, lost in reverie. The schoolyard was empty and all the waiting guardians gone, when I realised the patient taxi driver was looking quizzically at me over his shoulder. There was nothing to do but return to the hotel.

After a disturbed night's sleep, I rose early the following morning. I looked at the telephone longingly, wishing there was someone I could call, but it didn't allow long-distance connections, although international calls could be put through to the room from the front desk. There was no way I could heed Señor Morales's advice. So I formed another plan. I had brought the basic elements of a disguise with me. The mirror in the hotel bathroom was small and I realised it was not the best quality as I struggled to make the short, curly blonde wig, covering my long brown hair, look as natural as possible. The beige Burberry trench coat that I donned was appropriate for the cold overcast winter morning but the dark sunglasses were a little out of place! In my superficial disguise I left the hotel and ventured into Plaza Cataluña to find a taxi in the midst of the early morning rush.

As I crouched down as low as I possibly could in the back of the taxi I asked the driver to park opposite the entrance to the school and just wait. How I prayed that he had understood my poor Spanish and would go along with my odd request. As the children started to arrive I searched their faces to see if I could recognise Tanya. Child after child filed through the school gates but for me there was no recognition. Then I spotted the familiar car again.

I watched as it pulled up right in front of the school entrance. My heart was thumping but in spite of my immediate instinct to jump out of the taxi and run to Tanya, I knew I had to hold on for just a little longer. The car, as if on purpose, interfered with my view. As the passenger door opened, all I saw was the back of Tanya's navy school uniform, which all the children wore, and a dash of brown hair. Then she had disappeared. The car remained waiting at the entrance for what seemed an unusually long time and I was afraid that, in spite of my disguise, Hadi had spotted me. But after Tanya had completely disappeared the car slowly drove away down the hill. In a tiny trembling voice I told the driver to follow the Mercedes. I had no idea where it might lead us but I wanted to know how Hadi would fill his day.

To my surprise, after just a few blocks the car indicated it was turning off the road and into a driveway. The poor taxi driver must have been very confused as I urgently shouted at him to stop. The car disappeared down the drive of a multistorey apartment block. Clearly it was the entrance to the owners' underground car park. This must be where they lived, the address that Señor Morales had discovered. It was an opulent-looking building and in the best part of town.

After a short but safe distance, outside a parade of shops where I had spotted a cafe, I summoned the driver to stop and gave him a handsome tip. Luckily there was a vacant table inside the front of the cafe where I was able to sit at the window and watch the exit of the underground car park. I had almost consumed my third cup of coffee when I saw the silver car leaving. Should I wait for its return? And then do what? No, I had a better idea.

After a quick trip to the hotel to discard my disguise I went back to the school. By now it was mid-afternoon. I found my way to the general office and sent a message via a teacher to the headmistress that Tanya's mother would like to see her. I then waited. Finally one of the staff members came to collect me.

In spite of my well-practised ability to hide my emotions, I was conscious of my legs and arms shaking uncontrollably. The thunderous beating of my heart blocked out all my attempts to think. I stumbled behind the teacher who led me to the headmistress's office. It was formal and dark, with heavy Spanish furniture, a large wooden desk, leather chairs and, lining two walls, bookshelves full of heavy academic-looking tomes. There were framed certificates on another wall and a sombre oil painting of an elderly grey-haired gentleman, who had probably been the school's founder.

Señora Burgos was an elderly woman of about sixty years, with grey hair pulled back in a neat French roll. She was tall in stature, comfortably round but decidedly spinsterish in appearance. In my broken Spanish and with the help of my wad of documents I tried my best to explain who I was. To my surprise, with a forceful swish of her hand she pushed all the papers back across her desk and declared, 'I do not need all this. I can see just by looking at you that you are Tanya's mother'!

My heart took a great leap. This was the very first confirmation that Tanya was alive, that someone had seen her and knew of her existence. Even if she was not at this school, the woman sitting in front of me knew who she was, and more extraordinarily, had admitted that she recognised me as Tanya's mother.

Señora Burgos told me what a delightful student Tanya was, happy, intelligent and loved by all her teachers. However, there was one enormous problem. Did I know that Tanya believed, as everyone had been told, that her mother was dead?

At first I thought I must have misunderstood Señora Burgos's Spanish and so repeated in my own broken Spanish what I thought she had said. I could not believe my ears when she re-confirmed her statement. This was a thunderbolt I had never imagined. How could Hadi be so cruel to tell Tanya such a lie?

Señora Burgos, seeing my shock, continued in Spanish but I was no longer listening. When she finally attracted my attention I realised she was inferring that this misconception presented quite a stumbling block. The conversation was extremely intense and I became conscious of resorting to a nervous habit of flicking my hair. Even though I had been made to feel at ease by the Señora, I was acutely aware of the importance and possible consequences of this interview. We struggled to converse for a little time, impeded by the language barrier, then Señora Burgos invited me to leave her office and wait in an adjoining room. My anxiety increased. Was she getting an interpreter, was she calling Hadi, or did she just want time to evaluate the situation in which she found herself? Now there was this unforeseen element – Tanya did not know I existed.

Would I now have what I was looking for and end my search or would the door be slammed shut in my face once again? Could I withstand the tension any longer? Something told me I had to remain calm and present a figure of composure and discipline.

Surely this would be important in the headmistress's decision as to whether she should side with me as opposed to Tanya's father, who after all was paying the school fees.

The room I had been ushered into was dark and richly furnished in the trappings of the Spanish middle classes. I struggled to contain my nerves and emotions and without thinking, there I was again, flicking that stray piece of hair that hung beside my face. It wasn't in my eyes, it wasn't interfering with my vision, it wasn't even tickling me, but I felt the compelling need to remove it. I paced around the room, totally ill at ease and completely out of my own environment. If I had been in the counterpart of this room in England, surrounded by familiar English furnishings from the same period, I would have felt more comfortable. It was not just the language barrier that was foreign to me here.

All the time I was wondering what I should say to Tanya first, especially in the light of this new situation. How would she react? What would I do if Tanya no longer spoke English? How would we deal with Hadi?

Before too long, Señora Burgos escorted me back to her office. My excitement and anticipation rose to new heights but then fell as the Señora explored the possibilities of how we could proceed. She was anxious to help and sympathised with the extraordinary situation that both Tanya and I were in. She again told me of Tanya's ability as a student, and how everyone adored her. But she also informed me of her concern about Hadi smothering Tanya. She was obviously troubled by this and believed it unnatural for a father to be so protective and adoring of a girl of nine.

The major problem we had to face was that Tanya had believed, for many years, that her mother was dead. When Hadi kidnapped her, that event would have been an enormous trauma for her to deal with. However, she had apparently dealt with it and was to all appearances a happy, well-adjusted girl. If we now traumatised her again, by my sudden appearance, it could be very dangerous. Señora Burgos was clearly concerned about this issue and assured me she would speak to other professionals on the matter and seek their advice.

Seeing my devastated reaction to her view that she shouldn't risk traumatising Tanya further by allowing me to see her at this stage, she kindly asked if I would like a photo of Tanya. She produced a class photograph and pointed out Tanya. My heart almost stopped at the first sight of my daughter in nearly five and a half years. What a beautiful young girl – light brown hair and taller than all the Spanish girls. I could not see any resemblance to myself except possibly the height.

Where should we go from here? By this time the Señora was displaying great warmth towards me and had been gentle and understanding with my periodic emotional outbreaks. She finally suggested she would call Tanya into her office on the pretext that I was a visiting school inspector from England, and she would ask Tanya to communicate with me in English. She would only do this on the strict understanding that I remain composed and not physically approach Tanya in any way. If Tanya recognised me then the outcome would be easy. However, if a negative outcome was the case we would have to think again.

When the door opened and Tanya entered, my fingers were white from the force of clenching the sides of my chair. I tried as hard as I could to make my breathing slow and rhythmical but to no avail. I couldn't take my eyes off my gorgeous daughter – I was mesmerised as I tried to take in the changes that had taken place in the appearance of this beautiful innocent being over the years. Tears welled in my eyes and I was relieved that Tanya was listening intently to whatever Señora Burgos was saying. She seemed very shy and listened while the Señora explained my presence. Not once did she look directly at me.

I was suddenly aware that Señora Burgos was waiting for me to make the next move so after taking a gasp of breath I finally asked Tanya about her English studies. Her response was slow and hesitant, her head remained bowed, her English was obviously basic in the extreme, and any recognition of me was non-existent. The Señora could see that I was not handling the situation very well and helped out with questions to Tanya in her more familiar Spanish language. We were getting nowhere and as hard as I tried to prolong those moments, I knew Tanya would be sent back to her classroom. Once again she would be out of my life, be it temporarily, and she would not have had a clue as to who I was. In no time at all Tanya was thanked by the Señora for coming and dismissed.

I could no longer contain my emotions. Tears cascaded down my face and I sobbed. My body felt like lead in the chair and no sound, no sight, nothing had any impact on me. Should I have hugged Tanya when I had the opportunity? Should I have blurted out who I was? Should I have shattered the lie that she had lived for the past five years? Was it too late, could I run to her classroom, find her and steal her away? How could I next see her? Perhaps I could hide in the school all day and see her again before she left? What would Tanya be thinking? Would she be excited or confused? Out of all her class, Tanya had been chosen to meet the visiting English inspector and undoubtedly she would talk about this experience with her classmates. Would she tell her father when she got home?

Señora Burgos was bending over me, offering tissues from a small cellophane packet. She was very formal in a gentle way, and her matter-of-fact manner eventually forced me back to reality. I didn't understand most of what she said until I heard her say we would meet again the next day. This would give us all time to try to think of a way to resolve the situation. I agreed that I would return the following morning with my lawyer. She walked me to the door and within seconds I was standing alone in the deserted street. Crestfallen, I returned to the hotel.

Later that afternoon I called my mother and my boss from the international telephone exchange opposite the hotel to give them an update. While out, I took my treasured gift of the school photograph to a studio and asked them to isolate one student from the group and blow it up several times to a larger image.

The following day Señor Morales and I were received by Señora Burgos in a cordial manner and together we rehashed the facts and tried to decide how to proceed. During the discussion, she advised us she had spoken to a couple of child psychologists and had related our dilemma. Unfortunately, they had confirmed her initial reaction – to suddenly produce a *live* mother to Tanya would be far too traumatic and this situation should be dealt with very carefully.

The Señora suggested a number of alternatives. The school was planning a skiing excursion to the Spanish Alps. If Tanya was allowed by her father to go, it could be arranged that I also be at the ski resort. At least this way, I would be in the same place and have unhindered access to Tanya and thereby rebuild a relationship. Another possibility was that as the school was Catholic, Tanya should take her first communion shortly and we could speak to the priest and try to arrange something through him. This last suggestion, being in the immediate future, was more palatable to me and we agreed this plan should be put into action.

When Tanya joined the school three years earlier, Señora Burgos was told that the child's mother was dead. Her plan now was to ask Hadi to come to her office on the pretext of filling in a form for the education department. During the interview she would ask him for details about Tanya's mother and in the process hopefully get him to admit that she was alive. This would enable her to talk to Hadi about the difficulties and the injustice of the situation.

I could just imagine the scene. Señora Burgos was in many respects doing what would be regarded in Spain at that time as a man's job. This was reflected in the decor of her office and also by the dark, severe clothes she wore. Her demeanour was serious but pleasant and I could imagine her being very business-like with all the parents. Hadi on the other hand had a warm and friendly manner for those he wanted to impress and was always ready for conversation and a joke. The attention to detail in his appearance was always evident. This was a man who dressed immaculately, wore only the best Italian suits made from the finest fabrics, tailored shirts, silk ties and expensive leather shoes. His colour coordination was to be envied and he could wear wonderful, bright colours in that unique European way – never looking ridiculous.

Pleasantries would be exchanged. Hadi would be his usual engaging self but Señora Burgos might lack her usual calm and confident manner, knowing the task ahead. She would be trying to get him to admit to a terrible lie as well as trying to elicit the real truth with all its ramifications.

How would she approach him, this urbane fee-paying father of one of her students? Would she be caught out during her questioning and let him know not only that I knew Tanya was at the school but also that I was in Barcelona? How would he react? Had she ever experienced his other hidden side?

The Señora suggested we leave it with her to think about further and she would contact Señor Morales once a meeting with Hadi was arranged.

At the end of the day, before I returned to the hotel I passed by the photographic studio. The photograph of Tanya was now a reasonable size and as I gazed longingly I tried to read the different aspects of her face. By blowing up this one section of the school photograph the image had become a little grainy and had lost some detail, but to me it was the finest photograph in the world. That lovely, gentle smile and those high cheekbones. Her shoulder-length brown hair, by its wispy fly-away strands, told me she had inherited the same baby-fine hair that my mother and I shared and had struggled to control over the decades. It was difficult to determine the colour of her almond-shaped eyes; they were not brown – possibly hazel – but with a definite touch of green. Thankfully, they were not at all sad but the happy eyes of a contented nine-year-old.

How I longed to be able to touch that fine, soft skin which was almost shiny in its innocence. Being in a Spanish environment and living in a Spanish home she would almost certainly be bathed in the familiar fresh-smelling eau de Cologne that Spaniards used so liberally. I wondered continually about her emotional state. Although I had been assured Tanya was a happy student who did well in her studies, I wondered if she ever thought about her mother who had supposedly died years before, what her mother may have been like, and if they shared any similarities? How precious this photograph was, the only tangible thing I had to hold.

After several days in Barcelona, with the support of Señor Morales and comforted by the feeling Señora Burgos was on my side, my confidence started to slowly return and I was certain we would find a solution. While we waited for Señora Burgos to call, I decided to do some of my own detective work.

There was no way of knowing who could have sent me the anonymous note but I had an extremely strong suspicion that it was Señora Valero, Hadi's de facto wife. The only way I could think of obtaining a sample of her handwriting would be on a receipt from her shop.

Señor Morales had managed to find the address of her dry-cleaning business. It was only a short bus ride from my hotel and within walking distance of the main road. Señor Morales produced an old navy blue and burgundy striped tie and suggested I should take this with me as it would be less obvious than an item of my own clothing. It was a slim camouflage but seemed a brilliant idea at the time.

His directions were clear and as I walked along the side street towards the shop I was trembling and full of apprehension. I had no idea what I would find or what to expect. The shop appeared sooner than I had anticipated and was on a corner. Without stopping I walked straight in. To my surprise and relief there were no customers in the shop and a lone woman stood behind the counter.

It was not the sort of place I expected – more of a laundry than a drycleaners, and after the modern, stylish drycleaners of Dubai, this was somewhat shabby and resembled a workshop.

Was this woman the Señora Valero I was seeking? She was older than I had expected, more Hadi's age than mine. She was average height, medium build, with short, permed, strawberry-blonde hair. She looked very much the mother of three grown-up children and her attire was appropriate for a drycleaner.

For a moment all I could focus on was her sad, dismal expression. Even the arrival of a customer did not change it. Those brown eyes were so sorrowful and her mouth, while not unattractive, was drooping with palpable misery. My heart went out to her. I had been there myself. How did she get to this stage? I suspected she would contemplate almost anything to change her situation.

She had obviously been married, but whether she was widowed or divorced Señor Morales had been unable to ascertain. Divorce in Spain at that time was highly unusual. Raising three children as a single woman would have been a great challenge in the culture of the time, not to mention the financial burden. However, from what little we knew it seemed she was financially comfortable. She owned the apartment in one of the best buildings in a very affluent district of Barcelona where she, Hadi and Tanya lived. She owned the dry-cleaning business.

How convenient for Hadi to find a pleasant, educated woman who owned her own home and her own business, and had raised three children. Here was the perfect surrogate mother for Tanya with an established home and income. Señora Valero, no doubt having had a lonely and difficult number of years, would have easily been seduced by Hadi's immense charm, sophistication and air of wealth. But now, after several years of living together, the outcome was etched on her lugubrious face.

I have no idea how many minutes passed while all these thoughts were flashing through my mind, before I realised I had to say something. In my best Spanish, I tried to ask how many days it would take to dry-clean the tie. At some stage I indicated my approval and waited for the receipt. It was as though she had been expecting me and read my mind. Instead of writing a receipt she simply gave me a numbered voucher and said it would be ready the following day. The tie was never collected.

Two days later, Señor Morales and I were seated in a restaurant where we had agreed to meet Señora Burgos. It was eight o'clock in the evening. We had chosen a rear corner table for a little more privacy as many people were filling the room on this cold Spanish night. The familiar smell of olive oil, fried food and red wine permeated the air. The noise level was high enough to remind me I was in Spain, everyone chattering and gesticulating in a characteristically European manner.

I looked up as Señora Burgos entered the restaurant through an adjacent door. Immediately I knew something had changed. Something was wrong. The look on her face was sour and her body language defensive and although she saw me, she looked straight past. Up to this point she had been sympathetic, compassionate and willing to assist me. Instinctively I knew this had changed.

As she approached the table Señor Morales rose to greet her. Instead of a simple friendly greeting, there was a lengthy exchange in Spanish, with Señora Burgos monopolising the conversation. Señor Morales was obviously concerned at what he was hearing but tried not to let it show. Eventually both sat down at the table and Señora Burgos greeted me in a perfunctory manner. Silly small talk was awkwardly exchanged and drinks were ordered. Señora Burgos gave a veiled excuse as to why she was unable to stay for dinner with us as planned.

Eventually the Señora told us that she had met with Hadi in her office that day. Now I knew why her whole attitude had changed. What was his story this time? There were many tales I had heard from various people over the years and I had shared these with the Señora. The most common were that I had abandoned Tanya; I had run off with all Hadi's money; I had run off with another man; I was the reason Hadi had left his home country; and I had more or less been taken off the streets by him and treated like a princess. None of these stories contained any truth but Hadi was extremely convincing. No doubt, to draw people's sympathy, he would also stress the fact that he was looking after his daughter alone.

Señora Burgos confirmed that while filling out the form and under close questioning Hadi had admitted that Tanya's mother was alive. At last we were getting somewhere. He had told her that Tanya, like her mother, was born in Australia, her mother's name was Wilcox, but he did not want Tanya ever to know this name. He went on to tell her that I had run off to London with another man, abandoned Tanya, had a bad car accident and he didn't know whether I was alive or not. He had brought Tanya back to Spain and lived in a hotel in Gerona for two years, where he met a Spanish woman whom he married and moved with to Barcelona. He also told her that although he had once been very rich I was responsible for him no longer having any money. There was little else that she conveyed to me, except that once again Hadi was threatening to kill me – or anyone assisting me – if I ever tried to see or have contact with Tanya. This was the one part of my saga I had not broached with the Señora in any of our previous conversations.

There was more hurried conversation in Spanish with Señor Morales while the Señora looked very uncomfortable the entire time. She clearly did not want to be in the restaurant or anywhere else in my company. I could only presume this was due to Hadi's constant threats of violence to anyone who dared help me. Then came the final blow. Señora Burgos looked at me and told me she had done as much as she was able and there was no way she could help me any further. With that she gulped down the rest of her wine and hurriedly excused herself.

Señor Morales and I sat silently. Even he was subdued. I was completely stunned by this turn of events, particularly the Señora's now unpleasant and hostile attitude. Had Hadi's threats and insinuations contained new unsavoury suggestions about me? I pondered this question with Señor Morales while we tried to figure our next plan of action. Could Hadi have said I was a drug addict, or a prostitute? Whatever he had said, it had to be a great deal worse or more frightening than his normal lies to warrant this complete reversal of attitude by the Señora.

I experienced another sleepless night. Any strategy I may have envisaged to bring about a reunion with my daughter had been completely shattered. In the course of the conversations with Señora Burgos I had been warned that Tanya should not be told of my existence until she was sixteen! The once-friendly headmistress was now blatantly hostile towards me, and Señor Morales, with his best intentions, was unable to advise me further.

Sitting in his office the following day we nevertheless tried to figure out our next move. Our only source of help, Señora Burgos, was now out of the equation. Hadi obviously kept Tanya under very close scrutiny, and Señora Valero didn't look as though she could withstand any more tension in her life.

My biggest worry now was the advice Señora Burgos had related to us from the child psychologists. This I had to hear for myself first-hand so I enlisted Señor Morales to liaise with Señora Burgos to find out who was the most senior and respected child psychologist in Barcelona. Señora Burgos did offer to arrange an appointment with the senior child psychologist in the local children's hospital. The following day Señor Morales accompanied me to his office.

The doctor, in his starched white jacket, took us to his small office at the rear of the building. The interview was in Spanish and although most of the conversation was between the doctor and Señor Morales, I more or less understood what was being said.

In spite of willing the doctor to offer me something positive, his advice was that Tanya should not be told, at this time, of my exist-ence. He suggested we wait until after puberty, and ideally not before she was sixteen. Somehow she had coped with the trauma of being separated from her mother and her mother's reputed death. How, he did not know, but she had. If another shock was now thrown at her, she may not be able to cope and it could have a dramatic effect on her for the rest of her life. This was neither the verdict I wanted to hear nor one I could believe. I had no doubt this was a plot by Señora Burgos in conjunction with Hadi.

We left the doctor and went back to Señor Morales's office where I asked him to find me another child psychologist, preferably one who spoke English, and make an urgent appointment. He telephoned me that evening having made an appointment for the following day.

Señor Morales collected me from the hotel and took me to an office in the centre of town where, full of hope, I found myself in the more familiar surrounds of an office with a doctor in a suit. The discussion took almost the same course as that with the doctor the previous day, and although I tried to implant my own ideas and feelings in this man's head, the outcome, to my astonishment, was the same.

Now I was really furious. It can't be true. It's because they are Spanish. They don't understand. They don't think the same as we do. Their medicine is way behind the times. There was no way I would accept this ridiculous advice.

Señor Morales, not wanting me to go back to the hotel and be alone, invited me to join him and his wife for supper. I could see that this whole ordeal was also weighing heavily on him. However, I had other plans. Assuring him that I would be fine, I arranged to meet him the following day.

On the way back to the hotel I stopped to telephone Norah, a friend in Dubai who had a great deal of experience in children's education. Norah had no idea of my story and like almost everyone else thought I was a single career woman. However, when I asked her to find me, as quickly as possible, a top child psychologist in England and their telephone number she did not question my request.

Still not accepting the situation I spent another restless night, confident I could prove the Spaniards wrong. The following morning I was awake very early. The curtains at my hotel window were purely for decoration; they were so thin they welcomed the sunlight as soon as it appeared above the horizon and the noise of the traffic in the square below entered the room unhindered. While going over and over the events of the past days, the telephone brought me back to reality. It was Norah and in her usual efficient manner she gave me a telephone contact for the person who I believed would solve the dilemma. He would be expecting my call between eleven and twelve o'clock.

Now that there would be no language or cultural barriers, I was very nervous about talking to this stranger about a discipline of which I knew nothing. However, Doctor Davies was skilled in his profession and made the conversation easier than I had expected. But no matter how high the level of skill or experience a professional possesses, there is no easy way for them to tell someone something they don't want to know.

As soon as I heard the words, 'I know this is going to be very difficult for you . . .', I automatically switched off. This was not the outcome I had expected from a competent English doctor. It wasn't possible that he was in agreement with his Spanish counterparts.

The pillowcase was wet from my tears and I could not control myself enough to answer the knock on my door. Someone tried unsuccessfully to enter the room but eventually gave up and left. I vaguely remembered my appointment with Señor Morales, and presumed he had come to check on my whereabouts.

After more than five years of searching and longing was I really going to have to walk away and leave my daughter? This innocent nine-year-old caught in the middle of her parents' conflict. I didn't want us to be like pirates, both fighting over the same treasure and not caring if it was destroyed during the battle.

The more I dwelt on this thought the more my anger grew. First it was aimed at Hadi, for all the cheating and lies he had continually told to so many people. He spread these lies without any thought as to what the effect might be. I felt anger at his ability to persuade everybody that his version of events was the true one; anger at his all-consuming hate for me, which prevented him from showing any regard for Tanya; and anger at the way, I believed, he was ruining three lives.

My anger then turned inward to hate of myself for letting this happen in the first place. If I hadn't been so naïve as to leave Tanya alone with Hadi this would never have happened. I was really the one to blame and would Tanya ever understand or forgive me for this? I also felt hate for a system that could ignore the welfare of a child by allowing one parent to engage in a criminal act purely because they were a parent. If the circumstances were otherwise, the law would immediately class this as a criminal act, but because the perpetrator had the same bloodline this atrocity was permissible. Even in countries where Hadi's actions were looked on as criminal, the legal system seemed to have no power to deal with him.

My love of Tanya and my longing to have her in my arms and in my life were paramount. But I was thinking of myself again. What I really needed to consider was Tanya's welfare. I was assured she was happy and a totally normal nine-year-old, playing with her friends and enjoying school. She was obviously well cared for and loved. She was in one of Barcelona's best private schools and lived in a safe environment. If I appeared now there was the possibility of psychological damage. In addition to that we didn't have a common language so how could I converse with her? I was now a complete stranger, so why would she even want to speak to me? She might even be scared of me. Taking her to Dubai, with its foreign Arab culture, could be terrifying for a small sheltered girl. She would be leaving her friends and everything familiar – even her hateful father who was her only constant and whom she must love. I could not possibly frighten my own flesh and blood in such a way.

I cried even more. As a mother surely I had my own rights. I had already been robbed of seeing my daughter grow and develop, missed being there when her first tooth fell out, and had been deprived of her expressions of joy at receiving surprise presents on special days. How many more Christmases and birthdays did I have to forego?

If I took her to Dubai where I now had an ample-sized house on the shores of the Persian Gulf, she would have a garden and swimming pool of her own. I had been told she loved to swim and was very good at it. The English-speaking school was of a high standard and I knew the teachers were kind and patient. Enrolling her there would be easy. Although my job was demanding I knew we could find a way to adapt it to suit my new circumstances. Yes, it was all possible.

Hadi would of course be furious but I was different now. I was successful and assertive, and could challenge him. The question was would he fight fair? I knew he wouldn't. Over the years the many lies he had told, one after the other, had taken on a certain currency, preventing people from believing my story. My whole body shook and I wanted to stop crying but my efforts were to no avail. Thoughts of what was right and what was wrong just kept spiralling up and down in my mind.

Supreme in all this were Tanya's rights. She should know and have the love of a mother. She deserved to experience the boundless love and joy of her grandmother in Australia. Even her aunts and uncles who lived in France and Switzerland were strangers to her. Who could she look to as a motherly figure at that important time when she was approaching puberty, or when she became interested in boys?

What concerned me greatly was how she would be raised as the daughter of an Arab who had such a crazy mentality. Would Hadi want her to be veiled at puberty? Would she be forced into an arranged marriage? Although these ideas seemed ridiculous I was no longer sure of anything. Although she was learning about Christianity at a Catholic school, might he later force her to become a Muslim? No, I couldn't bear the thought of all this. I made myself physically sick by these thoughts and had to leap out of bed to visit the bathroom.

The cold damp of the pillowcase made me think along a different tack. I had no idea how far Hadi's network extended in the

Arab world. When we were married I understood his contacts were numerous and strong but the details were never revealed. Would they include people in Dubai? Would I be safe if he found out where we were? But worse still, what about Tanya's safety? All these questions continued to whirl around and around in my head.

There was no way I could survive another six years without Tanya – precious years I would never regain, just as precious as the ones I had already lost. There I was again, thinking about myself. It was not about me. Although I loved Tanya with every ounce of my being and longed to be able to show and share this bottomless well of affection with her I was lost in a world of turmoil and confusion with no one to show me the way. I felt as though I was in an impenetrable forest; and every time I tried to go forward the dense branches barred my way.

I could not help recalling the time all those years ago when I escaped from Malaga and how it had been so clear which path I had to take. Reliving that earlier decision brought the fear of Hadi to the surface. Life under that fear and silent pressure, ever-present while we were together in Malaga, would have ultimately destroyed me. Although I regretted many things I had done, leaving Hadi was not one of them. Maybe I should have done things differently but the one thing I now knew was that I could never have gone back. At no time would he trust me again, my movements would be even more restricted, and I would genuinely live in fear for my life.

Knowing Tanya was under his influence was an enormous concern but I prayed the love and happiness of Señora Valero and her children would offset it. The thought of Hadi's domineering, possessive clutches made me physically ill again.

I thought about the idea of snatching Tanya and running off with her. The more I considered this the more my instinct told me it was wrong. I was overwhelmed by the knowledge that two wrongs don't make a right. The words of the three doctors kept haunting me – Tanya could experience irreparable psychological damage. She had survived her separation from me apparently unscathed but how many traumas could one small human survive? I would die rather than harm my child.

For two days the mental torture of these arguments circulated, non-stop, in my mind until it felt like my head would explode. My uncontrollable sobbing was only interrupted by quick visits to the bathroom to be ill.

Finally, on the third day, weak from raw emotion and lack of fluid, I knew I had to get out of bed and get some fresh air. The Gothic part of Barcelona is only a short walk from the hotel and I found myself in the old cathedral. Why had I come here rather than the small church in Plaza del Pi that I found so comforting? Maybe because I had a very big ask. I am not a Catholic but believe there is only one God, who can be approached through any one of the world's religions or religious houses. God is within each of us and how we reach him is a very personal thing.

Kneeling on the hard wooden stool, vaguely aware of the towering ceiling above me, and in the distance a few people coming and going, I prayed. Please God, give me the wisdom to make the right decision for Tanya, and please God give me the strength and fortitude to carry out my decision.

In a daze I found my way back to the hotel and the comfort of the bed. The telephone dragged me from the stupor into which I had dropped once again. Señor Morales was concerned that he had not heard from me. After I explained about the telephone call I had made to the English doctor, he asked me to visit him as soon as I could. The following morning in his office we discussed the whole situation again at length. Finally, we agreed that at this time there was only one thing for me to do – go home.

And what was Hadi thinking during all this? I knew only too well what Hadi thought. I was the evil one for escaping from him; I had outwitted him, causing him to lose face. He was the clever one when he found us. It was his right to confiscate Tanya and keep her forever from her bad and defiant mother. I had no rights and if I suffered, so much the better; this was my punishment for daring to challenge his authority.

Now at age fifty, Hadi had established a perfect life for himself. It generally consisted of meeting whoever might listen to him in the local bar over a coffee. Here in Barcelona, as he had done in Malaga, he would know the local barmen, lottery sellers and news-agents and have jovial and inconsequential conversations with them. They would consider him a happy, wonderful fellow, even though he probably told them how they should run their businesses and no doubt their personal lives as well. They would discuss local and international politics, the country's financial situation, and Hadi's latest bizarre business idea. This would be either highly impractical or need such huge capital investment that only an oil state could afford it. After this exhausting morning's work, Hadi would go home to a prepared lunch. Señora Valero met all his domestic needs and he was head of the household – as it should be. He would enjoy a siesta before he collected Tanya from school in the afternoon. He was happy, secure and confident. This was his right as a man.

After my two weeks in Barcelona I returned to Dubai far worse than when I had left. I was bereft and wondered how I would con-tinue. The only consolation was that once I went back to the office, the heavy responsibility of my work would face me and there would be little time to dwell on the devastation and disappointment I had just encountered.

The morning I returned to work Ian called me into his office and closed the door. From my mournful countenance he knew my trip had not been the success I had anticipated. He sat beside me on the beige leather sofa and gently took my hand. It was hard to explain the events of the previous two weeks as I had difficulty in making sense of them myself. With the utmost kindness and sympathy Ian assured me I had done the right thing.

A couple of days later Ian again asked me into his office. This time it was to relay a personal message. An Arab confidant and friend, with whom we had significant business dealings, had offered his private Boeing 707 and crew to fly me to Barcelona, snatch Tanya and leave. I was shocked by this bold offer and surprised at its suggestion. But as I became familiar with the idea, and knowing the force of money and power, I became excited by the prospect. If we flew in to Barcelona early in the morning, we could take Tanya from the school playground during the morning break. Cars, drivers, and ample bodies, I knew, would all be provided. Also, being familiar with the procedures for dealing with private jets, which were a frequent element in my working life, I knew as a passenger I could skip through the airport with a minimum of fuss and attention. With the renewed passport I now had for Tanya, valid until she was fifteen, obtaining a visa for her in Dubai would not be a problem. Yes, it could be possible.

Now I was really being tested. I had made a momentous decision while in Barcelona to walk away, albeit temporarily, from my nine-year-old daughter and only days later was being tantalised by an option to reverse that decision.

I had already done an enormous amount of soul-searching in Barcelona so it didn't take me very long to decide. To take Tanya by force – with her not knowing who I was and not speaking English – to a completely foreign environment without a single familiar face or surroundings was too much to risk. This was not about revenge or possession, but what was right for Tanya. If I did accept this offer and it was carried through, I also had to consider what Hadi would do. He certainly wouldn't just accept the situation but would try everything possible to get her back. And what means he had of doing this in the Arab world were unknown to me. He was a loose cannon and possibly dangerous. The so-called 'tug of love' could go on and on, hurting the one person I could not dream of harming.

I knew I was not equipped to be making these decisions so had to be guided purely by instinct as well as the unwelcome but no doubt well-intentioned advice of three psychologists. In the bottom of my heart I believed to 'snatch' Tanya back was wrong. Nevertheless, the earnest offer was one of the most humane and generous anyone could receive.

During all the years of my search, it had been a solitary pursuit. Even with the love and best wishes of my family and friends, the path I had trodden was a lonely one. Every decision and action I had made in isolation, without the comfort of a sounding board or the opportunity of listening to an alternative view. Now for the very first time someone was offering a plan and physical help. Even if it was not one I agreed with, it was a concrete offer of help. What I had lacked all these years was power. Now someone who had it was offering it unconditionally. If I refused, would I ever have it offered again? Could I ever achieve my quest without it? What if I had had this kind of input earlier? What if someone had come forward with a plan months or years before? Would Tanya now be with me so I could sleep soundly at night? By not accepting this offer would I be committing myself to travelling alone again on a road of desolation?

Tanya antes de cortarse
el pelo en el 84   4° EGB.
9años.

DUBAI – VIRGIN ISLANDS – DUBAI
Temptation in the Caribbean: 1984

Back in Dubai, what I needed was to be kept busy, and in regard to reuniting with my daughter I needed to be doing something constructive. Although I had the mysterious anonymous note, there was still no proof of where it had originated. If I could obtain this, the writer could become an accomplice and help me get close to Tanya. My efforts to obtain a sample of the handwriting of Señora Valero, my main suspect, had been thwarted. Where else could I go?

During a cruise of the Caribbean on board the *QE2*, a year earlier, I had attended a lecture on graphology. I learned that experts, given a sample of handwriting, could determine the gender, age bracket and possibly ethnic background of a person. All I had to do was track down a graphologist.

I contacted Señor Morales and asked him if he could please try to obtain a sample of Señora Valero's handwriting. Several weeks later I received a dry-cleaning receipt. I marvelled at the ingenuity of the 'customer' as the receipt stated '1 tie', then continued, 'pale blue', and on the next line were a few additional words, which I could not interpret. Had Señor Morales cleverly engineered this generous specimen of Señora Valero's writing, and was he running out of ties?

At least I now had the sample I needed. A few days later the manager of DUBAL's London office was visiting Dubai. John had been involved in the DUBAL project from its inception and was living and working in Dubai when I first arrived, but had recently repatriated to England to run our London office. We had become close friends over the years and he was one of the kindest people I had met. He always had an amusing story to tell and fortuitously, on this occasion, one of his tales involved a friend, Martin, who was a detective at Scotland Yard.

At an appropriate time later that day I asked John, 'Do you think your friend could arrange for the analysis of a handwriting sample?'

'Martin is able to arrange almost anything in the detection area. Why do you ask?'

'Well, I have a document that I'd like analysed and wondered if he could help?'

'I'll ask him as soon as I get home,' John replied in his usual helpful manner.

The day after John's return to London I received a telex saying he had spoken to Martin, and if I wished to send the article, plus a covering letter explaining what I required, he would be willing to do what he could. My letter, the anonymous note, and the dry-cleaning receipt were dispatched that day with my request for a graphologist to examine the two articles. I made the added request that the anonymous note and dry-cleaning docket be fingerprinted. As far as I was aware nobody, besides my mother and myself, had handled the note other than the writer. I also enclosed a clean sheet of paper on which I was careful to place my own fingerprints before sealing all this up in a personal and confidential envelope.

The daily mail delivery became the focus of my day. When several weeks later I finally saw the large brown couriered envelope, bearing John's familiar scrawly writing marked 'urgent' and 'personal', I knew the answer had arrived.

I tore open John's brown envelope only to find another envelope also marked 'personal' and in an unfamiliar hand – obviously Martin's. My letter opener suddenly seemed inexplicably blunt as I struggled to open the envelope that had been well secured with adhesive tape. As I quickly read through Martin's handwritten letter my shoulders slumped and my anticipation rapidly dissipated. There were no matching fingerprints detected on the anonymous note and dry-cleaning receipt. Also, because the note had been printed and the receipt handwritten, one in pen and the other in biro, it was impossible to make a comparison. Finally, the samples were far too scanty for professional analysis.

There seemed little else I could do except accept the psychologists' advice and wait.

Overlooking the peaceful blue of the Persian Gulf, my bedroom always gave pride of place to the photograph of my mother. It was only a few years old and showed her not so much as the beautiful young woman I remembered from my youth, but as a mature woman with glasses, which only emphasised the beauty of her piercing blue eyes and could never detract from her brilliant smile. I found the love that emanated from her photograph gave me the strength and courage to face each day.

Although this whole nightmare had been hard on me, at least I had a job that occupied a great deal of my time, frequently demanding my attention seven days a week. In addition, there was the international travel, the glamorous entertaining, and the many new friends to distract me. But for Mummy, who no longer worked and had lost my father many years before, there was little to divert her mind from the fact that her only grandchild was in an unknown and possibly strange or dangerous place. She could not experience the joy of her friends as they talked and swapped stories of their own grandchildren, only the gnawing pain of wondering where her little princess might be. Not that she ever complained or even mentioned the situation to me. She was always very happy and bright and continually anxious to know about my welfare and what my life entailed.

Even when Mummy visited me each year while I lived in Dubai, very little was ever mentioned about Tanya, the subject being so painful. As none of my colleagues – apart from Ian and my friend Ann – were aware of my situation, the topic never arose.

To fill the little spare time that I did have occasionally, I looked for something enjoyable to do. I was out of the country so often I didn't feel I could join team sports, so diving seemed an ideal pastime. Deep down in the still water I was unrestrained and alone. I did not have to keep up any pretence or participate in social activities for which I had no appetite. Here I was completely free to wonder at the beauty of everything around me: the small clown fish, darting flashes of orange and white, playing among the tendrils of coral; the brilliance of yellow and black butterfly fish as they dashed about; and the electric blue of the slower-moving parrotfish. The underwater world comprised such amazing life forms, of every shape, size and colour. This was where I loved to be.

On these occasions I was always sorry when I had to return to the surface. Slowly I would inch my way up the firm supportive rope towards the boat, aware of the change in environment as soon as I emerged from the depths. As I rose higher and higher, bubbles both small and large would escape from my mouthpiece and dance around my body. The shafts of sunlight would grow stronger as the surface drew nearer. The dark shadow of the dive boat's hull would come into view. My rate of ascent would quicken as the thinner air left my lungs, replaced by heavy oxygen. As soon as my scalp broke the surface two heads and four grasping arms would be there ready to heave me from my 'lost world'. The loud shouts of 'Are you okay?', 'How was the dive?', 'Any surprises?', 'Are you ready to go again?', were an unwelcome assault on my senses. The peace was broken. I was part of the real world again.

My pale-blue cotton overalls sagged and clung to my salty skin. What would the DUBAL labourers' supervisor think of this? The overalls bearing the DUBAL logo, with their ample legs and long sleeves, were perfect protection from the sharp coral. Scratches could lead to nasty infections and were potentially deadly.

I had been employed by DUBAL for five years; my employment number was thirty-seven and the payroll number had now reached its optimum of thirteen hundred. Many of our employees had school-aged children who were enrolled at the Jumeirah English Speaking School (JESS). I knew very few of these colleagues as they worked out of town at the smelter. At the school, there were more children of DUBAL employees than there were from any other company in Dubai and, this being the case, DUBAL was expected to have a representative on the school board. Ian had held this position up to this time but due to his frequent absences on overseas business trips, I was asked to be his proxy. Although I knew nothing about schools or how they were run I was assured the governors were there to oversee the school's financial and administrative welfare. It was just the same as running any other business.

JESS was a purpose-built primary school planned to accommodate up to one thousand expatriate children and was erected on land donated by the ruler, Sheikh Rashid. Jumeirah was a beachside suburb of Dubai where most of the European expatriate population lived, and was the heart of expatriate activity. The school, a single-storey structure, was built around a series of courtyards, with a swimming pool, sports grounds, a splendid library, and an indoor sports hall that doubled as an auditorium for various performances. It had a proper stage and professional overhead lighting, and could be transformed into an effective theatre when required.

As the newest recruit to the board I was its youngest member and the only woman. Governors were invited to all the school functions and I vividly remember the first concert I attended. It was just prior to the Easter break and when I arrived at the hall there was an air of tremendous excitement, both from the children about to go on stage and from the parents about to witness performances by their upcoming Lawrence Oliviers and Sarah Bernhardts. I felt totally alien in this family atmosphere. The other governors were married and had children, and all the mothers and fathers seemed to know each other. Being a single, working woman was still a rare thing in Dubai at that time.

A signal was given and everyone filed into the auditorium. To my surprise I was seated in the centre of the front row. The lights dimmed, the noise level dipped noticeably and *The Wizard of Oz* was about to begin. It was an adapted version of the Broadway musical to accommodate several hundred primary-school children. There were small scenes from the musical with children playing the roles, interspersed with large groups of children on the stage singing. Every child in the school took part in some way and I soon learned it was normal practice for the kindergarten children to perform first, then older age groups, leaving the grand finale for the ten- to eleven-year-olds.

Patient teachers made a great effort to encourage the excited little ones, some struggling with their costumes, onto the stage. They were all shapes and sizes, many different nationalities but with a preponderance of fair-haired British boys and girls. Some slipped, some had fingers or thumbs still in their mouths, some were waving frantically to their parents, and others were looking anywhere but at the music teacher standing at the front of the stage. After what seemed like a very long time they were all assembled. The music teacher gave a nod, the piano broke into its melody and the show began.

All was proceeding splendidly until I realised tears were filling my eyes. I clenched my hands and bit my lip in an effort to gain control. This was the first school concert I had ever attended as an adult and it wasn't even for my own daughter. Was she performing in a similar pageant somewhere? Was she being taught music? Was she even in a Christian environment or eagerly awaiting the Easter bunny?

By now the tears were pouring uncontrollably down my cheeks, gathering on my chin then falling in a constant stream to my chest. I did not dare wipe them away in fear someone might notice. What about the plain cobalt-blue silk dress I was wearing – would the tears dry before interval? Would I have black streaks from mascara all down my face? How could I explain my grief to others? Why, people would wonder, was a responsible, sensible adult breaking her heart at a joyous children's musical entertainment?

At the end of the evening I couldn't wait to get home, totally exhausted but relieved that nobody had noticed my grief. For all future school functions I had to steel myself in advance, and while seated in the audience try to think of other things such as problems in the office or how I was going to word a complicated document the following day.

It was now 1984, seven years since Tanya had been taken out of my life. During those latter years in Dubai I was painfully marking time until Tanya became a teenager and I was constantly thankful for the comfort given me by close friends.

On one occasion, my dear friend Eleanor and I were on one of our regular power-walking trips through Saffa Park. This was a new park situated in Jumeirah. It was a large flat area where we could walk in private and away from the noisy congested roads. The tracks were sandy, the trees small and frail in their infancy, and the likelihood of grass seemed a long way away. However, a park in those early days, irrespective of its infancy, was quite a novelty and pleasure.

My inner sadness must have been showing and as we walked around the park Eleanor detected my fading morale. The conversation took an abrupt swing to plans for a family holiday that she was arranging in the Caribbean and next thing I was being invited to go along. I had met Eleanor's parents and one of her sisters several times, either when they were visiting Dubai or when I was visiting the Far East, but the other family members who were to make up the group were unknown to me. I instinctively raised the normal excuse of not wanting to intrude on a family holiday but Eleanor immediately shot this objection down with the retort that I was considered family anyway.

The idea of a relaxing holiday, carefree atmosphere and the warm sun of the British Virgin Islands certainly was appealing. Even more enticing, this was to be a sailing holiday, an activity I had loved since my teenage years on majestic Sydney Harbour – and more recent times on the sparkling waters of the Persian Gulf. Eleanor's invitation was too tempting to refuse.

Charles, one of Eleanor's brothers, who lived in New York, kept his yacht moored in Tortola, the capital of the British Virgin Islands, and by chartering a second boat from the local marina the family would have its own small flotilla.

There was an air of excitement and adventure when we all arrived in Tortola. Willi, Eleanor's partner from landlocked Germany, who had never sailed in his life, was to captain the second boat! Before leaving he had been given much instruction by a yachting friend in Dubai and that was his entire knowledge of boating. However, he was a competent and intelligent fellow, and with further instruction from Charles, did a splendid job. The sun was shining on the aqua-blue water and the gentle breeze dictated a leisurely pace as we headed for Greater Thatch Island. Fortunately for Willi, most of our moorings were offshore in natural bays or harbours, where all he really had to do was drop anchor and maintain a discreet and safe distance from any neighbouring boats.

As it turned out, all was well until our final day when we returned to the busy marina in Tortola. Charles sailed our boat in first and Willi was instructed to copy everything Charles did. Just as we were to pull alongside the marina a large boat manned solely by young, noisy, gorgeous bikini-clad girls was leaving the adjacent mooring. Knowing how easily Willi was distracted by the opposite sex, Charles immediately screamed out to him to cut the motor. Willi, while not amused at having his attention diverted from the bevy of beauties sailing past, only just missed a major collision with the jetty!

It was a most enjoyable two weeks. To my initial relief I was billeted aboard Charles's boat together with a cousin, Mim, who had never sailed before, and Jim, Eleanor's brother from London. At first I felt a little uncomfortable being away from Eleanor and not knowing the other three. However, once we were under sail I discovered that Charles had an unruffled disposition like Eleanor. He was also an experienced and competent sailor, and I soon felt much more relaxed.

Charles had the same dark hair and mischievous eyes that were so appealing in Eleanor. He wasn't much taller than me and his slim suntanned body showed evidence of daily visits to his local gym in New York. His five o'clock shadow gave him an air of ruggedness. He was always decked out in crisp white shorts, but the skimpy T-shirt with 'victim' emblazoned on the front suggested a bold sense of humour.

During the entire holiday, as Eleanor had predicted earlier, I was made to feel like a member of the family. Paradoxically this made me feel sad, emphasising as it did what was sorely lacking in my own life – my own family unit.

Charles and I developed a close relationship by the end of the two weeks, discovering that we shared many interests, as well as a mutual sense of adventure, and the same zany sense of humour. The only difference was that Charles had never been married and was looking to the day when he would have his own family.

Our relationship continued to blossom and although many miles separated us geographically we managed to meet at least twice a year, sailing the Caribbean during summer and skiing in Europe in winter.

One of the first things I learned about Charles was his love of flying – not the 747s or private jets I was accustomed to as a passenger, but much smaller single-engine planes that he flew himself. During one of my visits to New York we took off to one of Charles's properties in Philadelphia. It was a handsome two-storeyed house with ample garden and two garages. The house had been rented but the tenants were only permitted to use one garage. The second, almost the size of a small warehouse, was where Charles and I were to stay for a few days. It was not the smart, well-fitted bachelor pad I had expected of my architect friend, but a genuine workstation. This was where Charles was building his plane! There was very little spare space around the plane now that it was well into production. We slept in sleeping bags, had nothing much more than a kettle in the way of modern conveniences, and worked solidly for several days before returning to New York. As I stood there sticking pieces on to the fuselage I secretly hoped I would never have to fly in it. I knew Charles was an excellent architect, sailor and pilot – but building an aircraft?

There was never a dull moment during those happy times with Charles. In September 1985, after flying into Tortola in the dark of night, we went straight to the boat ready to set sail the following morning. We hadn't been on board very long and fortunately had not unpacked when the commodore of the yacht club came by. He knew we were planning an early start the next day and wanted to let us know of a hurricane warning. Under no circumstances should we leave port until we were given the all clear. The following day hurricane Gloria was still on course, heading directly for the Virgin Islands. By the second day we were told to tie up the boat and check into a hotel as Gloria was on her way. Charles was not happy until we had obtained the front room of the hotel closest to the coast – so we could watch the hurricane! Imagine his disappointment when the hurricane shutters were boarded across our window. Fortunately at the last minute Gloria decided to change course and headed directly north. However, the gale-force wind continued to blow and the sea around Tortola took a couple of days to subside sufficiently to allow us to venture out of the harbour to a nearby island. A week or so later on our return to New York we discovered that all of Charles's friends who kept their boats moored in Long

Island were chasing insurance claims. Gloria had hit Long Island with full force and small pleasure craft had been reduced to little more than matchwood.

Our relationship continued to strengthen over a couple of years and all was fine until one day Charles unexpectedly arrived in Dubai. At first this unannounced arrival was a happy bonus. I was delighted to see him and assumed he had made a detour from a business trip to visit me. However, one of the hardest decisions I have ever had to make soon followed. Charles produced a diamond ring, making it obvious that he had definite plans for our long-term future together. Here was my chance for happiness.

It is extremely painful to reject someone you love and even harder to convince them your decision is final. Every time I tried to explain to Charles why I could not commit to his proposal he would offer a solution. The only way I would marry anyone would be to give myself wholly – bodily and mentally. This I knew would not be the case. Finding Tanya was the first thing I thought about every morning and the last thing at night. Tanya would always come first. What if a situation arose where I had to choose to either rush off and follow a lead in Europe or do something important for Charles? I knew what the answer would be.

My passport and papers were always ready to fly to any city should I receive some new information. The convenient aviation crossroads that Dubai offered made this easy and within seven hours I could be in Europe. America was on the other side of the world and a long way away. The invisible line that I envisaged between Europe and America was an insurmountable bridge in my mind. I needed to be where I could move quickly and with ease. In addition to the physical distance of America, I also felt there would be a communication chasm, while in Dubai everything seemed simple.

I knew Charles wanted a family of his own, but the idea of

having another child while the whereabouts of my first-born treasure remained unknown was unthinkable for me. Nothing gave me the right to deny Charles the family he so wanted while I continued the search for my own daughter.

It was a tortuous decision. Here was a real chance of happiness with someone I cared for deeply, who I knew cared for me and had a definite plan to ensure our happy and successful future. Was I making another huge mistake? The emptiness I felt making that decision was monumental but I knew that until I found Tanya I could not possibly commit myself completely to anyone else. Tanya would always be the foremost thought in my mind, so how could I make a long-term commitment to someone who would only be granted second place? Certainly I would not expect them to understand the daily torment, or the unpredictability of my movements as I rushed off to follow up a lead.

Thankfully over the years Charles and I have remained good friends, and although we live on opposite sides of the world we remain in contact. If I had moved to America, the events that unfolded at a later date would not have taken place and the outcome of my search may have been very different.

*Margaret &
Eleanor*

BARCELONA
A new private investigator: June 1990

The last week in May 1990 was a busy few days, some things happening on a regular basis, some not. I had deported my houseboy after finding him entertaining a woman in his quarters and it was my godson Adrian's first communion. I attended Sheikh Mana's wedding at the Jumeirah Beach Palace and had a JESS board meeting. I danced at the annual Viennese Ball in Dubai and laughed during Derek Nimmo's performance in *Private Lives* at the Intercontinental hotel.

But the day I had been dreaming of – 30 May 1990, Tanya's sixteenth birthday – had arrived. My waiting period was over. I could go to Barcelona and without fear of possible damage make myself known to my daughter. I knew she would have moved from Señora Burgos's school, where I last saw her, and would now be in high school. Finding her would entail some investigation. I certainly could not approach her at home on Hadi's territory.

I needed to visit the Spanish Consul once again. The first free day I could get away from my office I drove the two hundred kilometres to Abu Dhabi. I explained to the consul my need to find a private investigator in Barcelona – after seven years I had lost touch with Señor Morales – to help me locate Tanya's school, and could he recommend anyone? His bemused expression was followed by a suggestion to look in the telephone book and make a selection. This advice also came with a warning to be very careful. He folded his hands and leaned further across his desk as he told me to make sure any person I hired was registered. I should ask to see their licence, and request them to prove or at least guarantee they could deliver what they promised. There were a lot of unethical people operating in this field.

This was not quite the response I had hoped for. However, I scanned the embassy's telephone directory and chose three companies. Not knowing when I would next get the opportunity to leave Dubai and visit Barcelona, I faxed all three a lengthy letter explaining the background and my requirements. One didn't answer. One answered but didn't address my requests. Thankfully the third one sent a brief reply that sounded professional. Of course he requested a handsome down payment but I was used to this procedure. Payment up front, irrespective of the results, if any, was normal. I was well aware why the consul had cautioned me.

The money was transferred and I waited. Four weeks went by with no communication from the company and my follow-up faxes commenced. What was happening? There was still no response. My telephone calls proved just as unsuccessful – either they weren't answered or if they were the manager, Señor Paredes, was not in the office. Had I just lost another three thousand dollars?

During one of my regular business trips to London a few weeks later, the alarming news broke on 2 August that Sadam Hussein had invaded Kuwait, placing the entire Western world on red alert. After his invasion of Kuwait the Iraqi leader announced that his army would continue its march into Saudi Arabia then down the Persian Gulf to the Strait of Hormuz, thus gobbling up Dubai in its path. The only stable things in my life by this time were my job and my home in Dubai. Both of these and consequently my livelihood were now threatened.

When I returned home from London, Dubai was a changing place. It was being prepared as the central mustering area for the Western allied forces. Ships from the British, American, French, Italian and Australian navies were heading for the Persian Gulf and many of them were to be moored in Dubai. Runways for allied jets were being prepared and field hospitals erected in the desert on the outskirts of town, all with incredible speed. The atmosphere in town remained relaxed; everyone continued with their daily tasks and generally made light of the situation. Homes were opened and hospitality given to men of the multinational armed forces, and a general camaraderie pervaded. Luxury hotels, normally full of businessmen, were now inhabited by wealthy Arab families fleeing from Kuwait and other areas near the north of the Gulf. Expatriate wives and families were preparing to evacuate from Dubai.

The most exciting thing on my return, however, was a seven-page fax from Señor Paredes. My pursuit of him for many weeks had paid off. The fax told me Hadi and Tanya no longer lived at their previous address, and Hadi did not have a car or driving licence but had a business – a café bar – in Via Laietana near the cathedral in Barcelona. Managers were running this business but when questioned they denied any knowledge of an address or telephone number for Hadi. They said he visited the business a couple of days a month, all bills were settled with cash and no banks were ever involved. They also offered the observation that Hadi was a strange, difficult person, and in their opinion a Mafioso. In the local trade register his old home address was still listed and he was shown as stateless.

Señor Paredes had no confirmation but suspected both Hadi and Tanya were in Marbella. Through further enquiries at the ten banks in Marbella, the investigator learned that Hadi had incurred debts with one bank and had a debit account with another, where an agent visited to collect amounts of cash from time to time. It was almost certain that Señora Valero, the woman who Hadi had previously lived with in Barcelona, was owed money by him and was in debt. The final comment from Señor Paredes was that further investigation would require more money. I immediately faxed a three-page reply suggesting other avenues to follow and things to double-check, together with more funds.

While I waited for further information business carried on as usual in Dubai and it wasn't long before I had to make another trip to London. With the prospect of war almost at our front door, and the closure of the Persian Gulf, alternative plans had to be made for the delivery of DUBAL's raw materials and the shipment of our finished product. Not to mention contingency plans for the possible repatriation of our thirteen hundred employees who came from twenty-eight different countries, many of them accompanied by their families. The Christmas decorations in some of the London shops reminded me we were almost at the end of another year. There were fewer decorations than usual and a dearth of festive spirit. No one felt like celebrating, least of all me.

There was no welcoming fax from Señor Paredes on my return to Dubai this time, in spite of my numerous reminders. I decided to take a couple of days off and visit Barcelona at the first opportunity. The chance came with the advent of Dubai's national day on

2 December, which in 1990 fell on a Sunday. If I took the Dubai weekend (Thursday and Friday) and added Saturday and Sunday I would have four days – plenty of time to get to Barcelona and back if I flew out on Wednesday night or very early Thursday morning. A quick call to the Hotel Monegal confirmed they were still in business and could provide me with a room for three nights. Now that it was mid-winter I only hoped they would have adequate heating.

Although the journey was long and tiring it was a relief to be away from Dubai and the tension of the ensuing war. Those who remained were stockpiling as much as possible – non-perishable food, fuel and most importantly, water. The Persian Gulf was now full of naval ships from the participating coalition countries, air-bases had sprung up in areas that previously were open desert, and the Gulf was like a volcano ready to erupt.

The advice given to their citizens by many embassies varied in nature, from 'leave immediately' to, in some extreme cases, the supply of gas masks. There were very few Australians in Dubai and our closest embassy was in Saudi Arabia. As a result Australians looked to the British Embassy for help and advice during any emergency in Dubai. I recall obtaining from a third party one or two pieces of photocopied paper outlining the precautions we should take, but as they were typically British and stiff upper-lipped these didn't amount to much. The most bizarre advice I remember receiving was how to react in the case of a chemical attack. You were either to lock yourself under the staircase – I did have a staircase but had no means of getting underneath it – or fill the bath with water, completely submerge yourself and breathe through a straw! Not an option I fancied. In fact the whole situation caused a great deal of humour as we casually went about our everyday lives in the normal fashion, ignoring the fear and terror that seemed to have gripped the rest of the world.

Flying above the Swiss Alps in December can be turbulent and this trip was no exception. As the aircraft swayed and dipped on our descent to Zurich I wished I could end my journey here and visit my friend Esther. From frequent business trips to this lakeside city I knew it well and my friend lived only a short distance from the centre. However, I was only in transit on my way to Spain.

Things might be different this time. Eleanor, always trying to be helpful, had come up with a contact for me in Barcelona. Willi had been in touch with a Spanish friend from his schooldays who now ran his own business in Barcelona. He had an American wife and three children under the age of five. With a personal introduction to Olivier and Elsa I arrived feeling a little more confident.

As I sat in the back of the taxi from the airport to the hotel in Barcelona I remember my astonishment at seeing shop windows displaying anti-chemical overalls and gas masks on full-size models! Why on earth did the Spaniards think chemicals, even if they were used, would reach them all the way from this as yet undeclared war in the Persian Gulf? I soon learned that aside from these obvious signs of preparations for chemical fallout, supermarket shelves were practically empty and bottled water almost impossible to find. Were the Spaniards paranoid or were we in the Gulf being totally stupid?

On arrival at the hotel, and before I even unpacked, I telephoned my new contact, Elsa. She was expecting my call and we agreed to meet at a nearby KFC. I had never before been into a KFC and will never forget the overpowering smell in the thick air of fried chicken and salty chips. The bright red and yellow plastic interior looked out of place in conservative Spain. The hollow noise of the chairs clanking on the floor grated on my tired mind, but Elsa had three small children to keep entertained and it proved a perfect location.

Elsa was easy to spot. Her small frame was casually clothed and her round face was fringed by soft, fly-away blonde hair pulled back with a tortoiseshell clip. Her welcome open smile was infectious and

I felt warmed by her friendly blue eyes. With a mother's efficiency she already had the children seated and enjoying their afternoon treat.

As I explained my reason for being in Barcelona as briefly as possible I could see the colour drain from Elsa's face. How old and tainted I felt in this young innocent mother's presence. In spite of her confusion she immediately offered any help she could give. The fact that she spoke English was more comfort than she could have imagined. Elsa suggested we meet again the following morning when the children would be at school or day care. They had already finished their second round of snacks and had started to get noisy and restless. A grumpy struggle with jackets, gloves and hats followed before we faced the winter chill and walked to a nearby multistorey car park. As I stood and waved goodbye to Elsa and her children, tears burned the back of my eyes and a hollow feeling filled the pit of my stomach. Anonymously I walked through the busy streets back to my empty hotel room. I couldn't erase the vision of the happy confusion of this young loving family and wondered if Tanya had enjoyed the silliness and spontaneity of such things, or if she had been restrained all her life by the rigours of correct behaviour and Hadi's disciplinarian style.

It was such a pleasure to see Elsa's friendly face the following morning. The first thing we did was call Señor Paredes' office in order to make an appointment, only to be told he was in Galicia. He didn't appear to have an assistant or anyone else who could help us. We asked that he contact me at the hotel immediately on his return. Not sure where to go from here we decided to pass by the address we had for Hadi's café bar in Via Laietana. Maybe he would be there, or we would see him in the area. I had mixed feelings of relief and disappointment when there was no sign of him.

Elsa suggested we go to her house to devise a plan. With Olivier's advice and guidance Elsa made numerous telephone calls to a number of government offices and eventually discovered that Hadi did have a driving licence, which was issued in Malaga. Although she was unable to get any further information it confirmed my lack of confidence in Señor Paredes. The plan we had hoped to formulate hadn't materialised so I returned to the Monegal.

In the cold grey afternoon I aimlessly walked the streets, the dull burdened faces I passed doing nothing to improve my spirits. Nobody looked at me, but all those grim expressions were anathema to my soul. Men and women rushing to their next endeavour made me wonder what torments they harboured and what loads they bore. Dejectedly moving over a pedestrian crossing as the light flashed red I stumbled up the gutter, kicking an empty cigarette packet. I felt the breeze of a taxi rush past too close to my back. More faceless people, more featureless buildings, more empty doorways.

The meeting I had anticipated with Señor Paredes was preying on my mind and I wondered how he would receive me. Would he be as dismal as I had imagined from his correspondence?

My mind flashed back to Dubai. What if war broke out while I was in Barcelona and I was unable to return? That thought was opening up a new hornet's nest and I had to dismiss it. I could only deal with the situation at hand.

The smell of strong bitter coffee filled my nostrils as I passed a dimly lit bar. It was a relief from the fumes of the ceaseless traffic but held no appeal. I had no desire to mingle closely with other people.

The following day I waited to hear from Señor Paredes. Passing time in a faceless hotel room was what I had done more times than I cared to remember. Barcelona was a city I knew reasonably well from previous visits, when I had passed the empty hours visiting museums, churches, the Gaudí buildings, the port and of course Las Ramblas, but I felt far from comfortable. Not knowing whether

Hadi was in the vicinity made me ill at ease and apprehensive. The boutiques had nothing new to offer, not even the scores of splendid shoe shops that punctuated the broad tree-lined streets.

Suddenly Gaudí's Sagrada Familia struck me as a likely place to pass a few hours. An unfinished work – sometimes dubbed Barcelona's third cathedral – it had created extraordinary architectural challenges and puzzles for those trying to interpret Gaudí's vision after his sudden death in 1926. Everyone wanted the complex structure to be completed – building had first started in 1882 – but there was disagreement on the execution of the task and no-one had any idea how long it would take.

I likened this to my own situation – an unfinished quest that had already taken far longer than I ever dreamed, but one I would never abandon until it was finished. The cathedral's numerous soaring towers, with their intricately stone-carved twists and turns, were linked at the base by the recesses of a large dome. The high-reaching towers, with additional ones still to be erected, seemed to symbolise the different pathways I had taken on my own journey. All my paths had so far culminated in a dead end, thus throwing me back with a thud to the dark recesses of despair to embark on yet another climb. Whether I would finish up with a magnificent work of art or simply continue on a journey without end I didn't dare contemplate. I feared I was going to be reduced to a crumbled mess.

Another day slowly passed. There was still no call from Señor Paredes and when I checked with his office I was told he was still away. Nothing remained but to return to Dubai feeling I had wasted more time and more money, and was no closer to finding Tanya.

Margaret

BARCELONA
Reliable help at last: February 1991

Two weeks later, towards the end of December, I received a fax from Señor Paredes. He had discovered Hadi did live in Barcelona and provided me with an address. However, he added there was no sign of Tanya and getting information about schools was very difficult. If I wished he could travel to the capital, Madrid, and try to get information from the education department. This of course would be expensive and the outcome was unpredictable.

If nothing else, I now had an address for Hadi. Knowing all businesses in Europe close down for at least two weeks during Christmas and New Year I again patiently waited. By early January commercial air traffic in the Gulf had virtually ceased. The fifty-three airlines normally servicing Dubai were no longer doing so.

But there was still one flight a day – Emirates to London.

It was quarter to six in the morning and I was woken by the telephone ringing at the side of my bed. A young American marine who we had entertained on several occasions during the preceding weeks wanted to let me know the first strike had been made. It was 17 January and the Gulf War had started. The telephone rang non-stop from then on for several hours, all friends and colleagues in Dubai making sure I knew we were at war. There was certainly no more sleep that morning, or for the next couple of days while we worked as normal during the day and watched CNN and listened to BBC radio at night. Frantic telephone calls came from family in Australia and friends around the world pleading with me to leave the area. They were far more concerned than we were in Dubai. It always intrigued me that being in the middle of a conflict was a little like being in the eye of a storm – relatively calm and peaceful.

As days passed and Operation Desert Storm intensified we became used to hearing and seeing in the media the damage done by the long-range Scud missiles with their incredible power and deadly accuracy. The bombing of Iraq's military sites was relentless with up to two thousand sorties a day. Late at night we would sit in our gardens and watch the allied jets pass overhead on their way to Iraq. A couple of hours later we waited for their return, counting them one by one, to make sure they were all accounted for.

Our working days were a little more fragmented than usual and one Friday I had gone to Ian's house to catch up on some paperwork. Working on the weekend was not unusual for me and was almost mandatory for Ian – the workaholic. The house was large and airy and Kate's flair for decorating was evident. The duck-egg blue and apricot furnishings were cool and relaxing, belying the heat outside. Persian rugs added a warm feeling to the black slate floors and took the edge off the air-conditioned environment. The green lawn, visible through the glass sliding doors and large windows, was bordered by petunias and pale pink bougainvillea, and the clear water in the sky-blue swimming pool sparkled in the sun. Ian's study was large with a wall of glass overlooking the lush garden outside. We worked all day, and after accomplishing our goal, enjoyed a couple of gin and tonics brought to us on a silver tray by the Indian houseboy clad in his customary sparkling white shirt and white slacks.

We sat back and relaxed and without warning Ian asked me how I was getting on with my search for Tanya. I relayed the frustrations I was experiencing with the private investigator in Barcelona and how difficult it was to make any progress. Ian then took me by complete surprise and offered something I had never imagined. He was friendly with a very influential businessman in Europe who, as well as owning a number of properties in Spain, frequently conducted business there. Would I like an introduction to this gentleman's legal firm?

Within twenty-four hours after Ian's request was made a fax came through giving us the name and contact details for the senior partner of the law firm. Although I had expected the office to be in Madrid, I was delighted to find it was located in Barcelona, a city I was now familiar with and could easily find my way around. With an introduction from this substantial client I knew my case would be taken seriously and not put to the bottom of a pile. Things immediately looked better.

The day after my forty-seventh birthday in early February, DUBAL again sent me to London on business. I had been working in our London office for less than a week when I saw an opportunity to get away for a few days, and booked a flight to Barcelona.

Before leaving Dubai my ever-helpful friend Eleanor came up with another contact for me in Barcelona. She gave me details for Lola, an English-speaking Spanish woman who Eleanor had learned of through an old college friend.

Although the Hotel Monegal was inexpensive and convenient I felt I could not spend any more time in its bare, depressing environment. A quick look in my Frommer's guidebook resulted in a call to the slightly more expensive Gran Via Hotel where I booked for a few days. My next call was to Elsa to say I would arrive the following day.

Elsa met me at the airport and took me to the hotel. When I saw the foyer I was pleased I had made the change. However, when I opened the door to a tiny windowless box with nothing but a bed, a side table and a rickety wardrobe I questioned my hasty decision. At least it had wall-to-wall carpet but how long was it, I wondered, since it had seen soap and water?

Not wishing to keep Elsa waiting, I rushed back to the foyer and we left for Señor Paredes' office. I had finally managed to speak to him from London and made an appointment for immediately after my arrival. After the formal introductions and the exchange of the necessary niceties, he calmly announced that he had no further news. I lost my patience at this point, and my raised voice and forceful gestures must have had some effect because he telephoned someone to enquire if Hadi was currently in Barcelona. Of course this request would take time to be answered and he would call me at eight o'clock that evening to let me know. There was no call at the appointed time but Elsa called me much later to confirm Hadi had been seen. Señor Paredes would collect me at seven o'clock the following morning to go to Hadi's address.

Huddled in a small dark blue Fiat opposite the apartment building where Hadi lived we sat and waited. February in Barcelona can be extremely cold and whether it was simply the weather, or the early morning temperature combined with my fear, I trembled for almost three hours.

Suddenly Señor Paredes whispered, 'There he is.'

'Where?'

'There, coming out of the building.'

'You mean the one in the green coat and hat.'

'Yes.'

'No. That's not him!'

'Yes it is. We have followed him several times. It is definitely him.'

'Are you absolutely sure?'

'Yes.'

'I can't believe it. I would never have recognised him.'

Hadi had put on a great deal of weight – I could see it wasn't just the winter clothing. His hair, what little he had, was almost down to his shoulders and very grey. The Austrian-style hat covered most of his face but his gold-framed glasses caught the glint of the morning light. He walked a few doors along the street and went into a bar. Señor Paredes then told me that when Hadi was in Barcelona he went there every morning for a coffee. A few minutes later he left the bar and went to the bus stop.

Although I still had difficulty in recognising Hadi my heart was pounding at the thought that he might see us. A number sixteen bus approached and Hadi got on. The little Fiat jerked away from the curb and we sped after the bus. We followed, at far too close a distance for my liking, and once in the heavy traffic in the centre of Barcelona it was very difficult to see who was getting on or off the bus. Our chase continued and, after tedious jerking in and out of traffic, to my surprise Señor Paredes announced that we had lost him. I was relieved that our pursuit was temporarily over. Señor Paredes delivered me back to the hotel and asked me to telephone him in the afternoon. In the meantime he would try to arrange for me to meet with Señora Valero, Hadi's former de facto.

That afternoon Señor Paredes told me that Tanya had not been included on Hadi's residency papers for the past five years and that the driving licence issued in Malaga showed his new address in Barcelona. This latest information was an alarming discovery. Why was Tanya not listed on Hadi's papers? Was she not in Spain, did he have her there illegally, or was there something worse? Señor Paredes departed saying that I should phone him the next day.

Sitting in the gloom of my hotel room I remembered a name I had heard from Señor Paredes during the past few days. It was the family Villalobos. They had three children of similar ages to Tanya, had lived in the same building where Hadi and Tanya had lived with Señora Valero, and were close friends of theirs. The family had recently moved to a different building but in the same street.

Visiting each building took time but with the help of the concierge in each new location I was able to establish where the Villalobos family were not living. By the time I located their new address there was no response to my persistent ringing of their doorbell. Not knowing what else to do I boarded a bus to the waterfront and walked along the shores of the Mediterranean, desperately trying to find solace in the gentle lap of the cerulean water and the cool embrace of the breeze.

The following morning I returned to the Villalobos home, trembling with fear as I rang the bell. If Señora Villalobos was close to Tanya she may also have been told in confidence by Hadi that Tanya's mother was in fact alive, as well as all the ugly lies that he had repeated to so many others. How would she react when I told her who I was?

It seemed a very long time before she finally opened the door. I had completely forgotten that nine-thirty in the morning was very early for Spanish women of a certain class. There she stood in her cream satin negligee and matching house coat, matching high-heeled slippers, blonde hair still swept high obviously from the night before, a slight trace of old make-up and expensive French perfume, and one of the heaviest-looking gold bracelets I had ever seen. The conversation was difficult, with my faltering Spanish and her surprise and confusion in her first waking moments.

Finally I was invited in to the dimly lit but lavishly furnished living room. I sank into a luxuriously overstuffed sofa and the routine, which by now I had down pat, followed. I produced my marriage certificate, Tanya's birth certificate, Tanya's passport and earlier photographs of Hadi, Tanya and me together. Señora Villalobos's confusion turned to bewilderment. She had always believed Tanya's mother to be dead, but now was convinced I was who I purported to be. She happily told me about Tanya, what an adorable child she was and that Hadi was a wonderful father. What I expected to gain from this meeting I wasn't sure but it was another link to Tanya.

Señora Villalobos excused herself to ask her maid to bring us coffee and I worried that she might be trying to telephone Hadi. No-one had ever found a telephone number for Hadi but I couldn't believe he didn't have one – what if Tanya was ill in the middle of the night and needed a doctor?

Señora Villalobos came back to the sitting room, followed by the coffee, and we continued our now laboured conversation. She told me she hadn't seen Tanya for a long time and didn't know where she was. She also promised to look for some photographs she had of Tanya and give them to me, together with a copy of a video taken at her daughter's birthday party. I felt there was nothing else I could achieve by interfering further in this kind woman's morning, so thanked her and left.

Completely frustrated with the lack of progress, the following morning I telephoned Estrada & Martos, the legal offices to which, through Ian, I had received an introduction. That afternoon I stood momentarily in front of a large baroque mirror that graced their entrance area. The mirror was decorated with gold leaf, suggesting the offices belonged to serious lawyers – not the unreliable appointees I had dealt with over recent years.

I met with the senior partner plus another colleague and outlined my story. I felt very comfortable with these two gentlemen and when Señor Huerta said he would be handling my case I sensed a renewal of strength. They explained that Tanya's legal status in Spain was important in how a case would be viewed, and at this stage it appeared that she was in the country illegally. The next thing they suggested was that I change my private investigator. They knew someone they thought could help and suggested I meet with her. They were not only recommending someone they knew to be reliable but that someone was also a woman. This was music to my ears.

On leaving the offices of the distinguished firm I revisited Señor Paredes. He confirmed that Tanya was definitely not living with Hadi and he could not contact Señora Valero as she was now living in Palma de Mallorca.

The following day I telephoned the Australian Consulate in Barcelona to see if Hadi had applied for a passport for Tanya, but was told the consul was out of the country for three weeks. After some pleading, his assistant, Maria Antonia, agreed to speak to my contact, Mavis Saul, at the Australian Embassy in Madrid. Mavis knew my case well and confirmed to Maria Antonia that Hadi had applied to the embassy many times for a passport for Tanya. These applications had been denied but as soon as Tanya turned eighteen she would be entitled to apply in her own right and would have to give a home address. On the basis of this information from Madrid, Maria Antonia agreed that I could visit the consulate and she would check to make sure an application had not been lodged in Barcelona.

Once I was in her office Maria Antonia said we could start by looking at the receipt book for the previous six months. I could not believe the number of receipts for Australian passports issued in Barcelona in a six-month period – there were literally hundreds. She laughed at my surprise and said they were mainly due to muggings, snatched handbags and hotel theft. It was hard to believe that in such a beautiful city there was so much crime. After a couple of hours of searching without success, we decided there was no point going back any further through the records.

It was now Friday and I telephoned Señor Paredes. Again he was not in the office. I telephoned Señor Huerta but he had not been able to contact his private investigator and would let me know as soon as he had done so. My frustration was building by the minute.

Elsa, Olivier and the family were busy all day Saturday and I toyed with the idea of calling Lola, Eleanor's new contact, but kept finding excuses not to do so. I always had great difficulty calling people I had not met but in this instance it was even more awkward. The first thing I would have to do was explain to this stranger why I was in Barcelona. How embarrassing. How does a mother explain to a stranger how she 'lost' her child and hasn't been able to find her? My strength had dissipated by this stage and I didn't want to go through the exercise. However, I was marooned in this tiny, windowless room of what appeared from the foyer to be a commodious hotel. With no television, my own radio that wouldn't work in the room, and no concentration to read, I decided I needed to talk to someone even if it meant explaining myself to Lola.

A very clipped voice answered the phone. Lola, obviously surprised by my call, suggested we meet the following day for coffee. Although grateful to have found someone with whom I could easily converse, the prospect of again having to face a whole day and night by myself was very depressing.

As I lay full of lethargy on the hotel bed the shrill of the telephone jolted me. On lifting the receiver I recognised Lola's heavily accented voice announcing she had discovered there was an English film showing at a nearby cinema that afternoon, and would I like to go? Never before had I been so excited about seeing a movie and even the thought of *The Fountainhead*, the 1949 film adaptation of Ayn Rand's novel, starring Gary Cooper, immediately lifted my spirits.

Within half an hour I was in the hotel foyer waiting for this most welcome stranger and mentally thanked my thoughtful friend Eleanor for making the introduction. Soon a woman of small frame was approaching me. Her dark, straight hair was extremely short, her glasses looked very academic and her suntanned skin had not seen a great deal of make-up. She wore a black leather jacket and grey trousers over sensible black shoes.

'You must be Margaret?' were Lola's first words.

As we left the hotel, me in my straight skirt and high heels towering over Lola's one hundred and fifty-two centimetres, I had to smile at the comical picture we must have presented.

'I hope you don't mind, I've brought my motorbike,' she announced.

My stunned silence must have made some impact for Lola hastily queried, 'You have ridden a motorbike before haven't you?'

'No. Never!' was all I could manage from my shocked height.

'You'll be fine,' she said, adding matter-of-factly, 'it's so much easier to get through the traffic.'

'But I can't even ride a bicycle!' I confessed pleadingly.

'All you have to do is hang on.'

And close my eyes and pray, I thought.

I have rarely felt so stupid and conspicuous – trying to get onto her motorbike in a lady-like manner wearing totally inappropriate clothing. I decided to abandon my shoes, which Lola efficiently placed in a pouch on the front of the bike, and rode with stocking-clad feet to the cinema. All the way I was conscious of truck drivers and people in buses paying more than due attention to my exposed legs, but the fear of weaving in and out of the traffic replaced my embarrassment.

After the film Lola suggested we have a drink, to which I happily agreed. Dutch courage for the ride back to the hotel, I thought. But then Lola added that her favourite bar was in the old part of town, which I knew to be some distance away from where we stood in front of the cinema, and nowhere near the hotel. Well, we had made it this far without incident so why should I worry about mounting the black machine again? At least by now it was almost dark.

Over our cocktail and olives I learned a little more about my companion. Lola taught mathematics and science at the university, had never married, and lived in her own apartment in the same building as her father. Her mother had died some years before but their housekeeper, Maria, had stayed on to take care of her father.

Lola and I came from very different worlds. My corporate life-style of private jets and five-star hotels in countries throughout Europe and the Middle East was the complete antithesis of Lola's quiet, academic life in downtown Barcelona. But in spite of this bizarre juxtaposition of lifestyles, and due to Lola's generous and understanding nature, a warm and lasting friendship was born. In fact Lola immediately offered to help in my enquiry by asking a friend of hers if he could find out if Tanya was registered in any of the high schools in Barcelona.

By Monday morning I was feeling positive again and relieved to receive a message from Señor Huerta requesting me to be in his office that afternoon as he had arranged my meeting with the private investigator.

Señor Huerta introduced me to his charming assistant, Alejandra, who would also be working with him on my case. Alejandra was probably in her late twenties, tall and slim with long blonde hair. The three of us went into a meeting room where Maite, my new private investigator, greeted us. She was a very large woman, her girth almost equal to her height and not camouflaged by the navy-blue coat she wore. Her hair was short, black and masculine in style. I was immediately glad she was on my side.

My initial interpretation of her unusual name was 'mighty mouse' and in living up to this sobriquet she was not to disappoint me. Maite was a no-nonsense woman and her English was equivalent to my Spanish – not very good! However, with the help of the young Alejandra, we communicated well and quickly built a working rapport. Maite was not shy in showing her disgust that Señor Paredes, in the many months past, had not accomplished anything regarding Tanya's whereabouts. If I wanted to employ her, she was confident she could find Tanya.

Elated by the professionalism of this group, and confident that Maite would find Tanya for me, I went straight to Señor Paredes' office intending to terminate his services. Unfortunately I found that he was in Madrid and when I requested a copy of my file was informed this would have to be cleared with Señor Paredes first. Nothing had changed.

The following day with little else to do I busied myself writing letters. One to my mother telling her the good news about meeting Maite. One to Tanya that I would leave with Señora Villalobos in the hope that it might one day be passed on. One to Señora Villalobos thanking her for the hospitality she showed me in her home, assuring her that I would not do anything if I thought it would harm Tanya, and finally thanking her for all she had done for Tanya over the years. The last letter was to the Australian Embassy in Madrid requesting Mavis to give Tanya my address should she apply for a passport. I also asked Mavis if she could possibly find a way to let me know, if the application were made, when Tanya was due to collect her passport so I could be at the embassy at the same time.

At my next meeting with Maite she brought two colleagues along: Fernando, who was an expert in finding missing children and who would be doing a lot of the investigative work; and Joanna, a young English girl who spoke excellent Spanish and was able to interpret for us both. I gave Maite the report I had finally received from Señor Paredes. I also outlined the details of my visit to Señora Villalobos and gave Maite her address, with the hope that being Spanish Maite might be able to glean more information than I had done. Maite was very confident they would be able to trace Tanya and asked if I could stay on in Barcelona for a few more days.

Lola phoned to apologise for not being in touch but her father had had an accident and was in hospital. There was no word from her friend regarding a registration of Tanya in any of the schools in Barcelona. I told Lola I was staying on for a few more days and she insisted that as she had a spare room I move out of the hotel and stay with her. This was happily arranged for the next day.

The following morning I was packed and ready to leave the hotel but the reception advised me that finding a taxi would be impossible. As a result of the war a demonstration was taking place outside in Gran Via and Plaza Cataluña. While I waited I watched the news on television in the guest lounge and was relieved that the Iraqi army had not marched beyond Kuwait. By mid-afternoon the streets had cleared and I made my way to Lola's apartment.

My days were by no means full, mostly spent waiting for telephone calls or attending meetings. But after I moved into Lola's apartment I was at least able to spend part of my day at the supermarket then go back to prepare a home-cooked meal for us.

During dinner the first night Lola told me she was due to fly to Canada the following week to address an international conference. She had completed her science and mathematics paper in Spanish and would I help her translate it! I had never studied science and my mathematics training had terminated at year ten. Admittedly my understanding of written Spanish was marginally better than my spoken attempts, but the combined level was not much beyond kindergarten. In spite of my objections and protestations Lola insisted I could do the job.

Not much later we were in her study. Where the rest of the apartment was minimalist and modern, with the liberal use of bright pastels and modular lines, this room was a different story. The walls were lined from floor to ceiling with dark-timber shelves, overflowing with serious books. A quick appraisal told me they were all in Spanish. Boxes, piles of books, and rows of videotapes cluttered the floor. Two tall filing cabinets and Lola's desk, which you could hardly see for papers, were by the narrow wall next to the door. Everything was cramped and congested with a heavy smell of old books. Lost somewhere among the bookshelves there was a small opaque window, looking onto a gloomy light well, through which the occasional clatter from a neighbour's kitchen could be heard. A lonely light hung from the ceiling, but fortunately a small lamp on the shelves above the desk illuminated the mound of papers. A heater with its flickering electric bars added a little warmth to the room. The old dark carpet had witnessed many years – this was a serious room and I felt out of my depth.

Lola pulled up a second chair next to her desk and once we were seated opened a manila folder and produced her speech, together with its half-finished English version.

After several tedious sessions over the following days, much reference to Spanish–English dictionaries and a lot of freewheeling, the task was completed to the best of my ability. Neither my mathematics nor my science skills had improved, and I cringed every time I anticipated how an English-speaking academic audience would receive this oration. I prayed that this generous young woman would not be made to look foolish by the stroke of my pen.

To my great relief when I saw Lola some months later she said her paper was well received and she had been enthusiastically congratulated!

The following day Maite telephoned to say she had spoken to Señora Villalobos, who had agreed to help in any way she could. However, as a result of their conversation Maite thought Tanya might be in Switzerland. She also wanted me to make an appointment with Señor Paredes, a meeting she and Joanna would attend. I didn't feel comfortable with this at all but I had to put myself in Maite's hands now. Maite and Joanna arrived thirty minutes before Señor Paredes was due. Maite advised me as to how she would run the meeting and what I should say. Señor Paredes arrived and, after introductions, informed us there was no further news, except that he had made contact with one of Hadi's neighbours who promised to let him know when Tanya returned to Barcelona. I then paid Señor Paredes' account to date and he left us saying he would keep on top of the case. Maite had suggested that I keep him onside and not fire him as we might still use him if the need arose. However, Maite understood that I would have nothing further to do with him.

Maite then advised me that Hadi was stateless and was trying to get Spanish nationality. She also confirmed that he had a car registered in his name.

The next day I met again with Maite and her team of two. She showed me a copy of an embargo that had been placed on Hadi's Mercedes but was unable to find out who had placed the embargo or when. Maite had again spoken to Señora Villalobos, whose husband had stated that in no way should his wife get involved. Maite had also spoken to the first psychologist I had visited, seven years earlier, who said because he did not know Tanya's disposition he could give no advice as to what approach I should make if she still believed I was dead.

Maite said she now believed Tanya was in Marbella but as there was a fiesta all that week in Malaga, which meant all schools were closed, Fernando was unable to make any enquiries.

I paid Maite the agreed down payment for her services. She warned me to be prudent in whatever steps I took, and as she encased me in a warm bear hug she whispered she was praying for me. I said goodbye to Maite, Fernando and Joanna and hoped I would see them again before Easter.

All that was left now was to pack and return to Dubai.

I believed the many years I had patiently waited before reuniting with Tanya were now coming to an end. My plans for meeting her were at last being put in place but – and this was my biggest concern – there was still the problem of how to alleviate Tanya's shock at finding out her mother was alive.

Through my connection with the local English-speaking school in Dubai, and as a member of its board of governors, I was ideally placed to find what I was looking for. However, I had to remain mindful that I was known in the community as a single woman, and any questions about a local child psychologist would have to be discreet. After numerous enquiries, the same name kept being mentioned as the preferred choice. Surprisingly, and to my delight, the person was female. Also she was Scandinavian, which I considered an excellent omen, believing those countries to be more advanced in this science than any other.

Making an appointment to see Christianne was the easy part; going for the meeting was nerve-racking. Firstly, I would have to reveal that

I had been lying about being single and rely on her professional ethics to keep this confidential. Secondly, this was the most important undertaking in my life and would she have the professional expertise to give me the correct answer?

Her first words were reassuring.

'Margaret, I know you have a high profile in Dubai, know a lot of people, and frequently represent your company. The first thing I want you to know is that I will never acknowledge you in public or at any gathering unless you greet me first. Whatever is discussed within these four walls will remain between you and me and nobody else need ever know that we have met.'

Much relieved, I thanked Christianne.

As I related the history of events to her she gently asked a number of questions. It seemed as though I was doing all the talking, which was not what I had expected. After what must have been at least an hour, Christianne asked if she could see me again in a week's time. She had said very little so I assumed she might need time to consider what I should do and say on my first meeting with Tanya.

The following week I felt more confident about our meeting, but impatient for Christianne to get to the point and tell me what to do. She talked in general terms about teenagers and more specifically about sixteen- and seventeen-year-olds. She also discussed how adopted children always wanted to know about their parents, irrespective of who they turned out to be. By the time children reached their mid-teens they were quite resilient and had a better capacity to deal in an adult manner with information and trauma, no matter how surprising or shocking.

Somehow the focus had returned to me and I was aware of still answering what I considered a lot of irrelevant questions. When I pressed Christianne on exactly how I should approach Tanya and what I should say there was a long silence.

Finally, she softly said, 'Margaret, it's really you, not Tanya, I'm worried about right now. I'm far more concerned about you.'

What on earth was this woman talking about? I thought. Here I had been wasting my precious time hoping she would help me prepare to meet Tanya, but she didn't seem to have understood me.

After a short pause Christianne continued, 'Have you thought about what you will do if Tanya doesn't want to know you?'

My initial reaction was that the woman in front of me was being absurd. How could she possibly imagine such a thing? Her soft, gentle voice continued, compelling me to listen, and for the very first time the suggestion she was broaching appeared to have some credence. Christianne had found a chink in my armour of steely determination and before I realised it I was sobbing uncontrollably.

Up to this point many fears had plagued me about my imminent reunion with Tanya, but none of them as alarming as this latest possibility. I would put the thought out of my mind immediately. It just couldn't happen.

Christine
May 1991

MARBELLA
Playing the sleuth: May 1991

A line of reliable communication was now established and I knew Maite would reply to my faxes and telephone messages. This was an enormous comfort after years of unreliable associations. It didn't in any way allay my impatience, but it helped minimise my frustration.

As the weeks passed Maite updated me on her progress. She was sure Tanya was in Marbella but her enquiries there were slow to be answered. Eventually in early May a fax arrived from Maite giving me the name and address of the school in Marbella where Tanya was enrolled. I telephoned Maite to ask if she would come with me to Marbella but unfortunately she was about to leave for Madrid, where she would be working on a case for several weeks.

I knew I no longer had the strength to make this trip alone.

I was desperate to get to Tanya but I was afraid of what repercussions there might be if Hadi was also in Marbella. Over the years his threats to me directly and through other people had taken hold. The thought of staying alone in another spiritless hotel room for an indefinite time was also too depressing to contemplate. Deciding to bare my soul, I made a humble plea to my friend and neighbour from my days in Libya.

After so many years of going off alone to foreign places, hotels, legal offices, government offices, courts and the like, the thought of meeting up with Christine again was both exciting and emotional. Christine was a perfect choice. First and foremost she was a mother, she knew me well, and unlike other close friends – Ann or Eleanor, for example – did not have the restriction of full-time employment to hinder her availability. Her staunch friendship and sharp wit presented the perfect travelling kit. Although we had not seen each other for sixteen years we had corresponded regularly as we each drifted from country to country. Christine had been one of the many people I contacted in the early years of Tanya's disappearance because Bill, her then husband, was a friend of Hadi's and I hoped there had been some contact.

Now twelve years later my telephone call to her in England asking if she would join me on this trip was totally unexpected. Without a second's hesitation she arranged for time off work and booked her air ticket to Malaga. Because it had been many years since we had seen each other, I was a little apprehensive about our reunion. In those intervening years Christine had had a son, now thirteen years old, she had divorced Bill, and was back living with her parents in England. Although she and Bill were very close friends of ours when we all lived in Tripoli, the intervening years and experiences could have inflicted changes on us both.

When I finally saw her great beaming smile above outstretched

arms in the din of the arrivals hall in Malaga airport I knew nothing had changed and I had a sudden surge of guilt for ever thinking
such thoughts. We rushed to each other and any idea of awkwardness that I had imagined was immediately forgotten. We both spoke
at once, firing questions, giving compliments, crying, laughing and
hugging each other all at the same time.

Immediately I was reminded of the happy times we had shared
in Libya. When Hadi and I left the country to live in Spain, Christine and Bill had remained. By that time all the better restaurants
had closed because of prohibition, the shops were virtually devoid
of goods, and the supermarkets frequently lacked the most basic
necessities. Life had become difficult and tedious. Four years later
when Christine and Bill's son was born, Christine moved to Malta,
where caring for a small child was more feasible. From Malta she
eventually returned to Sheffield as a single parent.

I had arrived in Malaga on an earlier flight from Zurich and taken
delivery of a hire car, which was waiting for me in the car park. Imagine the horror when I discovered it was canary yellow. Not quite the
colour of a vehicle to be used by a couple of novices in a daring
sleuthing expedition on the Costa del Sol. By the time Christine and
I arrived back at the car I had forgotten my initial reaction; we joked
about our little yellow peril and took off for Marbella.

Through a friend in Dubai I had arranged to rent a small villa
that fortunately, as we later learned, was close to the school. It was
well hidden among a row of similar two-storeyed Spanish-style
terraces in a housing estate just off the main road. All the villas
were clad in white stucco, with the arches and heavy wooden trim
so typical of Spain. The rich red bougainvillea cascaded down the
walls and curved around the arches.

The first evening, Christine and I had much catching up to do
discussing events of the many years since we had last met. When

Christine went to have a shower, I prepared to open the champagne and a tin of Iranian caviar I had brought with me from Dubai. And then I heard it – the familiar, high, professional operatic notes that emerged when Christine was relaxed and happy. Over the splash of the cascading water her clearly articulated aria flooded the room. It had been many years since I had last had the joy of being serenaded in this way! It reassured me that Christine was obviously not as worried as I was about the ordeal we were facing.

Our prime objective for the following morning was to locate the school. After a fitful sleep we left early in our cramped yellow car. After only a couple of minutes on the main road we spotted a yellow bus with the name of the school written on its side. Perfect. All we had to do was follow the bus and we would find the school. The bus stopped and started all along the route, collecting children, and each time it stopped I searched the faces of the schoolgirls to see if one could possibly be Tanya. How stupid for any mother to be looking into the face of a young girl, not knowing whether it was her daughter or not. The old feelings of frustration, fear and helplessness temporarily flooded back.

The bus finally turned off the main road onto a narrow winding lane that led into the hills behind Marbella. The small dwellings on either side soon disappeared and we found ourselves in an undeveloped area. After the thick traffic and burgeoning construction along the corridor of the main road this change of environment was a surprise, and made us more conspicuous. After several kilometres and at the end of the bitumen road we reached the school. The bus stopped on the edge of the narrow roadside. As soon as we could we slipped by and followed the meandering dirt track that continued into the hills and took us out of view. The road seemed to lead nowhere in particular and, as soon as we had travelled a safe distance, we stopped. Even though the car was very small it took several tight manoeuvres to turn it around on the narrow track, with the escarpment of the hill on one side and a slight drop and thick scrub on the other.

'Do you think they will have gone into school yet?' I asked Christine.

'Yes, I think we'll be safe to go back now.'

By the time we returned there was no sign of the children or the bus. The widest part of the road happened to be at the end of the school fence, not too close to the entrance, but in this rural area there was nowhere to hide.

The school was a large, white single-storey building with sparse dry acreage on the side where we were parked. This was in total contrast to the green terraced playing areas that dropped down to horse stables on the other side. The painted white wooden fence that surrounded the entire school was an unusual sight in Spain but was clearly intended to indicate it was private property.

To our surprise some kind of sporting activity was taking place with some girls and boys in green tracksuits and others in maroon uniforms. We walked slowly towards the playing field area and I looked intently to see if I could recognise Tanya. We beckoned to a couple of the girls and when they came to the fence asked if they knew Tanya. We directed the question to other girls as well but none of them seemed to recognise her name. Following the fence a little further we spotted two adults whom we presumed were teachers. Strolling as casually as we could, with eyes searching for anything that might be useful, we passed the noisy coterie of students clad in their colourful uniforms.

Clearly we had not managed to appear as casual as we thought, and one of the teachers walked in our direction and asked if we wanted something. With big smiles and rapidly losing our bravado, we thanked her, shook our heads then turned and fled back to the car.

'What should we do?' Christine nervously asked.

'If we wait a while they might finish and go inside. Then we could look around a bit more,' I suggested.

Our optimism eventually faded as there was no sign of the game finishing and we were very conspicuous sitting in a car in the middle of nowhere. It didn't take us long to realise this was not the right approach.

'Why don't we wait at the bottom of the hill, on the main road, this afternoon? We can follow the school bus and maybe see Tanya getting off,' I said.

The morning had turned out to be a wasted exercise.

That afternoon we waited at the junction of the main road. When we spotted the bus approaching from the direction of the school we braced ourselves. However, when we looked again there were at least four buses, creating yet more confusion in our minds. Which one would we follow? There was little time to decide so we followed the first bus, stopping each time it halted to allow children to get off. None of the children appeared to look like how I imagined Tanya to look, and finally when the bus was empty we had to admit defeat for the day, feeling more disillusioned than we had earlier.

On our return to the villa there was a handwritten note on a small scrappy piece of paper wedged under the front door. Would I please urgently call the car-rental company? With no telephone in the villa, we made our way to the nearest bar. This was only a short drive and when we pulled up outside we thought twice about going in. It was small, not very well lit and had a down-at-heel look about it, as did most of its customers. We decided that because we only wanted to use the telephone it would do. On entering this dingy, smoky establishment with a television suspended from the upper corner of one wall, we temporarily attracted the customers' gaze away from the small screen. As two conservative foreign women we looked totally out of place in this male domain which, had it been located in a different area, could have passed as a truckies' cafe.

Christine asked in her best Spanish if we could use the telephone. Without speaking, the swarthy, rotund barman pointed to the end of the bar. As we moved towards it all eyes remained glued on these two strangers who unwittingly were interfering with the football match in full swing.

I dialled the number displayed on the crumpled piece of paper and after announcing myself the young man asked if we still had the car? He seemed surprised when I, equally confused, said that we did.

'Well that's funny,' he continued, 'because it's been reported to the police. It was seen parked outside a school for no apparent reason and the unknown occupants were lingering suspiciously in the area for some time.'

After a prolonged silence on my part he asked if I was still there.

'Yes,' I replied, trying to take as long as I could to utter the word, and trying to think at a million miles an hour.

'Oh, yes,' I eventually offered, 'my friend and I are looking for a school for her children to attend when she moves to Spain.'

The old story, which I had found useful before when trying to gain entry to a school, had come in handy again. Meanwhile Christine was giving me very quizzical looks.

'Oh, well that explains it, but you'd better be a little more careful next time,' he suggested.

'Well, while we're talking about the vehicle,' I continued, 'I was going to telephone you in any case as there is a problem with the size of the car and my long legs. I wondered if we brought it in tomorrow, could we change it for something a little bigger?'

After obtaining his agreement to look for a suitable car for the following morning, the conversation finished on a friendly note.

Christine was looking more and more puzzled and noticed my trembling hands as I replaced the receiver. After I relayed the message to her that we had been reported to the police for loitering, we unanimously agreed we both needed to sit down with a glass of wine before doing anything else.

'But what was that about the car being too small?' Christine reasonably asked.

'It was the only excuse I could think of for changing our very conspicuous yellow peril.'

'Well done, my friend!' Christine exclaimed.

Seated in a remote corner, as far away from the television as possible, and having just been accused as loiterers, we tried our best to be inconspicuous.

The barman, a little confused by our presence, gingerly offered us a menu, which we graciously accepted. Slowly our eyes glossed over the menu and, not having the strength or inclination as wanted criminals to move much further, we placed our order, choosing a Spanish omelette for Christine and the daily fish for me. The food was unexpectedly delicious and this little haven off the beaten track became our regular retreat, keeping us sustained for much of the following week. Each time we entered we were greeted warmly and welcomed as part of the small community.

On arrival back at our little villa we knew we had to make a plan. The roller-coaster ride of emotions during the day had exhausted us and we had made no progress. Christine's eyes brightened.

'What about if we use the story you gave to the hire car man? We pretend we are moving to Spain, need to find a school for our children, and want to check out Alboran School.'

'Brilliant. We can make an appointment to see the bursar.'

'Or the headmistress!'

With new hope I said, 'We'll phone first thing tomorrow morning.'

'Yes.'

'Christine, could you please do the talking. Your Spanish is really good. I'll only confuse them,' I pleaded.

With a definite plan of action I slept a little easier and full of hope.

The following morning, after a coffee in our newfound *tasca*, we asked the now-friendly barman if we might again use the telephone.

The secretary who took our call was very obliging, but said the earliest the headmaster could see us would be twelve o'clock the following day. Now we had twenty-four hours to fill. We were able to spend the rest of the morning at the car-hire office, where we took delivery of a slightly larger, and thankfully grey-coloured, vehicle.

The next day, with ample time before our noon appointment, Christine and I lingered over a breakfast of coffee and half a slice of bread. Our stomachs were not fit to handle anything more substantial and I, in fact, questioned the sense of consuming the little we had.

Dressed in a lightweight woollen Jaeger suit with geometrical patterns in blue, green and turquoise that blended in with the Mediterranean surroundings, I checked numerous times to make sure I had all the necessary documents: one wad for the headmaster to prove my identity; a second bundle for Tanya including photos from our days in Malaga with her next-door playmates; and a letter to leave with her should our meeting be interrupted prematurely. Before we left the villa I went back just one last time to make sure my hair was in place and my dress was appropriate.

As Christine drove up the now familiar twisting road to the school I kept checking my watch and tried not to fidget as my anticipation mounted. First we had to overcome the language barrier with the headmaster and convince him to allow me to see Tanya. Then I had to make myself understood by Tanya. Although all the reports said she spoke English, they were from non-English-speaking people. From experience, I had learned this could be very unreliable and really depended on their own English-speaking ability.

We confidently parked our newly acquired, less conspicuous car outside the school, took three deep breaths and walked through the gates and up the path. Although I thought it was too early for the Spanish lunchbreak, many students were in the well-kept grassy grounds on our left-hand side. All were in animated conversation, laughing, shouting and generally engaged in the careless chatter of teenagers. Was Tanya part of this and was her mood about to change?

The secretary's office was just inside the main entrance and when we entered I was surprised to see a fresh-faced young woman not much older than the girls outside. Although we agreed Christine would do the initial talking we hadn't rehearsed what she would say. To my surprise I heard Christine announcing I was Tanya's mother! To my even greater surprise, and before I had time to worry too much about what I considered a blunder, the secretary replied, 'Would you like to see her?'

Trying not to show my astonishment, I stammered, 'Si, por favor.'

Christine sat me down on the nearest chair while the secretary went to the door and asked a passing teacher to fetch Tanya. I couldn't believe what was happening. Here, without any planning, this young woman was bringing Tanya straight to me. Could it really be this easy? Good heavens, what will I say? I knew what to say to the headmaster but that step had just been miraculously avoided. Will they have told her she is coming to see her mother? Perhaps she'll be too nervous to come? Maybe she'll tell the headmaster. Where will I start?

Some minutes passed while the eye contact between Christine and me was intensifying. A teacher entered and said they couldn't find her, apologised and said they were still looking. Was this a fabricated story to prevent me seeing her, or was she even at school today?

The secretary, spotting the English teacher passing by in the corridor, called her in and introduced us. The Spanish woman in her mid-thirties was beautifully groomed, very friendly and talked freely in heavily accented English about Tanya, saying that she was her best student. This delighted me because if her English was good at least we would be able to communicate when we finally met. It wasn't until I tried to get a little more information about Tanya and her father that the woman closed up completely and hurriedly excused herself to get back to her class.

Several more minutes passed. Then, without warning, Tanya breezed into the office, asking the secretary if she wanted her.

'Your mother is here to see you,' was what I understood to be the reply.

Tanya looked at both Christine and me, clearly confused and not knowing what to do. She did not say anything, but looked back and forth at our faces, not recognising either of them and evidently not knowing who was her mother.

The greatest restraint was mustered from the depths of my boots. I must not alarm her. I must remember she thinks I'm dead. I have to be calm and speak slowly. I stood up and ventured closer to where Tanya was standing. Instinctively I feared our time would be short, being vaguely aware that in the background the secretary had answered the telephone and had engaged in rapid conversation, while a serious expression rolled over her face. I launched straight into my practised account of how I had been searching for her for many years. At the same time, I slipped the two-page letter I had carefully written telling her how I had looked for her ever since that dark day in London, and how I longed to have her permanently in my life, into her pocket, saying it was to be read later. With the small photo album at the ready I asked Tanya if she remembered when we lived in Malaga.

With the speed of light we were interrupted by a female teacher rushing in and advising us in broken English that Tanya had to go back to her classroom immediately as she was missing her lesson. She wheeled a bewildered Tanya out of the office and I was left in mid-sentence.

Nervously, the secretary stuttered that the headmaster would see us shortly and would we please be seated. I sat frozen in the chair. This was my own flesh and blood and I had not recognised her. But the picture of her wearing a green tracksuit was emblazoned in my memory. She was almost as tall as me, with her hair still long, and pulled back in a neat ponytail. She appeared calm and composed.

She had not said anything except the occasional 'yes' or 'no' to my questions. Did she understand what I had said? Where were they really taking her? Was she now totally confused? And what had she thought of this nervous, emotional woman she had just been confronted by? Should I run after her?

'What should we do?' Christine asked.

'I don't know. Wait for the headmaster I suppose. What else can we do?'

As we sat huddled in the small space watching a few students coming and going in the corridor outside I saw Tanya again. She mischievously appeared in front of the open door and gave me a little wave and a huge beaming smile, and just as quickly disappeared.

'She obviously sneaked off somewhere and read my letter,' I whispered to Christine.

'Yes, I'm sure you're right,' Christine agreed.

'Oh. I hope she understood it all,' I wished aloud.

Christine held my trembling hand.

While entombed in the tiny office, trying desperately to get my thoughts in order, through the window above the secretary's head I saw Hadi entering the school. Now my heart and breathing really stopped. This was the first time I had seen him in years. Then I heard his voice – very friendly as it could be when the mood or need took him – from outside the secretary's door. Fortunately he did not come into the office and didn't see Christine or me. Whatever he said was beyond my comprehension but the secretary cheerfully replied and he was gone.

Christine and I, our eyes growing larger by the minute, frantically looked at each other. What would happen now? The wait seemed like an eternity before we were taken to the headmaster's office.

Señor Gonzalez was a large man, in his early forties, but of mild manner. He was alone in his office. I started on my usual spiel but was cut somewhat short. He clearly knew who I was and informed me that Hadi had come to the school and taken Tanya away. After a number of my requests it was clear that he was not going to answer any questions or give me any information about Tanya or Hadi.

The rest of that meeting remains something of a blur except I recall how kind and understanding Señor Gonzalez seemed. He told me how he had tried to persuade Hadi to meet with me, at least for Tanya's sake, and come to some solution. This of course had been refused outright. He had also voiced his belief that every child had the inherent right to know and have contact with their mother, but this was also ignored. Hadi reiterated that he would kill me if I ever tried to see or make contact with Tanya again – and, no doubt, this threat extended to anyone who tried to help me.

Confirming that there was no way of reasoning with Hadi, Señor Gonzalez suggested I pursue the matter through the court, at least for access, and also asked if I had considered making a *denuncia* against Hadi. At the conclusion of our meeting the headmaster promised to keep me informed, but I knew from previous experience that loyalty was given to the person paying the bills and that, unfortunately, was not me.

Back at the villa Christine made a pot of tea in an effort to calm me. My chin was trembling and as hard as I tried to control my tears they flooded down my face. How could I have been so close to Tanya for so little time then have Hadi take her again? At least now Tanya knew I existed and I was sure she had read the letter that gave a little of my side of the story. Just in case the letter fell into Hadi's hands I had used my mother's address in Australia as I certainly did not want Hadi to know I lived in Dubai, with all the possible dangers that might incur. Maybe after our brief meeting Tanya would not want to see me again, especially after all the poisonous thoughts I knew Hadi would now be injecting into her mind. Also, because Australia was so far away she might not even try to make contact with me. At this thought I lost control completely.

Christine tried to hug my grief away. Thank goodness I had not come to Spain alone as there was still a lot to be done. Would Hadi just keep Tanya away from school for a few days or would he take her out of Marbella? They could drive in any direction or even fly to another country. I had to start making enquiries right away.

Knowing I would get no information from the school and that by now Hadi would have Tanya hidden in a secure location, I struggled with the question of where to start. If only I could find someone who knew Tanya. Then I remembered something. Maite had told me Tanya was friendly with a girl of British parentage whose mother taught English in a local school. Somehow we believed this family lived in Ojen, just outside Marbella on the road to Coin. That would be my next step. We would try and find this English mother who would surely be able to help me.

The following day, with our road maps, Spanish dictionary and my brown leather folder containing my 'identity' papers, Christine and I set off to Ojen. The winding narrow road twisted slowly towards the Sierra Blanca behind Marbella. As we left the lush cultivated gardens and green foliage of the coast, the landscape became drier and the dusty heat clung to our throats. The dull countryside was occasionally relieved by a small, whitewashed farmhouse, but there was little sign of life. We bumped along the narrow potholed road, without the aid of signposts, hoping we were still heading in the right direction. With no warning, we drove over a crest in the road to find a small, seemingly deserted village.

'This must be it.'

'Can you see anything that says Ojen?'

'There are no signs on anything, let alone the name of the town.'

Not knowing the English family's name didn't help but I was sure if a foreign family lived in this tiny place, which was suspended in an era from many decades past, they would be known. There was not a soul on the street so we pulled up in front of what we hoped was the general store. A grey-haired, severely bent man shuffled to the counter. It took several attempts to make him understand our question. After rubbing his chin and screwing his wrinkled mouth for several minutes, while not taking his pale watery eyes off Christine's face, he shook his head and told us he didn't know of any foreign teacher or family living in those parts.

Doubting that he really understood, I suggested we move on and ask someone else. We passed a man working by the side of the road in what we assumed was his small farm. Again, we were met with a shake of the head and something like, 'No foreigners in these parts, you need to go to the coast.'

A short distance further I noticed a woman sweeping the steps of her small two-storeyed house. It was a shabby dwelling, probably no more than three or four rooms, and antiquated like everything else in the vicinity. The steps came directly onto the road, not the place to sit and admire the sunset. She squinted at us through her old-fashioned glasses and after leaning on her broom for a while shook her head, turned her back and went inside. It appeared she also didn't know, or even want to know, a foreign family. There didn't seem to be another living soul in the town so we made our way back to Marbella.

It was still only mid-afternoon when we arrived so I decided we should return to the school and ask to see the headmaster again. Señor Gonzalez was very sympathetic to my situation. He told me he was under strict instructions from Mr Senussi not to have any-thing to do with me or any communication whatsoever. He told me he had again tried his best to reason with Hadi, especially for Tanya's sake. He had requested Hadi to speak to me at least, even if it was through a third party. This of course had again been refused, followed by Hadi advising that he was taking Tanya away, and reit-erating that if I tried to find her or communicate with her he would kill me.

Señor Gonzalez was clearly upset by the whole episode and sug-gested the best thing for me to do was to engage a lawyer to file for access through the local court. Knowing Tanya was now in her final years of high school I prayed her father would not move her again at such a crucial stage of her education. Señor Gonzalez had already told me how happy she was at the school, that she did well in her work, and loved the horse-riding activities the school offered. She was also one of their best swimmers.

At the end of the following day we returned yet again to the school, planning to watch the students leaving in the hope of see-ing Tanya. On our arrival we were shocked to find all the students gone and the school closed. Perhaps because it was a Friday they left early or had sporting activities away from the school. The sheer disbelief stopped us in our tracks. But then we decided to have a closer look around the school at our leisure, without any prying eyes. As we walked around the dusty perimeter fence I noticed that one of the windows had been left ajar.

Quickly I pointed this out to Christine, telling her that I had seen a card index in the secretary's office the previous morning and if these cards were for the students we would be able to get an address for Tanya.

Christine laughed and asked, 'You're not seriously thinking of scaling the wall and breaking in?'

We were hardly dressed for such an escapade – Christine in her floating floral voile skirt and high heels, and me with a straight linen dress and heels. From the determined look on my face she understood, and immediately offered her hand to help me scale the perimeter fence on the far side of the school, where the grounds were untended, dusty and dotted with dry spiky grass. The school building was situated on unlevel ground and the side we were on sloped away slightly. Once alongside the building, the open window was at a level just too high for us to reach, but by going to the lower end of the building we were able to get onto a ledge that ran along the wall. We gingerly walked back along the ledge to the open window. Without too much effort I pushed the casement up far enough for us to scramble through. Modesty flew out the window as skirts were hitched up around our waists and high-heeled shoes quickly removed. We stumbled through the window, each helping the other to regain balance once inside, and found ourselves in a classroom lined with desks, chairs and a large blackboard and table at the front.

We quickly headed for the door, stopped, listened and not hearing anything but our own heavy breathing, took a left turn down a corridor. I prayed that the mental plan of the building in my head was accurate and that we were heading in the right direction. From our earlier visits I knew the secretary's office was next to the main entrance. We passed several doors and another corridor branching off to the right, but kept quietly running in what we hoped was the direction of the secretary's office.

Finally the entrance foyer and main door came into view. We dashed into the secretary's office, which was neat and tidy with no sign of registers or boxed card files. As my eyes scanned the room I prayed that all those cupboards and desk drawers were not locked. Christine started opening the cupboards on one side while I took the other. Just then we heard excited voices. They were muffled and in Spanish so I had no idea what they were saying. We stopped where we stood. The voices didn't appear to be coming in our direction although we could tell they were close by. Very quietly we continued our search, furtively looking at each other every time the sound level of the voices changed.

We were having no luck until in a long slim cupboard behind the secretary's desk I found the small, wooden card-index box. My fingers were trembling so much I could hardly open it and, when I finally did, couldn't remember where 's' came in the alphabet – at the beginning or the end? Then there it was, 'Tanya Senussi', complete with address. My temptation was to grab it and run but I knew as soon as the card was missed from the box, the culprit would be obvious.

Christine whispered desperately, 'Margaret, just take the bloody card and let's go!'

In spite of her pleadings, I knew we had to find a pen and paper and copy the details. This is not normally too difficult in a secretary's office, unless you are an unwanted intruder in a strange and frightening environment and your brain is not functioning rationally. My writing was completely illegible, looking more like marks made by the inky legs of a spider that had danced across the page, but I copied what I needed. After carefully replacing the box, and returning the pen, we huddled by the door to listen to the voices and determine where they were. While crouching against each other I heard the hollow clang of a bucket.

'It's the cleaners,' I whispered in relief, and off we ran out the main entrance and through a side passage back to our car.

Somehow with trembling legs, shaking hands and thumping hearts we managed to drive away from the school and down the hill to the main road, and pull off into the nearest car park to recover.

Armed with an address, Christine and I then started our search for its whereabouts. The area we had pulled into was the shopping complex for a housing estate, so without hesitation we went into the small general store and asked if they knew the location. To our amazement the apartment building we were looking for was on the opposite side of the main road where we had parked.

In front of the store was a building of three or four storeys still under construction that offered a perfect view across the highway. We climbed the stairs to the top and walked to the front where we could overlook Tanya's building. It was located on the seafront, and stood alone on the other side of the road with a large car park at the front and along one side. There was only one car parked in the area and we suspected this was a building occupied primarily by holidaymakers during the summer months and other holiday periods. It somehow looked deserted.

Could anyone see us spying on them? Would anyone recognise us? I stood looking at the building from every angle for some time, trying to will Tanya or Hadi to appear through the door or alight from a car. Eventually we decided we should go back to the safety of our little villa and return under the cover of darkness.

After a strengthening cup of tea and draped in black sweaters, we drove back to the building. Still there was no sign of life and only one solitary car parked adjacent to the entrance. We snapped out our headlights as soon as we turned off the highway into the car park where, except for the reflected light from the main road, the only other light came from the main entrance at the side of the building. We drove in the dark along the front of the building, which faced the main road, until we reached the far side. We could see that the side area was occupied by service shafts and air-conditioning units. Nowhere to hide and nothing to be discovered there.

We slowly drove back to the main entrance on the other side of the building, where I decided to get out and see if there was a list of names on the door entry system. As I was examining this I heard the noise of the lift descending. With jelly-like legs I rushed back to the car, jumped in and drove back to the opposite side of the building, where we stopped and tried to hide in the dark. Within seconds we could see an Arab man and his family leave the building and head straight towards us. Our hearts were thumping and we didn't know what to do so we just sat in our stationary unlit car. The man approached us in a very aggressive manner and, almost shouting, wanted to know what we were doing. Stammering in limited Spanish we said we were lost and were going to look at our map. He muttered something about us being on private property and that we should leave. This we did without hesitation, no further advanced and certainly with no apartment number.

Saturday had arrived and it was time for Christine to return to England and the job she had managed to escape for a week to be by my side. However, her flight wasn't until late afternoon, which left us a little more detective time together.

We were anxious to discover the number of Tanya's apartment. The only people we had seen entering or leaving the building from our various viewpoints during the past couple of days appeared to be Arab, so there was no use quizzing them about Hadi. If we could get onto the beach somehow, and walk along in front of the building, we might see something on a balcony – washing or anything that could belong to Tanya – that would help to identify her apartment.

Off we set, entering the beach through the grounds of an exclusive hotel a long way beyond the apartment building. After our harrowing week we now had no shame and the fact that the beach was only for the private use of hotel guests didn't faze us for a second. We practically ran along the beach until we reached the wall of Tanya's building, where we slowed almost to a stop and sauntered along gazing at the balconies. All the doors seemed firmly closed and there was not a sign of anything significant on any of the balconies.

Not being faint-hearted, while still with my friend, I suggested we go back to the little shopping area in Calahonda and watch the building one last time for any movement. While Christine looked in the shops for a suitable gift for her son, I climbed to the top of the unfinished building and watched. Gazing into space, not having seen a single person enter or leave the building, my attention was aroused by Christine running up behind me, obviously alarmed.

'He's here,' she gabbled, almost incoherently.

'Who?' I queried.

'Hadi. Hadi. He's downstairs with some fellow, having coffee.'

'Are you sure?'

'I'm certain.'

'Is Tanya there?'

'No, just Hadi.'

'Do you think she's nearby?'

'No, I've already looked,' came Christine's lowered response.

Christine suggested if we went and sat in the car we could possibly see them in the café. I sat in the driver's seat with Christine next to the curb. As we watched Hadi and his companion of Middle Eastern appearance, they talked uninterruptedly while making frequent hand gestures in the Latin way. We continued watching and then they stood up ready to leave. To our disbelief they started walking along the footpath towards our car. Christine hid behind a newspaper she had just bought; I pulled the sun visor down and was very grateful for my sunglasses. They came closer and closer, all the time talking, gesticulating, stopping and then coming nearer. Then unbelievably, and to our dismay, they stopped by the side of our car. I was so relieved to be on the far side but quickly lowered my head and didn't move a single muscle. To our great relief, after what seemed an eternity, they moved on.

Where was Tanya? Where had he sent her this time?

Sadly that afternoon I drove Christine to the airport and tearfully bade her farewell. Compassion was written all over her face. She instinctively knew how alone and desolate I would feel after she left and was also aware of the tasks I needed to complete before return-ing to Dubai – finding and appointing another lawyer for a start. Without hesitation she offered her help at any time and insisted I telephone her should I have the need.

With tears in my eyes and a very heavy heart I drove back to Marbella.

That evening and the following day I was violently ill and could hardly lift my head off the pillow. My head was giddy and my whole body trembled. The feeling of nausea just wouldn't go away and every time I tried to get up the horrible swimming sensation in my head returned. Thankfully I slept a great deal of the time but I knew by Monday morning I would have to be able to get up and continue.

Still feeling weak and somewhat insecure, now that I was alone, I had to make a new start. When Monday dawned I forced myself out of bed and tried to swallow some weak black tea but quickly reverted to water. My first step was to appoint yet another lawyer. I telephoned Señor Huerta, my lawyer in Barcelona, to see if he could recommend a lawyer in Marbella. After my previous disastrous experiences with lawyers in this town I was loath to trust anyone. Señor Huerta could not recommend anyone in Marbella, which did not come as any surprise to me but was very disappointing. However, the firm did know someone they could recommend in San Pedro, just over ten kilometres away.

I immediately arranged an appointment and took off to San Pedro that afternoon. Señor Barrido was charming and very sympathetic but explained this wasn't quite his line of work and a little out of his territory. He finally gave me the name of someone he knew of in Marbella who dealt in family court matters and, although it didn't come as a recommendation, it was an avenue to pursue.

The following morning I was in the office of Señora Paloma Cardenas. What a brilliant stroke of luck to be introduced to a female lawyer. She would no doubt be experienced in my type of request and sympathetic in dealing with it. Mature female lawyers were scarce in Spain and this was surely a good omen. There were the usual powers of attorney to sign, the request for authenticated copies of birth certificates and marriage certificates to be supplied, and payment up front for my case. Señora Cardenas was confident of the outcome and assured me that my case would be heard in about three months time. This news buoyed my spirits and I left her office to prepare for the work I now needed to do – including arranging her payment, getting authenticated copies of all the documents, updating my lawyers and Maite in Barcelona, and confirming my return air ticket to Dubai.

The last thing I did before leaving was to visit El Buen Gusto, the best patisserie in Marbella. There I made arrangements for a birthday cake to be delivered to the school on Tanya's birthday at the end of the month. I chose the style of cake carefully and wrote the words 'Happy 17th Birthday Tanya, All my love, Mother' that were to be iced on the top. Unfortunately Tanya never received it.

Tanya

MARBELLA
Another setback: January 1992

After appointing Señora Paloma Cardenas in May 1991 to file a case for me in Marbella, eight months passed. She had informed me that a custody case of this nature, provided all our papers were in order, would take about three months and in the worst case a maximum of six months. I had an excellent chance of success. She had been paid a substantial amount of money to prepare the papers and lodge my case.

In spite of numerous telephone calls and faxes to her in those months I could not obtain a satisfactory reason for the long delay. After three months she told me that the courts were on summer vacation then two months later she told me the original documents were incomplete and had to be refiled, and so the excuses continued.

There was now no alternative but for me to make yet another trip to Spain to establish for myself the real cause of the delay.

Luckily at a dinner party a few days later a friend of mine was excitedly telling everyone that she had purchased an apartment in Marbella and was planning to visit in about ten days time. I telephoned Katherine the following morning and asked if she would mind if I travelled with her to Spain. Katherine at that time had no idea about my predicament or that I had ever been married. She was delighted to have a travelling companion and someone to whom she could show her new home, insisting I stay with her.

On the first day in Marbella I sat with Katherine in her small apartment in the Skol building. Skol was an 'apart-hotel', with a mix of some private apartments used as permanent residences and others rented back to the hotel side of the business to be leased to tourists. It was a large U-shaped building on the edge of the Mediterranean with a swimming pool in the centre. A band was practising by the swimming pool for that night's party, and the electronic sounds vibrated through my body. I found it hard to relate the atmosphere of partying tourists to my serious legal endeavours.

The thumping of the music pounded in my head and I knew I had to tell Katherine why I was really in Marbella. Thankfully, although surprised, Katherine listened to my story without any questions and offered to help if she could. Relieved that I was no longer harbouring secrets from someone I was travelling with, I relaxed a little.

After a restless night's sleep I went direct to the office of Señora Cardenas. I had purposely not made an appointment – she had not answered any of my faxes or telephone calls for some time so I doubted she would appear for an appointment. Sitting in the waiting room of her office, the atmosphere was electric. Her secretary, poised opposite me behind her desk, maintained an embarrassed silence, aware of my determination to wait for the Señora, all day if necessary, and yet she had obviously been told by her boss to try to get rid of me.

During those hours I tried to imagine why Señora Cardenas was being so evasive – apart from the obvious possibility that Hadi had either paid her off or threatened her. But then I remembered back to when Hadi first took Tanya, and I flew to Malaga to try to find them. All the Spanish women had berated me for leaving the family home and blamed me for the circumstances in which I found myself. At that time Spanish women were not normally employed after marriage and deferred to their husbands in most matters. Divorce was unheard of, deserting the family home was a crime, and female professionals were still in the wings. This was a country ruled by a strict Catholic church. Women simply had one future – to marry and have children.

The Arab occupation of Spain for seven hundred years had certainly left its imprint on the culture, particularly as far as women were concerned. Spanish women were not completely covered in the same way as Arab women, but after a certain age all wore black, and occasionally a black veil. Young women were not permitted to go out with someone of the opposite sex unescorted and chaperones were still very much part of a young person's life. Schools were segregated and I was unaware of groups of young people congregating anywhere. Even the beaches were only frequented by tourists and family groups. My bikinis had always drawn disapproving stares from Spanish women who did not wear such attire and – more uncomfortably for me – blatant ogling from the men. Franco's Spain of the early 1970s was still very conservative.

However, this was fourteen years later and democracy had come to Spain. Señora Cardenas was an educated woman so surely she would not exhibit those prejudices of the past? So I continued to wait and at the end of a very long morning I was led in to see her.

When I entered the Señora's elegant office, the face that greeted me was tight and the eyes were everywhere except on mine. While piously sitting upright in her brown leather chair, making irrelevant comments, she shuffled papers randomly on her desk. Her excuses for the delays, which I had anticipated, flowed unabated while I sat stony-faced and disbelieving. How could this woman, whether a mother or not, do this to me? As I continued to fire questions she searched for valid reasons for the hold-ups then abruptly lifted the telephone and tersely gave instructions in Spanish to her secretary. A short time later the secretary entered the room and announced the Señora was due at another appointment. This immediately gave her an excuse to end our meeting and she suggested I return the following day, by which time she would have more information. Our meeting was brief and heated – marked by my obvious displeasure at what I saw as her incompetence, and her terseness and discomfort at having to face a client that she had either kept ill-informed or had been persuaded by a third party not to help.

My next stop was the court to enquire when my hearing might be. Having no idea of the address I set off in the direction of the old town, assuming it to be the most likely location. I received directions and in a small back street, anonymously hidden among other buildings, I found the court entrance. I walked up dark stairs to the first level and into a room with a wooden counter along one wall and seating along two. Opposite the counter was a line of windows overlooking a low-level building. The cheerful sunshine filtering through helped brighten this otherwise drab, utilitarian reception area with its smell of old files and paperwork.

After ignoring my presence for as long as possible a young man finally asked me what I required. I guessed he was probably in his late teens, in his first job and inexperienced. He was slightly built, not as dark as the normal Andalusian local, and had a gentle expression. His white shirt was slightly too large and I couldn't help thinking it was probably his father's. Undoubtedly in this macho, legal environment he would have had few, if any, previous dealings with foreign women, particularly those who spoke little Spanish. Once he established the purpose of my visit, he asked me to be seated, saying he would make enquiries about my case.

Sitting in the hot stuffy room I listened to the almost constant noise of cars in the narrow street below, interspersed with the shouting and arguing of drivers who thought they had the right of way. The conversations of passers-by, and friends who had coincidentally met and stopped to greet each other, drifted up from the pavement. Inside there were only years of faded paint and dust adorning the walls to occupy my attention, and the windows revealed nothing in the way of a view except the brick walls of adjacent buildings.

Time passed very slowly but I pacified myself with the thought that I would soon know the status of my case and when I could realistically expect a decision. Other people came and went and still I waited. Surely I was not being thwarted yet again? After several hours the young clerk beckoned me and, in rather embarrassed tones, informed me that my case had never been lodged!

By the time I left the court that afternoon it was too late to visit the school; besides, I was so fraught with anger and defeat I could not physically drag myself the extra distance.

Katherine was not home and it was a relief to plonk my weary body on the warm bedcover. The oppressive afternoon heat had managed to invade the small apartment, pushing out any hint of fresh air. My head, my body and my heart were heavy as I questioned how Señora Cardenas could do such a thing. Did Hadi pay her handsomely to drop my case? Had he fabricated such a realistic and vilifying tale, which I knew him to be capable of, that she walked away voluntarily? Or did he personally, or through a third party, threaten her physically? My experience nine years earlier with Señora Burgos, the headmistress in Barcelona, flashed into my mind as well as other instances of a similar nature. Whatever Hadi was doing or saying was certainly having a visible impact on anyone from whom I was seeking help.

Tears of frustration drained the life out of me and I dropped into a shallow sleep until the opening of the front door roused me. Following a supper of tinned tuna with Katherine, and a patchy night's sleep, I set off early the following morning to see the headmaster.

After my visit eight months earlier, my face was known at the school and I sensed my arrival created a feeling of awkwardness among the staff. Señor Gonzalez was informed of my arrival and after a short wait I was ushered to his office. As always he was very kind and sympathetic and, as gently as he could, told me Tanya was no longer at the school. Her father had removed her after my previous visit. I was assured that Hadi had not disclosed where he had taken her.

Feeling as though I had been kicked in the stomach yet again, I headed straight for the public telephone box in the centre of town. Maite's voice was matter-of-fact but also gentle. She was used to my tears by now and assured me that a new search would be much simpler because the trail would be easier to pick up. Although it was disappointing, I should go back to Dubai and she would get on with the investigation straight away.

Margaret & Tanya

BARCELONA
Reunion: April–May 1992

At last it arrived, a fax from Estrada and Martos advising that my case would be heard on Thursday 30 April.

As promised, after my trip to Marbella, Maite had done her job and found Tanya again. The situation could not have been better; she was now at a school in Barcelona, where both Maite and my lawyers were located. At the time of receiving this news, Señor Huerta had sensibly advised me not to come to Barcelona, but to wait while they lodged a case on my behalf and tried to expedite its hearing.

Now that time had come. Without hesitating, and anxious to know every detail, I telephoned Señor Huerta to find out more information. He then told me the disappointing news – they considered it better if I did not attend the trial. There was no explanation why they recommended this but I had grown to have great faith in these people. On the assurance that they would keep me fully apprised I hung up, but not before once more reminding them that Tanya turned eighteen on 30 May. While she was a minor any decision handed down by the court would have to be honoured, but once she reached eighteen she would be entitled to make her own decisions. That in itself would not be a problem, but while living under her father's influence she would very likely be too intimidated to go against him, even if she did want to contact me.

To my surprise and delight several days later I received another fax, which recommended I attend the hearing. This was exciting news as my presence in court would allow me to explain any misunderstandings, gauge how the judge reacted to my deposition, and see how Hadi would try to defend himself. Hopefully I would also get a better indication of how long the judgement might take, always praying it would be less than the three months I had been told to expect. I quickly made travel arrangements, organised for leave from my work, and confirmed details of my travel plans with Señor Huerta.

I arrived at Lola's apartment in Barcelona on the evening of Wednesday 29 April, the day before the court hearing. My Spanish friend greeted me warmly.

'Welcome back. Your room is ready and Father and Maria are anxious to see you.'

My small suit carrier was soon unpacked then Lola led me by the arm downstairs to her father's apartment, two floors below, where she ate most nights. On our return, after a family dinner, I set my alarm and tried to sleep. A million thoughts were going through my head. It had taken years to arrive at the point where I was confident Tanya would soon be with me. How would Tanya react? Would

Hadi have completely poisoned her mind against me? Would she want anything to do with me? Would she like me? After the event would I still be in danger of Hadi's death threats, and would he still try to keep Tanya from me? I did not wish to contemplate, too deeply, the future prospects of being with Tanya as that could create an expectation too hard to bear if it didn't come to pass. However, I felt Tanya was now almost within my reach. The hours raced by and it was time to rise and prepare myself for the day ahead.

Before leaving Dubai and already showing signs of stress, I had consulted my physician who thankfully prescribed tranquillisers for me to take during the impending ordeal. Even though I am totally against taking most medication without a valid reason, I happily swallowed these magic little puffs of wonder, which managed to ease some of my shaking and calm my mind. Without them, I doubt I could have survived those emotional and energy-sapping days.

Anticipating the great stress I would be under in Barcelona, I had carefully chosen my clothes in Dubai so that dressing for court would be automatic. I picked a long-sleeved, jacaranda-blue woollen dress with high round neck and no visible trim, an opera-length string of pearls, matching earrings and plain black accessories. All this was easy to put on and nothing could go wrong or be forgotten.

I made my way to the offices of my legal firm early on the Thursday morning. This was the closest I had been in fourteen years to gaining legal access to my daughter. That joyous prospect, together with the worry of the court appearance and how the judge might rule – not necessarily in my favour – weighed heavily on me. Also I had no idea how Hadi would react to all this. What tricks would he have invented this time, and would he engage in screaming, abusive behaviour in court?

After a coffee in Señor Huerta's office and a briefing to update me on procedures, we were joined by the senior lawyer, Señor Diago, and my female lawyer Alejandra. We then left for the courthouse where my case was listed for eleven o'clock in court number sixteen. Señor Huerta reminded me it was not customary in Spain to bring children into the court, as was the case in England. Minors were not expected to participate in any way. More importantly, he also stressed yet again, that even after the case was heard it would take at least three months to obtain the judge's decision – this was the way it was in Spain and one had to be patient. I completely understood.

Once we were seated in a small anteroom outside court sixteen, I felt the walls closing in on me. My palms were sweating and I could feel the coffee I had consumed earlier rumbling around in my stomach. The temperature of the room seemed to be increasing and I hoped the aroma of my favourite Van Cleef & Arpels perfume would mask any body odour I might exude as a result. I wondered where Hadi was – should he be waiting in the same room as us? If he saw me he would undoubtedly create a scene. The minutes ticked by and we continued to wait.

Half an hour passed and we still waited. Even Señor Huerta was curious at this lengthy delay. Then my senior counsel, who had joined us at the courthouse, was called and led away by the court attendant. Confused conversation in Spanish ensued among the remaining members of my team.

Somewhat distracted, my counsel returned to advise that because Hadi had ignored the summons and had not appeared as requested, and had not even had the courtesy to send a representative, the judge had decided to postpone the hearing until the following Monday – Friday being a public holiday to celebrate May Day.

This was the first part of his information. The second was that when Hadi did not appear at court the judge telephoned the director of Tanya's school, asking him to send Tanya to the court immediately. The director flatly refused! Understandably, this double contempt of court did not please the judge. As a result, he ordered the issue of a warrant authorising the police to fetch Tanya from the school on Monday morning and bring her directly to the court. This I thought was both good news and bad news.

The good news was that the judge was angry on two counts: first that Hadi had completely ignored his summons; and second that the director of Tanya's school had also refused to comply with a court order. Therefore, bypassing Hadi and the director, the police would bring Tanya directly to the court. This newfound power was something I had been seeking for fourteen years.

The bad news was that it was the eve of a long weekend, giving Hadi three days to take Tanya and run. They may have even planned to go away for the long weekend in which case it would be easy for them not to return. Initially Hadi would have had news of the case through his summons, and now he would have been told by the school's director of the unconventional request by the judge for Tanya to attend the court.

The only option for me would be to appoint Maite and her merry men to keep watch on Tanya and Hadi, starting immediately. Twenty-four hours continual surveillance with three men being paid by the hour for almost four days would be very expensive, but I had no alternative.

My legal team stood in the long, otherwise empty corridor outside the courtroom, speaking rapidly in Spanish, and I understood sufficient to know they were very angry because of Hadi's non-appearance. I felt numb, my body heavy as if carrying some great weight, making movement impossible. He had won again. He was still walking free and successfully keeping Tanya from my reach.

Desperately trying not to dwell on the most recent setback, my immediate concern was maintaining surveillance over the holiday weekend. Alejandra dislodged herself from the group suggesting the sooner we got started the better. With my agreement, she telephoned Maite, who was put to work. Maite and her team would maintain a twenty-four-hour watch until Monday morning.

The group disbanded and I returned with Señor Huerta and Alejandra to their office where we discussed procedures and manoeuvres for Monday. With our plan agreed I reluctantly left and slowly made my way back to Lola's apartment, dreading the onset of the next three days. How would I pass the long hours? But there were urgent things to be done. Fortunately there was a bank near Lola's apartment and I rushed to change my travellers cheques so I could partially pay the additional fee for the weekend surveillance by Maite and her colleagues. The teller ignored my funny Spanish and continued to point at the clock on the wall. As I begged him to help, he kept saying the bank closed at two o'clock. It was two minutes past.

As I entered the apartment Lola saw the tears running down my face. She rushed to my side and was quick to assure me there was no problem. She knew a bank in the city centre that remained open until four-thirty. Before I had a chance to think about it we were both on Lola's bike heading for town. I was able to get the necessary funds and we delivered them straight to Maite.

That evening I was temporarily distracted when I joined Lola in her father's apartment for dinner. The happy, jocular atmosphere and sharing food and wine with these warm, hospitable people soothed me for several hours.

We returned upstairs a little after midnight and, while preparing for bed, were interrupted by the telephone. Thinking it was Lola's father from downstairs I was surprised when she called me to the telephone. Maite was at the other end and informed me that the girl they had been following all that day was the wrong girl! However, they would start afresh the following morning by keeping watch outside Tanya's house from six o'clock.

'But what if they have already gone?' was my agonised reply.

There was little else we could do at this stage but hope and pray we were not too late. Crestfallen I lay quite stiff and still in the dark bedroom wondering how so many things could continually go wrong, and why I was being tested in this way? Would it ever all end satisfactorily?

Friday passed slowly and the following afternoon Lola, trying her best to lift my sagging spirits, suggested we go to the movies. An English-language film was showing at one of the cinemas and she had read good reviews. My inclination was to remain curled up on the sofa and not do anything or go anywhere, but as Lola was trying so hard to help distract me I felt I had to make an effort. On the back of her bike we zigzagged through the Saturday afternoon traffic, weaving in between cars, buses and trucks. The film was a distraction but my mind kept wandering back to thoughts of where Tanya might be and whether Hadi had whisked her as far away from Barcelona as possible.

After the movies Lola suggested an aperitif so we sped to the old Gothic part of town. I was quite adept at getting on and off this mode of transport by now, in spite of having to wrestle my straight skirt up around my waist beforehand while at the same time trying not to let anyone see. However, I hated every minute I was on the bike and mostly kept my eyes closed as we dodged in and out of heavy traffic on the busy four-lane thoroughfares. I prayed several times as we headed for Plaza del Pi and a favourite bar of Lola's just behind the Espiritu Santo church. The bar was on a narrow corner overlooking the cobblestone square, which was filled with people at small tables drinking coffee or alcoholic beverages. Passers-by strolled to and fro at a leisurely pace, some with children, a couple with a small dog and occasionally a lone person moving more hurriedly.

A bright three-quarter moon was peeping out from behind the

building opposite, fringed by the leaves of the only tree in the centre of the square. Gazing at the wrought-iron balconies that adorned the surrounding buildings, I wondered what secrets were concealed behind the wooden shutters. There was no sign of life in those rooms, but I couldn't help but wonder who lived there and what might be going on behind those closed doors. The waiter appeared with our glistening olives, delicious *boquerones* (small fresh anchovies, marinated in oil and garlic) and glasses of chilled Spanish sherry. The alcohol and atmosphere worked its magic. Lola and I chatted while watching the passing parade until it was time to mount her little machine for our return home.

The weekend passed very slowly as I wished the hours away.

On Monday morning, after a sleepless, nerve-racking night, I rose early and again dressed very carefully in the same conservative blue dress which, although appropriate for court would also, I hoped, be appealing and attractive to a seventeen-year-old girl. I paid special care and attention to my hair, make-up and accessories. No previous date had ever been so carefully prepared for.

As arranged, Maite arrived to collect me from outside Lola's apartment building at seven o'clock. This was to make sure we would be at the school to see Tanya's arrival and thus confirm, after the confusion on Thursday, that she was still in Barcelona and that Hadi had allowed her to go to school. When I was ushered to Maite's little dark blue Seat, it was difficult to see how it could accommodate yet another person. My lawyer Alejandra and young interpreter Joanna were already seated, and by compacting themselves in a manner which would have done sardines credit, I was also able to squeeze in. The drive through the congested early morning traffic to the school, although only a short distance from Lola's apartment, seemed endless.

On our arrival the street was busy with heavy traffic, crowded buses and people coming and going in all directions. Maite pointed out several of her men strategically positioned at various bus stops and entry points at the school, together with a police car containing three officers parked on the opposite side of the road. They undoubtedly held the warrant enabling them to escort Tanya from the school to the court. In this way, even if Hadi again ignored the summons for his appearance, the warrant would ensure Tanya's presence at the court where the judge would interview her personally.

Hundreds of children seemed to fill the approaches to the school and as I eagerly searched every female face it became more and more apparent that I really wasn't sure of the face I was looking for. Apart from our very brief meeting in Marbella twelve months earlier, the only other time I had seen Tanya was nine years before in the office of Señora Burgos, the headmistress of the school in Barcelona. In the meantime the one form of identification I had was the school class photograph generously given to me on that occasion by Señora Burgos. Although I treasured this and it was always by my side it was not very clear and lacked detail.

By now Tanya would have developed into a seventeen-year-old so what changes might have occurred? Would she have changed the colour of her hair? How long or short would it be? Could she have grown any taller? Would she be fat or skinny? What kind of personality would she portray? Would she still have that beautiful smile? There were so many children, all very Spanish-looking. Would Tanya look foreign, or after all these years would she just blend in?

How jealous I was of Maite and her colleagues. They were the ones who found Tanya and had since kept her under surveillance. They knew what she looked like; they knew who they were looking for. How unfair that they were able to tell me how beautiful she was and how happy she looked when I had no idea what to expect.

I should have felt very safe surrounded by all these people who, although paid primarily to find Tanya, were at the same time protecting me. Even though I had as much right as anyone else to be sitting in a parked car in that bustling street I felt extremely vulnerable, as though I was in imminent danger of attack. To my surprise the threats on my life by Hadi over the years had certainly taken their toll. Whenever I went on a trip to search for Tanya, my secretary, Yasmine, knew that I would telephone her every day. If she did not hear from me or could not reach me then she would initiate the alarm system on which we had agreed. Also when I was on train platforms or bus stops I never stood at the front of the platform or close to the road where I could be an easy target. These things were second nature by now, but I questioned if I had the strength to face whatever the remainder of this day would throw at me? I was, as much as anything, still recovering from the events of Thursday.

Suddenly the signal came. One of Maite's men had spotted Tanya approaching from a different direction and saw her enter the school. The policemen waiting nearby were also advised to be at the ready.

Knowing that Tanya was safely in the school grounds and with no sign of Hadi, Maite suggested that we escape the confines of her car and go for a good strong coffee and cigarette. This seemed like a bizarre suggestion to me. Why didn't we go straight to the court? Why should we waste even more time? The fact that it was only eight-thirty in the morning and the court would not yet be open escaped me. I just couldn't wait to get there. That everyone had been up very early with no time for breakfast and might need refreshment was way beyond my mental capacity. I was shaking to such a degree there was no way I could hold a cup, but I did consider a cigarette even though I had never smoked and am an adamant opponent. However, the need for my team to regroup at this point and exchange information on what they had seen or learned slowly became apparent to me.

When we finally arrived at the court all my team members were present – my two senior lawyers, Alejandra, a barrister, and Maite and her men, making a team of nine including myself. After formal greetings and a very brief wait, the judge's representative came out to tell us that the director of the school had refused to let the police take Tanya from the school. The police, however, demanded she be released and they were now on their way to the court. The director had then immediately phoned Hadi.

I was invited to enter the judge's office. It was a large, solid-looking room wrapped in tones of sombre brown, with a large wooden desk in the centre. Behind the desk, on both sides, were orderly but well-stocked bookshelves. As I sat on the leather chair in front of the desk I felt comfortable and relieved. After the tension and anxiety of the morning I had immediate confidence in the man facing me. To my surprise, and relief, he was much younger than I had anticipated. The only judges I had previously encountered in Spain were well over fifty. This one I could imagine with a teenage family. He was wearing a blue-grey suit with white shirt and conservative tie, almost disappointingly casual compared to the formality I was used to in England and Australia. He appeared thoughtful and composed, but more importantly, he seemed very approachable in spite of his precise and proper manner. He also spoke English!

I was confident he had been well briefed on the background of my case and this became evident from his probing questions and easy discussion. He reminded me that the process of Spanish law was slow and it would be some time before a judgement was handed down. I also took the opportunity to point out to him that in less than four weeks Tanya would turn eighteen and any judgement delivered after that time would, in my opinion, have much less effect as Tanya would be free to make up her own mind. However, if an official document were in place it would take the burden off Tanya having to confront, and undoubtedly disobey, her father, in order to see me.

After approximately thirty minutes and a brief telephone interruption the judge advised me that the police had arrived at the court and had Tanya with them. He told me that after his meeting with Tanya he would ask her if she wanted to meet her mother. If she did, Tanya and I could use the private room that adjoined his office. We could stay as long as we wished and would not be disturbed. However, if she did not wish to see me he would be obliged to abide by her wishes. The emotional meeting I had with Christianne several days before I left Dubai came rushing back to me. The judge rose from his leather swivel chair and opened a side door to his meeting room. I shakily walked across the carpeted office and entered a sterile-looking space.

Before I realised it the judge had disappeared and I was left feeling vulnerable and alone. The room I was in was very informal and utilitarian. There were several long trestle-like tables in blond wood. The light from a large frosted-glass window made the white walls look stark, and the flimsy chairs did not look inviting. A long cupboard in pale timber stood in the shadow of a far wall. In contrast to the judge's office there was nothing plush or comfortable here. As well as the connecting door to the judge's office, from which I had entered, there was a second door at the end of a narrow hallway.

I sat rigidly in an upright chair and waited, knowing that Tanya had arrived in the judge's office and would be sitting in the same chair that I had vacated a short time before. I strained my ears, listening for her voice, but as hard as I tried I could not hear anything.

The judge had been very specific about it being Tanya's choice to see me or not, and I was confident he would be thorough in his interview. Meanwhile I rose from the chair and moved about fitfully, wondering where I should be standing if Tanya entered the room. Thankfully the pills I had taken so reluctantly took the edge off my nervousness.

Although I kept looking at my watch I really didn't know what time it was and lost track of how long I had been waiting, but I remember after forty agonising minutes thinking that something must have gone horribly wrong. Then finally, without warning, the door from the judge's office opened and Tanya was led into the room.

The judge announced, 'This is your mother.'

Then he left the room, closed the door and disappeared.

No longer able to restrain myself, I hugged and kissed her while the tears streamed down my face. Trying desperately to remain calm, I apologised that my Spanish was less than adequate. I also told her how sorry I was that the police had to bring her to the court, at the same time trying to explain why this had become necessary.

Tanya, I could see, was agitated and told me she was afraid her father would barge in. Thankfully I was able to reiterate the judge's promise that we would not be disturbed for the rest of the day. She relaxed and as we talked and shared our stories she gave me the beaming smile for which I had waited so long. As I learned later, the judge considered Tanya to be controlled and serene and he understood that although she wanted to see me she also knew her father would be furious if she did so.

We talked of the previous twelve months after our aborted meeting in Marbella, of my family, of my present life. Tanya told me Hadi wanted nothing to do with his family, not even Aminah. Tanya was now in her final year at school and had considered studying law, but without any identification papers she would not be able to enter university. In other words, to my horror, she was stateless. I assured her that we could settle this very quickly at the Australian Embassy, where they had been aware of her case for the past fourteen years. But she then explained to me the additional problem of having no Spanish papers allowing her to live or study in Spain. I wondered if she understood she was an illegal immigrant or had any idea of the repercussions of this crime.

As we sat arm in arm discovering small snippets of each other's lives we heard Hadi arrive at the court. I had no idea where he was, but by the level and furious tone of his voice he was very close. Immediately Tanya's body tightened and her worried eyes shot in the direction of his ranting. Again I told her of the judge's promise, and prayed it would hold. When Hadi's shouting eventually subsided she became calm again.

Later I discovered that Hadi had tried to use every trick he knew to persuade the judge to prevent me from having access to Tanya. He had also told the judge he thought Spanish law was stupid, he did not believe in it, and he would sue the judge and my lawyers.

Tanya eventually became more settled and we continued our easy rapport. We talked about her friend Señora Villalobos, about Christine, who had been with me at the school in Marbella, and most importantly about seeing each other in the future. This obviously worried Tanya enormously because despite her desire to continue seeing me, she had no wish to go against her father, with whom she still lived.

The door from the hallway opened and Señor Huerta and a woman, Hadi's lawyer, entered the room. They asked Tanya if she wished to remain in our meeting. She assured them that she did. Señor Huerta suggested we might like to go out for coffee but Tanya and I, knowing we would have to pass Hadi on the way, declined. It was hard to believe my own lawyer, who had come to know so intimately the history of my case and Hadi's unreasonable obsession, would even suggest such a thing.

Yet again Tanya and I were left to enjoy our tranquil space, to continue our journey of discovery of each other, our lives and our past. We both delighted in the familiarity that grew so easily.

Then, without any warning the door at the end of the hallway flew open and several people, including Señor Huerta, stormed into the room alarming us both.

'Quickly,' Señor Huerta blurted at me. 'There has been a bomb scare and we all have to evacuate the building.'

I sat bewildered for a moment and when I looked up Tanya was gone.

With Señor Huerta's help I was led into the main corridor outside the judge's office. There was no sign of Tanya, Hadi, or anyone else except my own team: Maite, her three detectives, Alejandra, Señor Huerta, his senior partner, my barrister, the judge and myself. They were all speaking rapidly in louder tones than I had heard before. None of them seemed anxious to move, and eventually realising that I was excluded from their conversation, turned to me and in unison said, 'Another Senussi trick!'

I couldn't believe my ears but slowly, trying desperately to gather my thoughts, I understood what was implied.

Aware that Señor Huerta and Señor Diago were on either side of me, each gently supporting an arm, we slowly walked through the now deserted court building. Through the corridors and down the sweeping circular staircase the only sound was our footsteps on the cold terrazzo floor. Nobody hurried, nobody spoke, but the silence was so profound it seemed to echo from the walls.

We exited through the imposing entrance onto the busy street, where people were rushing in all directions, and the noise of the traffic and the beeping horns was overpowering. An unseasonably brisk spring breeze quickened our lazy steps. I was being led back to Estrada & Martos's offices just a short distance from the court and on arrival was deposited in a meeting room. While Señors Huerta and Diago went to confer with colleagues someone kindly brought me a cup of coffee. The taste was hot and bitter and reflected my mood. Alone in this austere room I felt totally insensible. When Señor Huerta and Alejandra joined me their first advice was to cancel my flight booking to Dubai the following day. They neither told me how long they wanted me to stay in Barcelona nor gave me a reason for the change of plan, and I no longer had the strength to question anything.

Agreeing to telephone them later that day I left their offices and made my way back to Lola's apartment. Lola was still at work and I welcomed the solitude and privacy to vent my emotions. The events at court earlier in the day were unprecedented for my lawyers and I was in good company, having no idea what would happen next. When I telephoned their office at the appointed time nobody was available to take my call so I said I would try again the following morning. It was the following afternoon before I managed to speak to Señor Huerta, who suggested I come to their office immediately.

What on earth could be happening now? Señor Diago, Señor Huerta and Alejandra were all awaiting my arrival and greeted me, which instantly sent a chill of fear down my spine. With great compassion they informed me that the judge had already made his decision. It was in my favour! Before they could tell me that this would have to be put in writing and formalised I burst into tears. After I had sufficiently regained my composure they informed me that until they received a copy of the judgement, and had studied its exact wording, we could not act upon it. They could not anticipate its terms and conditions so we would just have to wait.

This formality did not bother me in the least. The most important thing was that I would be seeing Tanya again. Slowly I also began to realise the excitement that was being shared in that room by my wonderful legal team. This they assured me was the first time they had ever known a judge to deliver a decision so quickly. Furthermore, orders were in place for the document to be processed urgently. This was a groundbreaking event. Again I was told to go home and keep in touch with their office.

I walked aimlessly back to Lola's apartment, wandering the streets simply to pass the time, and I saw a small poster advertising a piano recital that evening. Classical music had always calmed me; and as I had been a student of piano in my childhood that instrument had become my favourite. I had inherited this fondness from my mother, who had been very disappointed with my youthful lack of perseverance. As an adult I also constantly regretted being so careless and neglectful as a student.

I thought no doubt the concert would be sold out at this late stage but I might be lucky – and I was. That evening I entered the large theatre and found my seat in the front row of the dress circle. There are some benefits of being alone, I thought – this excellent seat looked straight down at the shiny black grand piano, poised waiting on a round dais. The auditorium was a cavernous space with heavy wood-panelled walls, relieved by lashings of decorative gilt and stained-glass panels. In spite of its size, the theatre was surprisingly warm. The many seats slowly filled with a cross-section of Barcelona's music-lovers – young and old from all walks of life, everyone showing signs of anticipation and excitement. The lights dimmed and the muffled chatter of the audience subsided to a hushed silence. In the same moment, I experienced a feeling of complete isolation, as though I was the only person in the theatre.

A tall slim man entered the stage. His slightly wavy hair was light brown, long and gathered in a ponytail. There was no traditional black dinner suit and bow tie on the youthful figure, but rather a pristine white troubadour shirt, with its long puffed sleeves, cascading over coal-black trousers. Strangely enough this looked just as formal on the American musician, and certainly more romantic and passionate than the normal concert attire.

When David Lanz's fingers touched the glistening keyboard I was immediately transported to a higher, safer and more loving place and sensed this was a significant moment in my life. The music was so powerful, the tears streamed down my cheeks as my arms and legs began to quiver. At the end of the moving piece David Lanz announced he had written it for an estranged daughter with whom he and his wife had recently been reunited. I was transfixed, unable to move and hardly able to breathe. The musical recital continued, which gave me time to recover from the emotional impact of this overwhelming coincidence.

The following day I went to every music outlet I could find in Barcelona but regrettably none of them stocked David's soulful music. Some time later my cousin in America tracked it down and I now have my own copy of *Return to the Heart*, which is my favourite piece of music.

Many telephone calls later Señor Huerta told me the awaited document had been received. This was barely forty-eight hours after I had been seated with Tanya in the court. On arrival at the lawyer's office I learned the contents were brief: the judgement, to take effect immediately, allowed me access. Taking into account Tanya's schooling hours, I was permitted to spend from five to nine o'clock with her every single evening. The other news was that if Hadi took Tanya away again, or interfered in any way with our meetings, I could enlist the help of the police. Señor Huerta's expression then changed as he held my arm and told me to make certain I always stayed in a public place.

This judgement was also conveyed to Hadi through his solicitor. Without hesitation his reply came. Because Tanya's examinations were drawing near she would have to have additional tuition after school each day, and therefore the timing was impossible. I would not be able to see her. In addition, before he would ever allow me any contact with Tanya – completely disregarding the official judgement – I would have to reimburse him for all of Tanya's education fees and expenses for the past fourteen years, pay all her present and future school fees and living expenses, give all my jewellery to Tanya, and sign over my half share of an apartment that he and I jointly owned in Marbella.

Negotiations between my legal team and Hadi's solicitor began. Eventually it was agreed that I would meet Tanya after school at two o'clock and have time with her before she left for her extra tuition. At least this was a start.

Regarding Hadi's list of conditions my solicitors encouraged me to negotiate. I did not understand this tactic, and still don't. As far as I was concerned I owed him nothing. After a lot of persuasion to negotiate, at least on something, I agreed to sign over my half share of the Marbella apartment. Hadi had rented it out during all those years and I had little hope of ever seeing my share of it in any case.

The following morning, by now Friday, an arrangement was made for me to meet Tanya outside her school at two o'clock. I was at the entrance at a quarter to two and tried to be patient as I waited. By three o'clock there was no sign of Tanya, so I walked to a café opposite the school and had a cup of coffee. I returned to the school gate and waited until six o'clock but there was still no sign of Tanya.

First thing Monday morning I was back at Señor Huerta's office. By lunchtime Alejandra, with a copy of the court resolution, and Carmen, Hadi's solicitor, were both with me at the school. I was left to wait in a corridor while Alejandra and Carmen went to speak to Tanya. While I was desperately wondering what was happening the three of them came strolling slowly along the corridor towards me.

It was almost two o'clock and Tanya had to go straight to her tutor to prepare for her exams. Tanya and I left the school together and walked to the bus stop. Her bus came but she said she would wait for the next one. When it came I suggested I go with her. When we parted she said she would see me after school the next day. That night I telephoned my mother to tell her the latest news.

The following day I again went to the school. Two o'clock came, quarter past, half past and by quarter to three I doubted there was much point in waiting any longer. Just then Tanya came running up to me. She had been detained in a class unexpectedly, had to return to school for ten more minutes and could I please wait? After waiting fourteen years, travelling regularly to Europe, searching every possible avenue, paying out huge sums of money, and living with Hadi's threats on my life, not to mention the emotional turmoil – she obviously had no conception of the absurdity and hidden irony in that question.

Our first lunch was rather rushed, crammed into just one hour, and letting Tanya go at the end of it was agonising. On one hand I was ecstatic at having spent a whole hour with my daughter after fourteen years, but on the other I was terrified that she would disappear before I had a chance to see her again. We arranged to meet at a nearby restaurant the following day. This time she arrived promptly at two o'clock.

By now it was Friday and I was afraid to contemplate yet another long lonely weekend. But on hearing this Tanya, without any hesitation, said we should meet early on the Saturday and have lunch as usual. She suggested the Mandarin, a Chinese restaurant she knew well and where the food was good. After lunch the owner came to greet Tanya, and my heart felt as if it would burst when she introduced me as her mother! I didn't hear another word as the phrase 'my mother' kept exploding in my ears.

A couple of days later we were shopping and Tanya tried on a dress she liked. While I was waiting outside the cubicle I heard a voice saying 'Mummy, Mummy' but didn't take any notice. The sound persisted and then the thunderbolt struck – this was my daughter and she was calling me! I hoped Tanya was too excited about the dress to notice the tears rolling over my cheeks.

A pattern was now established and the times set by the court were completely disregarded. Hadi was still demanding one hundred thousand pesetas a month for Tanya's expenses, all my jewellery, and my share of the apartment. However, I left this to my lawyers to work out. I had more important things to do.

Tanya and I continued to meet at every snatched opportunity, and weekends gave us a much longer time frame than weekdays. Those weeks passed quickly and I was conscious I had to return to my responsibilities in Dubai. It was now well into May and Tanya was due to turn eighteen on the thirtieth of the month. At least if I stayed for her birthday we could celebrate this special occasion before having to say goodbye, albeit temporarily.

Nothing would stop me, after all the years of missing out, from celebrating this special day with Tanya as mother and daughter. I located a florist near Tanya's house and ordered a bouquet of specially chosen pink flowers to be delivered the morning of her birthday, and hoped that Hadi would not intercept their delivery before Tanya ever saw them. We had arranged to meet mid-morning in Plaza Cataluña to spend the day together.

Sitting in the park Tanya excitedly opened her gifts while throwing her arms around me and kissing my cheek. The years of waiting were worth every second of this moment. Our noisy chatter and behaviour attracted the attention of an elderly woman sitting on the opposite bench. She did not seem able to take her eyes off this unusual scene and I longed to rush over and tell her that this was my daughter whom I hadn't seen for fourteen years and now she was legally free to see me, and wasn't life wonderful. In fact I wanted the whole world to know.

We each nibbled a Belgian chocolate from the box I had given her while Tanya stretched out her arm to admire her birthday gift of a gold and pearl bracelet. The sun was beaming down on us as we strolled down to the port. Tanya knew of a popular fish restaurant, Can Costa, on the beach at Barceloneta. The waiter showed us to our table in the front by the window overlooking the Mediterranean. It only seemed moments before the waiter was standing at my side, clearing his throat and holding our bill. Everyone else had left the restaurant and the staff was setting up for the evening.

We had so much to catch up on. Tanya told me about her schooling, her girlfriends, her love of the beach, holidays she had in a friend's mountain home, skiing in the Pyrenees, the boyfriend she would like to have if her father would ever allow her.

Tanya's birthday came to an end, as did my stay in Barcelona. I had spent time with my daughter every day for three weeks but after a month away it was necessary to return to Dubai, at least this time with a full heart and plans to see Tanya again in two months. The only photograph I had of her was now nine years old and although we had taken dozens of snaps in those past joyous weeks I asked if she had a photo of herself that I could keep. My heart leapt the following day when she produced a large picture from a burgundy cardboard folder. It had been taken three years earlier, when she was delivering a lesson at a wedding service in one of the beautiful old churches in Barcelona.

It was a head and shoulders shot capturing her lovely smile, which reminded me how delighted I was that she had inherited her father's perfect teeth – always one of his best features. She was wearing pearl stud earrings – what a coincidence, I mused, because

I had worn pearl studs on a daily basis all my life. The white tailored shirt looked a tad too serious for her, I thought, but then it was a wedding and it was in a Spanish church. The shiny satin fabric was definitely too old for a young girl! Who could have chosen this? Her skin was flawless except for a small mark on her forehead – was this due to a childhood injury or was it the remains of a bad pimple? How little I knew. The fine baby hair that had been the bane of my life, as well as my mother's, had also found its way to Tanya. At least she had a great deal of it and it was a lovely glossy brown. Above all else in the photograph, the innocence and happiness of the moment shone through.

The underlying message that also came to me through the picture was that Tanya appeared to have had a normal upbringing. To have been asked to read at a friend's wedding in a Christian church meant a great deal to me. She and Hadi obviously had nice, normal family-oriented friends. There was no conflict with a foreign religion – this had really been a groundless worry on my part, as she had been educated for the most part in private Catholic schools.

Gazing at the photograph, the colour of her hair, the shape of her face, those little pearl earrings – yes, I could see a similarity. I had been thrilled and very proud when people said she looked like me but it was only now that I could see the resemblance.

Margaret + Tanya

LONDON – AUSTRALIA
Bliss and bereavement: 1992–2005

Before leaving Barcelona, I told Tanya I had to visit London in August and it would be wonderful if she could join me. Without hesitation she agreed. Knowing what Hadi's response would be I was doubtful, but Tanya assured me that as long as I arranged her ticket she would be there. She was so positive I felt inclined to believe it.

Back in Dubai I was able to maintain contact with the help of one of Tanya's school friends, Victoria, and her mother. I could telephone their home each Friday and speak to Tanya. This arrangement didn't always work but it was our only means of communication. When I telephoned Tanya on the day before her scheduled arrival in London, it was no great surprise to learn her father would not allow her to go. This news devastated me and I could tell from Tanya's monotone that she was terribly upset. I suggested that I would finish my business in London as quickly as possible and fly to Barcelona for a few days. Her voice immediately brightened and although we were both desperately disappointed that our arrangements had been sabotaged we now had an alternative plan.

When I walked into Barcelona's noisy, crowded arrivals hall I couldn't believe my eyes when I saw Tanya standing there. That she would go to this trouble took my breath away. My excitement was tempered within seconds when I started wondering where her father thought she was going on this occasion, and how long we would have together.

It was school holidays so we met as often as we possibly could during the next few days. Tanya took me to her favourite museums, including the small apartment in the Gothic area where Picasso had lived when he was an emerging artist. We went to her favourite shops, including some exclusive shoe boutiques, and we discovered new restaurants while also returning to our favourite, Casa Jordi, which Tanya had introduced me to on a previous visit. Located in a narrow side street on the first floor of an old building, its interior featured heavy wood panelling and rustic decor. It was a family-run restaurant specialising in the food of Cataluña and we always chose the specialties of the day, together with a spinach dish containing ham, pine nuts and sultanas, as well as a rabbit casserole when available. I longed for those shared hours to stretch out forever.

Again we made arrangements for our next meeting. This time it was a really bold plan; Tanya would come to me for Christmas. The festive season was a very happy time in Dubai with many visitors, lots of parties and weather that was not too uncomfortably hot for the beach. How proud I would be introducing her to my numerous friends and colleagues. There were lots of arrangements to make.

On 3 December I had a lovely surprise when, for the first time, Tanya called me. At the end of our brief conversation, she asked if I would come and collect her. I explained that her visa needed more time to be processed but it would be ready in plenty of time for her visit. Of course I could come to Spain and accompany her back to Dubai. After talking to me further, I suddenly became aware that Tanya was not afraid of travelling to an Arab country on her own, as I had first understood, but was asking me to go and get her because she wanted to come and live with me!

My shock and delight were immediate. My wildest dreams had come true in a matter of seconds. I could barely think. Tanya didn't say what had prompted this request but I assumed she had had an argument with her father and for the first time realised she now had alternative means of support. But was this proposal feasible? Now I had to think like a mother. Tanya had seven more months before her final examinations and there were no Spanish schools in Dubai. Also, there was no university in Dubai so even when she finished school she would have to go away again. Dubai was certainly not the environment for a naïve eighteen-year-old girl. There was nowhere a teenager could go for entertainment or to make friends as all expatriate children of her age were away at school or college. There was no public transport, and I worked very long hours. It was a hopeless situation.

In order to give myself time to think I arranged to telephone Tanya the following day. I toyed with the various options for hours until it became clear what I had to do. My monumental decision was easy to make. It would take time but my life would have to be dismantled. I would move to London and create a new home where Tanya could join me on completion of her examinations. Unfortunately, I could not consider Australia at this stage because I suspected Tanya would not want to be so far away from Europe.

How would I tell all this to an upset, emotional teenager? Would I be able to explain to her over the telephone, in a language in which she was not fluent, my reasons why she should not join me in Dubai but instead wait several months to join me elsewhere? Would she take this as a rejection? Could I take that risk? Tanya's whole future hinged on this decision.

I was distraught at the thought of Tanya's possible reaction and I cried myself to sleep. The following day, I steeled myself to make the call. Tanya was much calmer than she had been during our previous conversation, seemed to understand my reasoning and agreed to my plan. However, her voice was very flat and I could tell she was disappointed.

I took immediate action to arrange accommodation in London, find employment, start the heart-wrenching months of packing up my house, re-allocating my faithful houseboy and farewelling my friends and colleagues. Dubai had been my happy home for fifteen years, with a wonderful job, frequent travel and valued friends. It was very hard to turn my back on all this but my new future promised a great deal more, in fact, the fulfilment of all my dreams.

On 2 March 1993, I arrived in London to start my new life. Close friends in Dubai insisted I stay in their two-bedroom, fully equipped London apartment until I was able to settle in a place of my own. River Court was a secure high-rise building on the edge of the River Thames just beyond the South Bank theatre complex. Luckily, also through contacts in Dubai, I was offered a less demanding job managing a small office in Westminster. This allowed me time to prepare for Tanya's arrival in July, after the completion of her examinations, and to start looking for a permanent home. I knew how difficult it might be to find the right place, especially in a depressed property market, so I started my search at once.

On the other hand, some things were so much easier in London.

The first weekend after my arrival, I flew to Barcelona to spend time with Tanya. From London, I could do this on a regular basis and during each of my visits we excitedly discussed our future together. Although Tanya was never anything but positive, I always had that nagging feeling at the back of my mind that Hadi would somehow prevent her from joining me. Even though she was now eighteen and free to make her own decisions, I was aware of the hold he had on her. Meanwhile, with Tanya in mind, I busily looked for a special place where we could make our home, and continued to plan for her arrival.

In spite of my nagging doubts, Tanya arrived in London on 28 July and joined me at River Court. Those first weeks were the happiest days imaginable. There was a continual smile on my face and every day was like Christmas. Introducing Tanya to London, a city I loved and knew well, and to all my friends in England, was the most exciting time of my life. She was so beautiful and charming and I was exploding with pride. We visited art galleries, museums, antique shops and street markets as well as the famous tourist sites. We had centre front seats at *Phantom of the Opera*, Tanya's first live-theatre experience. We got drenched at an open-air charity concert at Hampton Court. Prince Charles, as patron of the charity, was under cover and did not get wet. On this occasion Dame Kiri Te Kanawa gave an amazing performance, protected only by a flimsy tarpaulin yet showing no concern for the weather conditions.

Many people living in the Middle East swarm to London in August, like bees to a honey pot. A large number of my friends from Dubai arrived and as we dined at the finest hotels and restaurants, I proudly showed off my beautiful daughter. Fortunately the months that it had taken to pack and leave Dubai had given me time to explain, to those who did not already know, my real circumstances and the reason for my move to London.

It was all so exciting and those months were like a new love affair. I hung on to Tanya's every word, learning what she liked, her interests, her taste, her favourite food, favourite colour, what kind of music she liked, discovering the many interests we shared, the things we disliked and the things that made us laugh. We were inseparable. We walked everywhere arm in arm, something we had always automatically done from the time of our first meeting in Barcelona fifteen months earlier.

Our weekends were frequently spent away from London staying with friends on country properties, or in quaint villages, which gave Tanya an idea of rural English life. We were enchanted by the landscape and the people, revelling in the history and architecture of the old market towns, the warmth and friendliness of the country pubs, the style and colour of the magnificent public gardens, and the bluebell-carpeted floors of the ancient forests, through which we took long walks. These unforgettable experiences enriched our time together.

One Saturday morning we had no particular plans. Tanya was keen to explore everything and loved shopping so I decided a trip to Camden Markets would be a new and different experience for her. Camden was arty and avant-garde. The items for sale were new and trendy, or if not trendy, definitely unconventional. However, I also had some misgivings. Tanya was quite conservative and although she loved all forms of art, I didn't know how she would react to the bohemian people who frequented Camden Passage. We ambled from shop to shop and my concerns were soon allayed as I watched her eyes darting from side to side, paying attention to every detail. Then that little frown would appear as it did when she was concentrating on something of particular interest; or I would see that familiar dreamy gaze as she focused on some minute detail, like the paint finish of a small, handmade wooden frame. The clothes, both on the people and in the stores, were outrageous in every sense. The fabrics, colour and style – or lack of it – were so different and although she didn't want to buy anything she loved looking. The contemporary artwork was beyond my comprehension but Tanya saw meaning in it that I could never imagine. It was so rejuvenating to see things through my daughter's eyes.

As the weeks passed all this joy and excitement was exhilarating for me and allowed little opportunity to think about the future. However, I did understand how new and foreign it all was for Tanya; she was faced with strange customs, different food, a colder climate and a struggle with the English language. She was also away from the father she had spent most of her young life with – I knew that she somehow had contact with Hadi in Spain, but I never knew when or how this took place.

Communication between father and daughter was important and to keep him happy I agreed Tanya should return to Barcelona for a visit. The week she was away seemed like years. I had no means of contacting her because Hadi did not have a telephone, but I remained confident she would manage to call me if there was a problem. Every day I agonised whether she would return to London or not. Would her father convince her to remain in Spain? Would she be happier in her old familiar environment with all her friends, whom she must miss terribly? One of my major concerns was despite my many friends in England, who all adored Tanya, I did not know any young people for her to meet. Once she started university that problem hopefully would disappear, but that was still almost a year away.

On the day of Tanya's planned return from Barcelona I stood in the arrivals hall at Heathrow anxiously examining every face. I looked at my watch a million times. Would I still recognise her? Would she ever arrive? How long should I wait if she didn't appear?

Could she have missed her flight? Did her father prevent her from leaving? Hundreds of people passed by me as the perspiration grew at the nape of my neck. But finally, there she was with her great big smile and an embracing hug. After this Tanya made regular visits to Spain and her absences gradually became less stressful for me.

Several months passed and we were still getting to know each other. Tanya's English was less than perfect and in some instances I struggled to comprehend what she meant. Occasionally I was left wondering if I had understood her correctly. Finding a college where she could study English became a priority. The Westminster School was perfect. Apart from its excellent reputation it was only minutes from my office, which enabled us to travel together in the mornings and even meet occasionally for lunch.

It was all very well learning English but I thought Tanya also needed to practise with other people rather than predominantly speaking with me. I also felt that because she had led such a protected and sheltered life it would help if she could widen her experience of the world. As luck would have it, a friend of mine was able to give Tanya part-time work in his public relations company. After several months as the office junior, she told me she was bored and wanted to do something different. Two days later she informed me that she had found herself a job with a florist, arranging plants in the window boxes of Belgravia and Chelsea. I smiled at her choice. This was a job I would never have thought of but was more in keeping with Tanya's artistic flair and gave her a wonderful opportunity to explore the area where I hoped we would soon live. My search for an appropriate property was ongoing and there seemed to be nothing to suit our needs.

One afternoon, even though my voice leaves a lot to be desired, I was singing *I Feel Pretty*, while carefully dusting the delicate crystal and china objects displayed throughout the apartment. Luckily, because of the thick walls, the outside traffic and the quietly tuned stereo, I was confident no-one could hear me. It was many years since I had shared my home with anyone so I was temporarily alarmed when I heard the door open.

'That sounds very nice.' Tanya's Spanish-accented English came floating over my shoulder and I was so happy I was tempted to believe her.

My days and weeks, full of contentment and light-heartedness, were nevertheless marred by the worry that Tanya might be lonely or homesick. I was conscious that she still did not know anyone her own age. Even though she frequently saw my friends, she needed the company of her peers like any normal eighteen-year-old.

An advertisement for drama lessons at Kensington Town Hall caught my eye. When I asked Tanya if she was interested she seemed enthusiastic but I could also tell she was apprehensive about going by herself. If there is one thing that terrifies me it is being the centre of attention, in the public eye, and public speaking. However, for my daughter I was prepared to do anything. The town hall was in the area where I hoped we would eventually live. When we arrived there were about a dozen people gathered, a mixed group of different ages, sexes and backgrounds. As the lessons progressed, I could see Tanya was confident and enjoyed the experience. I hated every minute and the easiest part was when I had to pretend to be a tree! After our first couple of sessions, I thought Tanya was comfortable enough to attend the lessons alone. One night she arrived home very excited with the news that she had been selected for a part in an outdoor performance of *The Marriage of Figaro*. Within a few weeks, I proudly invited my friends to watch her perform on the large stage in Holland Park.

That balmy night marked the end of the drama course and the group dispersed to return to their individual lives. I was again left looking for young people for Tanya. I knew she missed her friends, especially Victoria. Then I had an idea. What if Victoria came to London to spend a long weekend with us? All we had to do was get her mother's permission.

It was quickly arranged and Victoria arrived. It thrilled me to see Tanya chatting away non-stop and laughing with her best friend. If only I could understand just a little of their animated conversation, I wished secretly, especially when I saw Tanya tilt her head on one side as she did when she was really concentrating. And then she would flick her hair behind her ear and I could tell the subject had changed.

Naturally they wanted to explore London's night-life. I was well aware that this was what was missing for Tanya and was delighted that she now had the opportunity to go to clubs and discos with her best friend, but my motherly instincts rose to the fore. I was sick to the stomach at the thought of these two beautiful girls at the mercy of experienced, slick-talking young men. The girls were both sensible and responsible but those qualities alone would not necessarily protect them.

While they were out I paced the floor for most of the evening, wondering where they were and what they were doing. At last when I heard a key in the front door and their muffled giggling, I jumped fully clothed into bed.

'Are you girls okay?' I asked in the sleepiest voice I could muster.

Somehow I survived those few days but am sure I developed my first grey hairs.

Christmas was rapidly approaching and I made arrangements for us both to fly to Sydney for our first celebration as an entire family. It was hard for me to control the thrill of taking Tanya home to meet her grandmother and aunty – my sister, Kim, was now married with her own child, a three-year-old daughter, Rebecca.

That first Christmas was very emotional and I feared Tanya might be overwhelmed by the excitement and attention of my family and friends, all complete strangers to her. However, when I saw Tanya and her grandmother emotionally embrace for the first time, I cried – this time from joy. The love that poured from my mother was immeasurable and I saw the heartache she had carried for many years evaporate. Tanya and Kim had an immediate rapport and when they weren't chasing Rebecca, they were locked in conversation. In her casual, relaxed way, Tanya floated through all the euphoria, winning the hearts of everyone. Those three weeks with my family together as a unit for the first time was like a fairy story. I kept pinching myself to make sure it was not a dream.

Leaving Sydney was terribly sad but we had the exhilaration of London to beckon us. It was winter in Europe so we could add skiing weekends in France and Switzerland to our busy schedule. The love of skiing was one of the many interests we shared. We also had the joy of designing and choosing the decor of our new home. Just before leaving for Australia I had agreed to the purchase of an apartment. It would need a great deal of remodelling but otherwise was perfect. There were so many decisions to make and endless choices for us to ponder. Naturally I wanted everything to be perfect but Tanya always persuaded me to go the extra distance to find something a little better. This was sure to be the most beautiful home in London!

There was a reverse side to all this happiness. I had kept Tanya a secret from my friends and colleagues for many years and in doing so had suppressed a great deal of feeling. When we were reunited my emotions were, in some respects, completely locked down. I experienced a continual fear of losing her, which prevented me from being open about a lot of things. At times I felt like I was stepping on eggshells, too afraid of doing or saying something that she would misinterpret, or which might upset or hurt her and compel her to run away.

Trying to establish a natural mother-daughter intimacy quickly was very difficult. We did not have the luxury of getting to know each other over a period of years – in the way normal mother and daughter relationships develop – but were thrown together suddenly, with no time to adjust, and with the added complication of possible misunderstandings caused by language difficulties. How could I tiptoe successfully through the minefield of our different cultures?

Neither one of us lacked the will to make our relationship work, but it was the peripheral stuff that was difficult. I had not been a mother for fourteen years and didn't know how strict I should be, where to draw the parameters, what control to exercise. How much money should I give her? What time should she be home? How would I tell her to tidy the perpetual mess in her room? Should I ask for help with the household chores, which I was now doing for the first time after living in a world of housekeepers and houseboys?

I was aware that Tanya must be experiencing similar confusion. She was learning to have a mother. Life with me was obviously very different to life with her father and although she no doubt would experience greater freedom with me, perhaps she would miss his spontaneity. My life, through necessity, was fairly structured. I spent my weekdays at the office; her father had been around all the time.

There were small aggravations, such as her complete lack of regard for time. She had no sense of urgency. I came from a closely regimented, heavily responsible corporate background; Tanya was brought up in Spain where everything could wait until tomorrow. There were those wet bath towels that found their way to the bathroom floor or even on occasion escaped to the bedroom! And why would you go out without a front door key, or worse, lose it when your mother was at the office?

There were times when the undercurrents rose to the surface. One big issue on which we totally disagreed was her future career. Being very artistic, Tanya wanted to study fashion design. It was the only thing in which she was interested. On the other hand, I firmly believed that to succeed in the twentieth century a degree was paramount – I always regretted not going to university – and on this I remained firm. Our difference of opinion on this issue caused Tanya a great deal of unhappiness. I tried to explain that with a degree she could choose from a range of careers, whereas fashion design would allow her to do little else. I pointed out that she could always study design after she completed university.

In mid-1994 I was very proud when Durham University offered Tanya a place to study Politics, but it was with a heavy heart that I delivered her to the campus, three hours from London. We were to be parted again but at least this time I knew where she was, could telephone her, and we could visit on occasional weekends.

Meanwhile I had my work to fill my days as well as making all the necessary decisions on the major renovations of our new apartment. Settlement of the purchase had been protracted and took until March and time seemed to be running away. Over the ensuing months, whenever Tanya was back in London for a weekend or a term break, we took great care choosing the appliances, decorations and furnishings for our new home. Tanya spent ages choosing every item for her bedroom and walked for miles to find just the right coloured tiles for her bathroom.

At the end of 1994 we had celebrated Christmas in Sydney again but in spite of the happiness and excitement, my mother was not well, which cast a shadow on our visit. At that time we did not know specifically what was wrong; she just wasn't herself and seemed to lack any energy. Mummy was normally full of life, and she would never tell you if she was in pain or suffering any form of discomfort.

The following May I received a call from Kim to say Mummy was unwell. With only an overnight bag, I flew to Australia for what I thought would be two weeks, leaving Tanya at university. On arrival in Sydney, I discovered my mother had lung cancer and was terminally ill.

Tanya and I had only lived in our newly renovated home for three months before I left for Australia. The hardest decision of my life now faced me. Should I stay with my mother or return to my daughter? I had already deserted my mother when my father died. This was my last chance to be there for her.

Somehow I had to explain this to Tanya. We agreed she would complete the academic year at Durham, only a matter of a few more weeks, then join me in Australia.

In the meantime, I once again had to organise a move to a different country. I could not afford the time to fly back to London because I was taking my mother to doctors and hospitals on a daily basis. Apart from not being able to return to pack up our beautiful house in London, it would have been too painful. Once again, I called on my dear friend Maureen. She agreed to book the packers and supervise the shipment of our personal effects to Australia.

I longed to see Tanya, but more overwhelming was my concern at how she would react to living in Sydney. Most of my time was spent looking after my mother so how would I have sufficient time to spend with Tanya?

The nine months after Tanya arrived were a nightmare. I was

constantly torn between looking after my mother and spending time with my daughter, who found herself in yet another foreign country but without the excitement and lure of London or the friends and familiar surroundings of Spain.

Apart from my sister and two friends from school days, I knew no-one in Sydney. I had not lived in Australia for thirty years and everything was foreign. Luckily I found a job as office manager in a recently opened Dutch private bank. Here I was in yet another start-up situation where the workload was heavy and the hours long. I left the office at night and went straight to the hospice to visit my mother; when I arrived home, it was almost time to go to bed.

This left Tanya by herself most of the time. She did not feel comfortable about going to university in Australia, was desperately unhappy, marooned by an absent mother in a foreign country and with no friends. I knew she was lonely, didn't like living in Sydney and missed the sophistication and lifestyle of Europe. Eventually Tanya told me she wanted to return to Spain, which hurt me deeply and broke my heart. I understood why she was so unhappy but my great fear was that I would lose her again.

One thing I had to make clear was that if she returned to Spain she would have to rely on her father to support her. Although I was employed, my salary had halved since London, I had all my mother's medical bills to pay and money was tight.

Tanya flew back to Barcelona. Exactly six days later my mother died. I had lost the two most important people in my life. It seemed like I curled up and died also.

The months that followed were a blur. Months turned into years. Although we corresponded and I telephoned when I could it was July 1998, over two years later, before I eventually persuaded Tanya to visit Australia, but that was the only time she came during the long, lonely years that ensued. The tyranny of distance and only four weeks vacation a year restricted my ability to visit her as often as I wanted but I flew to Europe whenever I could. Maintaining a close relationship became more and more difficult and I was sure her father was again using his influence to turn her against me.

By 2005 communication between us had broken down completely and I didn't think our relationship would survive. Instead of visiting Spain, I suggested Tanya join me in London, a city I knew she loved and where we had enjoyed such happiness. Right until the very last minute I was not sure if she would arrive so when she telephoned my hotel to say she was on her way from the airport I took three very deep breaths, put my head in my hands and gently wept.

It was three years since we had seen each other and I was very nervous about our meeting. It was an unimaginable relief when the initial awkwardness was quickly overcome and I again had my daughter. My fears vanished. Tanya was no longer a student and since our last meeting had transformed into a woman. We had an amazing time together in London and I was determined we would never again be separated for so long. Before I even arrived back in Sydney I knew where our next meeting place would be.

India –
nov. 2006

INDIA
A gift of love: November 2006

The journey from Australia was long and tiresome. It was almost midnight as the aeroplane approached the runway at New Delhi airport and the thick, grey pollution at ten thousand feet was not welcoming. Was this an ill omen for the meeting that lay ahead?

The plane shuddered as the pilot applied the brakes, or was that my own body shaking in trepidation? My mouth was dry as I willed the plane to go faster and a mixture of excitement and fear ran through my veins. I had visited India many times but this was to be Tanya's first. Up to that minute I had assumed she would love the country as much as I did. Now, for the first time, the awful thought that she might hate India ran through my head, making our anticipated three weeks together all the more unpredictable.

Tanya was coming on a flight from Spain and, thankfully, our arrivals were to coincide within thirty minutes of each other. Knowing well the vagaries of airline schedules, especially during a European winter, this was a plan that could go horribly wrong.

The terminal at New Delhi was bulging with people from different points of the globe, a seething mass of humanity all wanting to get out of the building. It was impossible to know what flights had arrived and from where as I joined hundreds of people in a queue to go through the formalities of immigration. Why is it that one always joins the slowest line? There was still time before Tanya's flight was due but I was apprehensive about this first meeting in eighteen months. Horrible visions of us unable to find each other and thus spending the night in the bowels of Delhi airport flashed through my mind.

While I waited, watching the surly immigration officer at the front of the scores of people ahead of me, an announcement that Tanya's flight had arrived lifted my anticipation to a higher level. It was hot and sticky, the stale smell of India was already in my nostrils, and my weary jet-lagged body was objecting to the pushing and shoving around me. My queue did not progress and the minutes continued to pass as I imagined Tanya in the baggage hall by herself not knowing how to find me.

The thud of a stamp in my passport finally sounded and I rushed to the appropriate carousel to collect my bags. To my amazement, and that of my fellow passengers, there was no sign of our luggage. The empty carousel rolled around endlessly. By now I was beginning to think there was some vendetta against me. My tired, aching limbs slumped over the metal handles of the baggage trolley as I willed the luggage to arrive.

A tap on my shoulder brought me up with a start. It was Tanya, her beaming smile accompanied by 'Hello Mum'. She had sensibly travelled with hand luggage only, had zipped through immigration in a much faster queue than mine, and had tracked me down.

My heart, already racing with anticipation and frustration, was catapulted to even greater heights by a mix of joy and relief. The squeals and bear hugs that followed attracted no attention in the sea of confusion in the busy terminal. Up to this point, to see my daughter at any time was sheer delight but after eighteen months it was like seeing her for the first time. Her tall, slim body so delicately formed, her long, brown fly-away hair framing her beautiful face and cheeky green eyes. It was obvious why she stopped traffic.

We talked all the way to the Maidens Oberoi hotel, my jet lag and exhaustion miraculously gone. This was the same hotel where, thirty-six years before, I had spent part of my honeymoon. During my many return trips to India in the intervening years I had not once stayed here. What an amazing coincidence that the travel agent had booked this particular hotel for the return visit with my daughter. This I took to be a good omen.

There had been inevitable misunderstandings between us over the past few years, born out of problems of distance, language and Hadi's resentment. In fact, there had been a twelve-month period during which Tanya would have nothing to do with me and I feared I had lost her forever. I prayed that sufficient time had now passed, and the wounds healed, but I was not sure. Tanya's anger was very deep and I wondered if I would ever gain her forgiveness.

The planning for this trip had taken almost a year. I wanted somewhere very special to present Tanya with the book I had written for her. She had constantly been subjected to her father's point of view and had never really been privy to a considered account of my side of the story. I certainly had never burdened her with any of the detail. But now I thought it only fair that she know.

Most of all I wanted to make sure the manuscript was something

Tanya could keep and of which she would hopefully be proud. Searching through Sydney I found a traditional bookbinder, who bound my work in dark blue leather, placed the title in gold leaf on the cover and spine, and made a matching leather slipcase. After looking through countless shops I came across some blue, marbled wrapping paper – which perfectly matched the blue of the leather – and a suitably wide satin ribbon.

This letter of love was now carefully tucked away in my hand luggage waiting for the moment of delivery. The timing had to be right. We both needed a couple of days to recover from our long flights as well as time to calm down after the excitement and joy of seeing each other after such a long time.

By the end of day four, I couldn't wait any longer. We had travelled from Delhi to Jaiselmer, the ancient capital of Rajasthan in the heart of the Thar Desert, and booked in to the old Narayan Niwas Palace. The rooftop of the hotel, overlooking the sleepy desert and the lights of the medieval walled city, was a magic setting for our leisurely dinner. The golden glow of our surroundings coupled with the atmosphere, evocative of *The Arabian Nights*, warmed our hearts. At the conclusion of an exotic display given by swirling dancers, wearing vivid multicoloured costumes that twinkled like stars when caught by the candlelight, we walked arm in arm back to our room. It seemed time.

My book epitomised a lifetime of love and two years of hard work and now I would hand it over in the space of a couple of seconds. I was nervous about giving it, how it would be received, and what effect it would have on our future relationship.

The first thing Tanya saw when she carefully unwrapped the package was my name on the book's spine.

'Oh,' she said. 'How exciting. When is it to be published?'

'That is not really the idea. It is just for you.'

She browsed through the first few pages, turning them gently and slowly. Tears twinkled at the back of her tired green eyes and she encased me in her arms with a big hug.

She said simply, 'This is the most wonderful present I have received in my whole life.'

We were both exhausted from our long dusty trip that day and the uncomfortable, narrow beds beckoned. Many hours later as I rolled over in a half-sleep, half-awake state I was aware that the feeble bedside light was still burning. Tanya had stayed up reading her book until she had fallen asleep. At every opportunity she read some more, finishing it before we left India. We laughed about the silly things, cried about the sad things but, most importantly, I could feel the deep love we shared.

Tanya & Margaut

EPILOGUE

Tanya now happily lives in Spain, and works in sales and marketing. I live in Australia. Hadi lives by himself and Tanya sees him regularly. Unfortunately, he steadfastly refuses to have anything to do with me, which is difficult for Tanya. She is still the one being damaged. Do I hate him? No. The only feeling I have had for Hadi for a long time is one of great pity. Tanya and I are in constant contact and meet as frequently as possible. We now have many wonderful years ahead of us to share together.

My Two Husbands

Kathy Golski

When artist Kathy Golski fell in love with and married a handsome Polish medical student named Olek, her life changed forever. She was thrust into the chaos and passion of Polish culture, as well as the joys and struggle of motherhood. Life was full and happy: raising children, following Olek's medical calling to different corners of the world and establishing herself as an artist.

As foretold in a gypsy's prediction, ill-fated tragedy left Kathy and her three young children to face life without Olek – their foundation and inspiration. Amidst their grief they were sent a guardian angel in the form of Voy, also Polish, who, in time, won the hearts of Kathy and her children. Kathy and Voy married, and together they walked a new road that welcomed another son and took them to Sydney, to remote Papua New Guinea and to Poland, always somehow guided and inspired by the spirit of Olek.

In *My Two Husbands*, Kathy Golski reflects on the life that was her destiny – a life of love, loss, celebration and grief. A life filled with children, grandchildren, art, music and food, straddled between two diverse cultures. A life graced by the love of two husbands, and full of riches of a very different kind.

Tanya